The Education Ecology o Universities

Many universities around the world are finding that the structures and processes they have put in place to further their educational missions are being tested by rapidly changing circumstances. These changes involve new pedagogies, new course designs, new technologies and updating of the physical campus; reflecting diversifying student needs, growing student numbers, increasing competition and more demanding stakeholder expectations.

The Education Ecology of Universities examines these issues, starting with the challenges identified by university leaders who have responsibility for education, digital and campus planning. Sharing an analysis of in-depth interviews with more than 50 leaders, it identifies a range of conceptual and procedural gaps that undermine the full development and alignment of education, digital and campus strategies. The second half of the book provides practical ideas for taking a more holistic – indeed *ecological* – approach to understanding and improving university learning environments.

Setting out a case for a new applied science of educational ecology, this book offers foundational concepts and theoretical perspectives, introducing methods for analysing and evaluating teaching and learning ecosystems. It will be of interest to anyone who wants better ways of understanding how local systems function and can be improved. It is a must-read text for all leaders and researchers in education, and indeed for anyone concerned with the future of higher education.

Robert A. Ellis is Professor of Learning at Griffith University, Queensland, Australia. He is also Dean (Learning and Teaching) of seven faculties in the Arts Education Law Group.

Peter Goodyear is Professor of Education at the University of Sydney, Australia, and was the founding co-director of the university's Centre for Research on Learning and Innovation.

Society for Research into Higher Education Series

Series Editors: Jennifer M. Case, Virginia Tech, USA
Jeroen Huisman, Ghent University, Belgium

This exciting new series aims to publish cutting edge research and discourse that reflects the rapidly changing world of higher education, examined in a global context. Encompassing topics of wide international relevance, the series includes every aspect of the international higher education research agenda, from strategic policy formulation and impact to pragmatic advice on best practice in the field.

Titles in the series:

Enhancing the Freedom to Flourish in Higher Education
Participation, Equality and Capabilities
Talita M. L. Calitz

Student Plagiarism in Higher Education
Reflections on teaching practice
Diane Pecorari and Philip Shaw

Changing European Academics
A Comparative Study of Social Stratification, Work Patterns and Research Productivity
Marek Kwiek

The Education Ecology of Universities
Integrating Learning, Strategy and the Academy
Robert A. Ellis and Peter Goodyear

For more information about this series, please visit: https://www.routledge.com/Research-into-Higher-Education/book-series/SRHE

The Education Ecology of Universities

Integrating Learning, Strategy and the Academy

Robert A. Ellis and
Peter Goodyear

Routledge
Taylor & Francis Group

LONDON AND NEW YORK

First published 2019
by Routledge
2 Park Square, Milton Park, Abingdon, Oxon, OX14 4RN

and by Routledge
52 Vanderbilt Avenue, New York, NY 10017

Routledge is an imprint of the Taylor & Francis Group, an informa business

British Library Cataloguing-in-Publication Data
A catalogue record for this book is available from the British Library

Library of Congress Cataloging-in-Publication Data
Names: Ellis, Robert A., author. | Goodyear, Peter, 1952– author.
Title: The education ecology of universities : integrating learning, strategy and the academy / Robert Ellis and Peter Goodyear.
Description: Abingdon, Oxon ; New York, NY : Routledge, 2019. | Includes bibliographical references and index.
Identifiers: LCCN 2018054755| ISBN 9780815353645 (hbk) | ISBN 9780815353652 (pbk) | ISBN 9781351135863 (ebk)
Subjects: LCSH: Education, Higher—Aims and objectives. | Education, Higher—Effect of technological innovations on. | Universities and colleges—Administration. | College teaching. | Education, Higher—Aims and objectives—Australia. | Education, Higher—Effect of technological innovations on—Australia. | Universities and colleges—Administration—Australia. | College teaching—Australia.
Classification: LCC LB2322.2 .E46 2019 | DDC 378.94—dc23
LC record available at https://lccn.loc.gov/2018054755

ISBN: 978-0-8153-5364-5 (hbk)
ISBN: 978-0-8153-5365-2 (pbk)
ISBN: 978-1-351-13586-3 (ebk)

Typeset in Galliard
by codeMantra

Printed and bound by CPI Group (UK) Ltd, Croydon, CR0 4YY

Contents

Series editors' introduction

This series, co-published by the Society for Research into Higher Education and Routledge, aims to provide, in an accessible manner, cutting-edge scholarly thinking and enquiry that reflects the rapidly changing world of higher education, examined in a global context.

Encompassing topics of wide international relevance, the series includes every aspect of the international higher education research agenda, from strategic policy formulation and impact to pragmatic advice on best practice in the field. Each book in the series aims to meet at least one of the principal aims of the Society: to advance knowledge; to enhance practice; to inform policy.

As Robert A. Ellis and Peter Goodyear note in their Introduction, ecological metaphors and a focus on environment have a rich history in educational thinking. In this book, however, they significantly advance how such conceptualisations can inform our thinking on leadership and planning in higher education. Drawing on a large empirical project with leaders and managers in Australian universities, they use thoughtful interpretations of this study to propose a powerful new way of thinking about how universities can best respond to the multiple challenges they face in contemporary times. With an accessible style that does not diminish the sophistication of its contribution, the book will appeal equally to researchers, leaders and policymakers in higher education.

Jennifer M. Case
Jeroen Huisman

Foreword

Carol Nicoll

As I write this Foreword, I am in Beijing attending a doctoral forum that is part of a partnership between my university, Beijing Normal University and the University of Calgary. Yesterday I heard a presentation from one of the BNU students about her research into faculty development centres – a major initiative by the Chinese government to fund teaching and learning centres in its universities.

The Chinese approach is one which may not be adopted by other governments, but it did prompt me to reflect on how for many years Australian universities had benefited from significant government funding and policy interest to improve and innovate in teaching and learning. Indeed, Australia had been recognised as an international leader in teaching and learning policy and practice in higher education for many decades. In 2018, however, the policy carrots are long gone, replaced by sticks of various sizes and potency, and government rhetoric (rather than coherent policy) around budget constraints, accountability, performance measures and graduate outcomes.

The need to respond strategically to the multitude of external impositions on our universities is a complex task, as is planning for teaching and learning across a university. Whilst responsibility for innovation in and the quality of teaching and learning should rest with every academic, in reality, the people with the greatest accountability are the senior leaders in universities who are the focus of this book.

When I attended university as an undergraduate in the late 1970s there was no such position as deputy vice-chancellor education/teaching and learning. It is a creation of the late twentieth-century higher education landscape and is now part of the organisational status quo of Australian universities, and most universities around the world. Equally, in the pre-corporatised university, chief information officers, chief financial officers and facility managers either did not exist, or existed without any seat at the executive table or as prominent a role in the massive organisations many of our universities have become. This book brings the views of all of these people together to further our understanding of what the authors describe as the learning ecology of a university.

The emerging trends in teaching and learning, particularly through the intersection of education, information technology and university facilities, are highlighted in this book through the voices of university senior leaders. They expose considerable tensions for academic work, governance and effective management of universities. Universities are faced with a range of potential 'disruptions' to traditional teaching and learning delivery and governance, including adoption of third-party partnerships in teaching and learning, and large-scale curriculum renewal as a result of new course and credential designs. These challenge external professional accreditation, internal accreditation processes, and how these accountabilities fit within the current industrial context in universities.

There is a veritable tsunami of innovation in teaching and learning being offered to higher education providers, deluging each university with opportunities and risks. Yet whilst many of these innovations are being adopted and implemented, governance, strategy, policy and effective management are all lagging behind. We are in a state of perpetual catch-up, which the authors, and indeed many of the senior managers interviewed, argue requires university senior managers to take more deliberate, collaborative and consistent responses.

Beyond the changes to teaching and learning, the authors raise a number of issues that challenge the very nature of a university. They include the way teaching is and should be valued in the university; the importance of academic autonomy as expressed in individual control and delivery of teaching versus team teaching through collaborations involving academics, learning designers and third parties; the role of the faculty and its control and autonomy versus central leadership and governance; and the nature of academic work versus professional work and how that relationship might be constructed as an enabling service or strategic partnership. These are issues that go well beyond higher education standards set by governments and are about the very fabric and character of the university.

From their framework of the university and its educational ecology, the authors call for a holistic approach to educational leadership and management – an awareness that in the learning ecology of a university multiple factors must be considered by multiple senior leaders, in arriving at strategic directions, choices for teaching and learning and a grounded understanding of how process relates to outcomes. They offer service design and their own approach to educational design and analysis as an approach to address these challenges and provide practical suggestions to enable these to be applied.

The most disturbing section of the book is the ratings of the maturity of each university in capability and organisational alignment in strategy, governance, policy, management and funding. The relative immaturity of so many of the Australian universities in terms of readiness is a wake-up call for all university senior leaders.

The most important contribution of this book is the further development and application of the authors' conception of an applied science of educational ecology. This approach will be considered provocative by some academics and unhelpful by some policy makers as it critiques the unflinching outputs and outcomes focus of universities as they respond to higher education policy. It certainly reorients thinking about teaching and learning and the potential for delivering and managing it quite differently.

Whilst educational ecology has been applied in this book to only one domain in a university's ecology – teaching and learning – it clearly has salience for all aspects of the university and indeed other educational sites such as schools. It therefore has relevance for a readership well beyond the teaching and learning community.

This book is essential reading for aspiring and incumbent academic and professional leaders who wish to shape our universities and keep their sanity in the face of indomitable change. Individual academics will find much to inform their teaching and potentially refocus their pedagogy around a learning ecology underpinned by collaboration and creativity. The invaluable resources and strategies offered seek to improve the process, experience and outcomes of teaching and learning in higher education.

I felt a sense of optimism about learning and teaching as I read this book – the authors offer new ways to think about pedagogy, curriculum, the student experience, leadership and our work in higher education.

Carol Nicoll is Executive Dean of the Faculty of Education at Queensland University of Technology in Australia. She was the first Chief Commissioner and CEO of the Tertiary Education Quality and Standards Agency and before that was CEO of the Australian Learning and Teaching Council.

Acknowledgements

Enduring questions concerning the role and functioning of universities have fuelled the research collaboration that has led to this book. For their contributions to these discussions we are deeply indebted to the Australian university leaders we interviewed: people with leadership and management responsibilities in the fields of education, information technologies and facilities and estates. We celebrate their openness in sharing problems as well as insights, and are glad to acknowledge their decisive role in shaping the first half of this book. In turn, we hope that the ideas we have begun to develop in the second part of the book will prove useful to them and their colleagues.

Some of the chapters in this book have benefited immensely from close collaboration with other research partners, notably Nick Klomp, Bruce Meikle and Kenn Fisher. Nick Klomp worked with us on the interview-based research reported in Chapter 3. At that time, Nick was Deputy Vice-Chancellor (Academic) and Vice-President at the University of Canberra, and is now Vice Chancellor at Central Queensland University. Bruce Meikle and Kenn Fisher played similar roles in relation to Chapter 4 and Bruce also helped produce the synthesis reported in Chapter 5. Bruce was Chief Information Officer at the University of Sydney for over ten years. Kenn is an architect and academic with a well-earned reputation for work on the design and evaluation of learning spaces. Working with these three research partners has made it easier for us to engage with other senior people in Australian universities who have leadership responsibilities in education, technology and facilities. Our partners' participation in the research in the first part of the book does not mean that they necessarily agree with what we have written in the second part. For that, we take full responsibility.

The University of Sydney and Griffith University offer rich intellectual environments for anyone researching higher education. We have benefited from discussions with, and feedback from, numerous colleagues, and we are also grateful for the luxury of time and space needed to focus and test our thinking and writing. We particularly thank our colleagues, past and present, in the Centre for Research on Learning and Innovation at Sydney and at Griffith in the Arts, Education, Law Group and Institute for Educational Research. Special thanks to Lina Markauskaite, Kate Thompson, Lucila Carvalho and Peter Reimann at

Sydney and Paul Mazerolle, Gerry Docherty, Ruth Bereson, Stephen Billett, Jill Rowe, Lynda Davies, Karin Barac, Henry Cook, Michael Gleeson and Juanita Shaw at Griffith.

The book is an outcome of a Discovery project (DP150104163, Modelling complex learning spaces) funded by the Australian Research Council. Our Partner Investigator colleagues Kenn Fisher (University of Melbourne) and Alexi Marmot (University College London) have helped guide and animate a worthwhile and enjoyable project. Feifei Han and Pippa Yeoman have been outstanding postdoctoral researchers on this project and we are glad to acknowledge their many contributions. We thank Cristina Garduño Freeman for drawing the original of the ACAD figure used in Chapter 7.

We also thank the series editors, Professor Jenny Case and Professor Jeroen Huisman, for their support and for enabling us to share this research with a wider readership.

As promised to our partners and children in 2008, we have waited a decade before producing another book because of the sacrifices they make when we write. Special thanks, therefore, to Louise, Sonia, Jeremy, Emily and Michael. We promise not to do it again, we think.

Robert A. Ellis and Peter Goodyear
Brisbane and Sydney, September 2018

Introduction

> The concept of ecology has a subtle *ought-ness*. If an ecosystem is found to be impaired, then one has a responsibility to help to restore it to good health. And so it is with the university.
>
> (Barnett, 2018, 8)

Thinking ecologically about university learning and leadership

Ten years ago we wrote a book called *Students' experiences of e-learning in higher education: the ecology of sustainable innovation* (Ellis & Goodyear, 2010). Through that book we aimed to do two things. The first part of the book summarised the main findings from our empirical studies on university students' engagement in various kinds of technology-supported learning. The second part introduced a set of ideas for understanding and managing universities from an ecological perspective.

In particular, we argued that an ecology focused on *learning* stood the best chance of helping university leaders find ways of promoting innovation in response to rapidly changing circumstances. By this we meant that all the functional areas of the university should make it part of their core business to learn about contemporary conceptions of 'good learning' (Knight & Trowler, 2001; Goodyear, 2002) and orient their activities around better support for such learning. We reinterpreted concepts of ecological balance, ecological self-awareness, feedback and self-correction, and began to sketch some ideas about academic leadership in ecologies of learning.

Our focus in this new book moves – for a while – from students to university leaders. The first part of the book (mainly Chapters 3 to 5) reports on some empirical research we conducted over the last three years. With the help of some very experienced colleagues, we interviewed 54 senior staff from 39 of Australia's 42 universities. These included approximately equal numbers of people with leadership responsibility for education (deputy vice chancellors, education or equivalent), technology (chief information officers, technology directors, or equivalent) and physical infrastructure (facilities directors). In-depth, semi-structured interviews gave them an opportunity to talk about a range of issues that were salient for them in their leadership roles.

We draw on this rich corpus of interview data to cast light on some of the main issues that constitute the leadership work of these under-researched members of university staff. What becomes very clear is that – across education, technology and facilities – there are concerns about the ways in which university learning is understood, and support for it is managed. The leaders spoke about the problems arising from fragmented understandings of core activities. They spoke about the difficulties of thinking and planning holistically, of linking macro and micro processes, and of aligning educational and infrastructure planning. We go on to argue that some of these concerns relate to how 'quality' has been understood in some of the debates in higher education (HE): privileging outcome measures at the expense of understanding the processes that generate those outcomes. Without paying attention to both outcomes *and* the pathways by which teachers and students reach them, a university's ability to deal with dynamic change is compromised.

We use this evidence of deep-seated uncertainties, and a frustration with current conceptions and ways of working among the university leaders, to provide a rationale for the ecologically inspired approaches that we introduce in the second part of the book.

Since our previous book appeared in 2010, several others have been published that make educational use of ecological ideas and metaphors. For example, Cope & Kalantzis (2017) have recently brought together a useful compilation on 'e-learning ecologies'. Patterson & Holladay (2017) draw on systems dynamics and 'deep ecology' to reconsider complex teaching and learning activities. Bain & Zundans-Fraser (2017) have written about the 'self-organizing university' and Barnett has published what he says may be the apogee of his work on HE in a book called *The ecological university* (Barnett, 2018; see also Barnett & Jackson, forthcoming). Ecological terminology is also appearing in reports and commentaries on the current state and future prospects of universities generally, and the Australian HE system in particular (see, e.g., Mintrom & Gunn, 2018; Parker et al., 2018).

We are not, for a moment, deluding ourselves with the notion that we stimulated any of this work. The use of ideas from ecology to understand educational and psychological phenomena has a substantial history, going back through Bronfenbrenner and Gibson to Barker, Lewin and beyond (see, e.g., Barker & Wright, 1949; Lewin, 1952; Bronfenbrenner, 1979; Gibson, 1979/1986; Hannafin & Hannafin, 1996; Heft, 2005; Bailey & Barley, 2011).

There have been other substantial contributions that help frame educational institutions and their structures and processes in ecological terms, including Luckin's work on technology-infused learning contexts and the ecology of resources (e.g. Luckin, 2010) and research on human–computer interaction in educational contexts by Nardi & colleagues (e.g. Nardi & O'Day, 1999). More recently, Damsa & Jornet (2016) have been reconceptualising learning in HE as *coupled* change in people and their material and social environments: change in the complex entity (organism+environment) that Ingold refers to as a 'developmental system' (e.g. Ingold, 2000).

This associated idea of 'learning environment' also has a long and rich history in educational writing. 'Environment' was a key concept for Dewey:

> the only way in which adults consciously control the kind of education which the immature get is by controlling the environment in which they act, and hence think and feel. We never educate directly, but indirectly by means of the environment. Whether we permit chance environments to do the work, or whether we design environments for the purpose makes a great difference. And any environment is a chance environment so far as its educative influence is concerned unless it has been deliberately regulated with reference to its educative effect.
>
> (1938, 22)

Deliberately constructing and reconfiguring environments so that the young can learn by observing older and/or more skilful people, and occasionally joining in with their work, has a very long history: some argue that it accounts for the distinctive rapidity of human cognitive and cultural evolution (Clark, 2011; Sterelny, 2012; Rogoff, 2014).

The term 'learning environment' is now well established in the literatures of educational research (e.g. Walberg, 1976), educational technology (e.g. de Corte et al., 1992; Wilson, 1996; Jacobson & Reimann, 2010), educational architecture (e.g. Imms et al., 2016) and HE (e.g. Entwistle et al., 1991; Ford et al., 1996; Ashwin, 2012). But it can also be argued that 'environment' is under-theorised and unevenly used in much of this literature. It is often taken for granted; its meaning assumed to be self-evident even though quite different sets of connotations are drawn by different authors.

For some researchers in educational technology, for example, a learning environment is 'inside' a computer, whereas other researchers conceive of (say) a classroom learning environment as containing a multiplicity of digital devices. Some researchers use 'learning environment' to mean just the material world 'surrounding' a learner, while others include a much broader range of social, psychological, affective and pedagogical entities (Goodyear & Jones, 2002). So while much of this research has a relevance to understanding learning, teaching and technology in contemporary HE, some clarificatory work is needed to make the concepts and metaphor(s) useful. We offer a first pass over some of the key ideas in the next part of this chapter, and a closer examination in the second part of the book.

Environments, (eco)systems and ecology

We follow Ingold in defining 'environment' in a *relational* way:

> Just as there can be no organism without an environment, so also there can be no environment without an organism ... Thus my environment is the world as it exists and takes on meaning in relation to me, and in that sense it came into existence and undergoes development with me and around me
> (2000, 20)

Environments are never complete. They change, in part, through the actions of the organisms dwelling in them, and those organisms change and develop. Indeed, for many purposes, it makes sense to take as a single analytic unit the organism plus its environment as an indivisible totality: not so much a bounded entity as a process – a developmental system.

As researchers and/or as people with professional responsibility for educating others, we can think about, and act in relation to, the multiple developmental systems that comprise a class or cohort of students. While we too make sense of the world, and act towards it, within the constraints of what we perceive in our own environment, we can bring into that environment data, evidence, representations, ideas, tools and other resources that may be helpful – that may expand what we can readily come to know and strengthen our capacities for knowledgeable action.

Among other things, we can choose to represent a cohort of students (organisms+environments) as an *ecosystem*: a community of living entities and the many non-living things with which they interact – on some of which they depend for their existence. Some of these 'non-living things' are natural (air, water) while others are artificial products (buildings, computers). Some can be brought into an ecosystem intentionally, thereby changing each student's personal environment: enabling and precipitating changes in the developmental system that is each organism+environment.

Ecology – like history, geography and geology – has a double meaning. It can be used as a synonym for an ecosystem, just as we can say 'the geology of this area is predominantly sandstone'. But it also refers to a branch of scientific study. To practise ecology is to attempt to understand ecologies (or ecosystems). Barnett puts it like this:

> 'Ecology' is a double-barrelled term. It both refers to systems *in themselves* that have an internal unity, the coherence of which could be threatened in some way, and also refers to a *study* of such systems in the world. ... This dual headedness applies also to the university, for the university lives amid ecologies (they have real substance in the world) and also has helped bequeath the formation of ecology as an academic field of study
> (Barnett, 2018, 18, original emphasis)

In the same way, we can talk about 'an educational ecology' or 'a university ecosystem' as a complex tangle of entities with real substance in the world and we can also talk about 'educational ecology' as an academic field of study. (We describe the foundations for this field in Chapter 8.) And just as ecology can draw on zoology, botany, climatology and other fields of knowledge, so educational ecology can draw upon psychology, anthropology and more. Ecology is not the same as biology and there is more to educational ecology than the psychology of learning.

This 'dual headedness', as Barnett calls it, has an extra resonance in our work. It adds a reflexive, indeed a recursive, quality. One of the core purposes of HE is to help people become more capable, autonomous lifelong learners. A vital but rather neglected aspect of being an autonomous learner is knowing how to create for oneself, and one's colleagues, a well-furnished learning environment. In this sense, it helps if lifelong learners become their own educational ecologists, knowledgeable about how to create and sustain congenial sites for learning and enquiry, or in other words able to engineer appropriate 'epistemic niches' (Sterelny, 2012; Markauskaite & Goodyear, 2017).

It is one thing to take an ecological approach to achieve an academic understanding of how complex learning systems function. It is quite another to have responsibility for shaping them – for designing, creating and/or managing the complex sets of processes and artefacts, at multiple scale levels, that help constitute an educational ecosystem. Extra tools, methods and actionable knowledge are needed to discharge the responsibilities of education, technology and facilities leaders in contemporary universities.

To exercise leadership in educational work, or in the provision of appropriate technologies and learning spaces, we recommend shifting the focus of attention from the needs of individual students (whether seen as customers to be managed, apprentice scholars or employable graduates) to the requirements of whole *activity systems*. This is not to deny the variability in legitimate needs among students. Rather, it is an argument for making planning and leadership more effective by ensuring sufficient attention is paid to the needs of (collective) learning systems in action. As we will explain shortly, the defining characteristic of an educational ecosystem is the presence of *situated learning activities*: by which we mean the activities in which students are actually engaged in their work as learners. This raises two further considerations:

- how to frame, succinctly and clearly, what it is that education, technology and facilities leadership combine to offer to the main activity systems in each university; and
- how best to understand and evaluate the relations between what can be designed and provided by the university and the students' emergent learning activities and outcomes.

We approach these challenges in Chapters 6 and 7. Chapter 6 offers ideas from the field of *service design* as a way of integrating education, technology and facilities planning and aligning them to outcomes. In Chapter 7, we explain what we mean by *situated learning* and *activity systems*. The core purpose of Chapters 6 and 7 is to orient leadership to *the provision of co-produced educational services for and by activity systems*. A brief summary can be found below. We also introduce some ways of thinking about relations between what is designed and provided (on the one hand) and what students do and learn (on the other). We place student learning activity at the centre of educational service design, using an approach called activity-centred analysis and design or ACAD (Goodyear & Dimitriadis, 2013; Goodyear & Carvalho, 2014; Carvalho & Goodyear, 2018).

Service design

Ideas about how to design technology and spaces for students' learning are strongly influenced by fields like product design, user-interface design and architecture. This makes a certain amount of sense, but it places quite strict constraints on conceptions of what can be designed. Crucially, it makes it unnecessarily hard to *integrate* the design and management of curriculum, assessment, pedagogy, technology and learning spaces so that their combined contribution to outcomes can be conceptualised and managed.

In recent years, there has been a growing interest in an alternative conception of design – with a broadening of attention from product design to *service design* (Secomandi & Snelders, 2011). Service design has been making progress in a number of fields, notably in public services like healthcare. However, education is almost invisible in the literature on service design. Most of the existing studies of educational service design focus on ancillary areas like student administration or catering, rather than on core processes of learning (Carvalho & Goodyear, 2018).

Service design has ways of integrating both the tangible and the non-tangible aspects of services, and so lends itself to challenges of the kind we focus upon in this book. It also pays close attention to the idea of services as *co-produced*, which is a necessity in HE. We introduce the key elements of service design, and draw out some of the possibilities and implications for university leaders, in Chapter 6, at the start of the second half of the book.

Activity systems and activity-centred analysis and design

Human learning takes place within and between complex, continuously changing activity systems. Learning needs themselves are increasingly opaque. It is not at all clear just what needs to be learned to cope with the demands of complex activities and global networks in constant turmoil. Humans – practitioners, teachers, students – are intentional and interactive beings who keep interpreting and reinterpreting the challenges and tasks they face in their own, multiple, changing, and often unpredictable ways. They do not neatly obey the laws of linear causality. The practical usefulness and ecological validity of research on learning based on classical well-controlled experiments are more questionable than ever.

(Engeström, 2011, 599)

A core characteristic of the approach we describe in the second half of this book arises from our insistence on the centrality of *activity* in an ecology of learning. What the students actually do circumscribes what they can learn (Shuell, 1986; Biggs & Tang, 2007). This may seem self-evident, but other images are still powerful in discussions within, and about, the core functioning of HE. For example, some very influential consulting services and agencies still portray 'content delivery' as the core business (EY, 2018). The supposedly disruptive wave of interest in massive open online courses (MOOCs) was premised on the value of scaling up content delivery and expanding the reach of didactic teaching (Littlejohn & Hood, 2018). The idea that 'coming to know' is merely a matter of copying 'content' from one mind to another is remarkably hard to kill.

So we make no apology for promoting another conception of educational phenomena and processes – an *activity-based* and *situated* conception – nor for insisting on a way of framing the analysis of real-world university learning in terms of activity systems (Bligh & Flood, 2017). We draw on Greeno's definition of an activity system:

> The defining characteristic of a situative approach is that instead of focusing on individual learners, the main focus of analysis is on activity systems: *complex social organizations containing learners, teachers, curriculum materials, software tools, and the physical environment.*
>
> (Greeno, 2006, 79, emphasis added)

Looked at from a design, planning or management perspective, it can be helpful to distinguish between three dimensions of situatedness: physical, social and epistemic (Goodyear & Carvalho, 2014). Student learning activity is situated physically (materially and digitally), socially (through relations with other people) and epistemically (through tasks to be tackled and associated structures of valued knowledge). When activity is unfolding, tasks, knowledge, materials, tools, spaces, language, people are entangled together. But when consideration is being given in advance to the design of learning tasks or learning environments, it can be a helpful simplification to think in terms of discrete designable components that are physical, social or epistemic. We discuss this in more detail in Chapter 7.

For now, it is worth registering that different logics connect entities of these three different kinds. There are reasonably predictable relations between connected physical entities (such as devices in a network or the layers of a building). Relations between individual human beings and social groups are less predictable, but not random. Moreover, strong moral considerations apply when thinking about design and the social, which do not apply in the same way when designing sets of digital tools or learning spaces. Relations between tasks and sub-tasks, between areas of knowledge and between disciplinary ways of creating knowledge are not fixed, but neither are they arbitrary.

In sum, thinking about and discussing how a design (for learning) will function, or how it might be improved, depend upon an ability to weave together some rather different ways of knowing – about the physical, the social and the epistemic.

Knowing what can be designed in advance, and what must be left to emerge in an activity system at 'learntime', is important. So too is the capacity to build a shared sense of what is changeable and what is not, in particular places and timescales.

A major complicating factor with educational design and leadership arises from the need to connect macro and micro, or in other words to get coherence across levels. This applies in each of the three dimensions mentioned above. In the epistemic dimension is the familiar need for curriculum coherence: for example, to align the details of specific assessment tasks or class exercises with their higher-level intended learning goals and to ensure adequate curriculum coverage. Less familiar is the need to strive for *pedagogical* coherence, so that a common set of assumptions informs both the detail and the broad brush strokes of pedagogical action and teacher–student relationships.

To sum up, part of what we offer in the second half of this book is a connected set of ways of thinking about educational activity in universities by focusing on sets of *activity systems* – understood as entanglements of people, tasks, tools and places.

Understanding processes of influence and causation

A rational approach to the complex challenges of supporting student learning activity by leading and managing, designing and creating requires some intellectual tools for reasoning about causation. How does the environment that we help create influence what students actually do? What effects do tools and spaces have on activity and learning outcomes? What effects do pedagogical strategies or tasks have? Can we think about reliable or predictable effects without assuming some deterministic processes are at work? Where does student creativity and agency come into this? How can we expect them to exert greater agency – learn how to take more and more control of, and responsibility for, their own learning – if we surround them with oppressively tight structures?

It is sobering to observe that the everyday discourse of HE is virtually devoid of notions of causation – beyond cynical assumptions that students will always act strategically. ('Is it assessed?' 'Are lectures compulsory?') But if we have no sense of the relations of influence between what we, shapers of educational environments, can set in place and what students then do, how can we (in good faith) proceed? Or draw a salary? Clearly, what is needed is a way of thinking about such relations that positions them as neither deterministic nor random.

Structure and agency

In Chapter 7, we introduce ideas about 'structure and agency' as a way forward. We show how (partly designable) structures both constrain and enable students in what they do, allowing them to exercise and strengthen their agency. We draw on a variety of sources to investigate and explain this important area, which is strikingly underexplored in HE research (Ashwin, 2012). It is unhelpful to assume that structure and agency sit in opposition to one another, or are mutually exclusive forces, or that 'more structure' means 'less agency'. Rather, they depend upon one another.

On this view, the causal powers of social structures take effect through constraining or enabling what people set out to do (their 'projects'), so it is only through the exercise of agency that structures can have effects: 'unless agents did subjectively conceive of courses of action in society, then nothing would activate the causal powers of structural and cultural properties to constrain or to enable them' (Archer, 2003, 15). Or in other words, 'Social events, then, are produced by the interaction of *both* structural and agential causal powers' (Elder-Vass, 2010, 4; emphasis in original).

Ashwin (2012) provides a useful re-examination of teaching–learning processes in HE, using ideas about structure and agency. However, he refers almost exclusively to *social* structures. Like most of the sources on which he draws, he has little to say about the material world. This creates difficulties for people who also want to understand how material and/or digital structures influence students' activities, or teaching–learning processes. This lack of concern for the causal powers of material structures in sociological writing about structure and agency is steadily being remedied by organisational theorists, anthropologists, archaeologists, ergonomists and others involved in what can be described as a 'materialist turn' in social science (see, e.g., Barad, 2007; Orlikowski, 2010; Fenwick et al., 2011).

This is crucially important for people with a professional obligation to understand educationally productive integrations of curriculum, pedagogy, digital technology and learning spaces. To play a rational role in guiding developments in these areas, one ought to have a working knowledge of how complex socio-material structures enable and constrain students in their learning projects. How do the properties of specific learning spaces have effects on learning activity? How do specific digital tools enable or constrain valued activities? How do students translate the tasks set for them into practical activities? Answering these kinds of questions is made easier by a sharper sense of structural-agentic processes (Ashwin, 2012). Chapter 7 returns to this important topic and introduces some additional conceptual tools for thinking practically about the different kinds of causal relationships connecting people and people, people and things, and things and things.

Epistemic fluency in university leadership

It should be clear by now that we place a high value on ideas that help get things done in practical circumstances: 'working knowledge' or 'actionable knowledge'. This involves drawing ideas from a multiplicity of sources – from human–computer interaction as well as the philosophy of knowledge, from ecological psychology as well as software engineering. There's a clear danger of drowning in a sea of incompatible constructs, so this capacity for making use of diverse sources of knowledge has to be accompanied by a sense of where that knowledge comes from, how it gets produced and what counts as trustworthy. Being able to work skilfully with diverse kinds of knowledge and ways of knowing involves *epistemic fluency* (Markauskaite & Goodyear, 2017). We mention this here for two related reasons. First, people managing, leading, designing and creating components of educational ecosystems need epistemic fluency, including a keen sense of what kinds of knowledge are likely to be the best available for each kind of problem encountered. Second, the students we graduate also need to be epistemically fluent, to deal with unforeseen and 'wicked' problems in their future working lives. So it makes sense to share with them some of our reasoning about how we do our educational work.

We will briefly mention two further aspects of this here – revisited again in Chapter 9. The first of these concerns the need for managers, designers and others to view the systems for which they have responsibility from two vantage points. These are labelled in the literature in many different ways, but boil down to a 'view from above' and a 'view from within' (or outsider and insider perspectives). As we argue in Chapter 9, it is important for university leaders to be able to dwell within educational ecosystems – to take on the sensibilities of what Bligh (2014) calls 'denizens' of the university. But they also need to be able to switch to viewing systems from outside/above and to use abstract representations of significant characteristics of those systems in decision-making. Switching strategically between these views is difficult but important, and Chapter 9 shares some ideas and techniques associated with melding insider–outsider perspectives.

Chapter-by-chapter overview

This book falls into two main parts. Part I sets the scene and presents results from our interview-based research with education, information technology (IT) and facilities leaders. Part II shares a connected set of practical concepts aimed at finding better ways of integrating work across these three areas.

Chapter 1 provides an overview of the contemporary HE landscape, with a particular focus on recent trends that are raising new challenges for university leaders. In this chapter, we summarise some key points from the research literature, and statistical and policy documents, on matters of concern to education, IT and facilities leaders. We also provide a brief description of the Australian university system, to help readers who do not know that system in interpreting the results we share later in the book.

Chapter 2 explains our research methodology. Chapters 3 and 4 present the main themes arising from the analysis of the interview transcripts. Chapter 3 is based on interviews with education leaders. Chapter 4 is based on interviews with the technology and facilities leaders.

Chapter 5 does three jobs. It provides an overarching summary of the challenges mentioned by the three sets of leaders. It analyses the levels of capability and degrees of alignment in key areas of concern to leaders – the five 'organisational elements' of strategy, governance, management, policy and funding. And building on this analysis, we argue that stronger conceptual tools are needed to help leaders and others make shared sense of the complexities of learning, teaching, technologies and space.

For example, *educational leaders* are very focused on the student experience, curriculum reform and renewal, employability, quality assurance and the kinds and degrees of educational innovation needed to position their universities to meet foreseeable challenges – changes in demand, competition, and so on. *Technology leaders* are very focused on providing a reliable IT infrastructure, for a wide range of activities and clients, not just education and students. They also have to look forward, interpret and make sense of emerging trends in technology and workplaces and guide the university accordingly. *Facilities leaders* are very focused on efficient use of space, managing complex new build and renovation projects and meeting the emerging requirements of educational leaders for flexible spaces, and so on. Each of these three areas of responsibility is complex in itself. It is unsurprising that integrating the three areas throws up challenging intellectual and practical problems.

Chapter 6 starts the second part of the book. We shift gear from reporting research findings to offering conceptual tools and investigative methods aligned with understanding HE institutions and their work in ecological terms.

In Chapter 6 we argue that some of the difficulty of aligning the organisational elements arises from uncertainties and differences in perception of leadership and management roles. We therefore offer *service design* as a high-level conceptualisation that has the potential to connect education, technology and facilities leadership around a shared practical mission. Service design is not yet well developed or widely discussed in HE and the HE literature, so in Chapter 6 we provide an introduction to its core concepts and how these can be refined to apply in (higher) education settings. We also help fix the focus of attention (the 'object') of service design – moving away from the 'solo' student (whether understood as partner, client, customer or user) to *design for activity systems.*

Chapter 7 explains why activity systems are an appropriate unit of analysis when understanding and providing leadership for university education. This is not to say that the needs of individual students are unimportant – far from it. Rather, the argument is that:

(a) students need to be understood as learning and acting in ways that are closely coupled with their environment(s); and

(b) the nature of the environments in which they work have significant consequences for what and how they learn; so

(c) an activity-centred analysis of what students are actually doing and how they are using tools, spaces, assessment tasks, etc. provides important insights for (re)designing for their learning.

Chapter 7 introduces some tools for activity-centred analysis and design and helps make some crucial distinctions between what can be designed (for students; for activity systems) and what is necessarily emergent.

In Chapter 8 we take an important step: from talking about ecologies (in the sense of (eco)systems in the world) to ecology (as a discipline that studies ecosystems). We propose and outline *educational ecology as an applied science* – useful for understanding educational activities and outcomes and also for producing actionable knowledge – knowledge that is useful in designing, creating and managing those elements of educational ecosystems that are susceptible to such leadership work and understanding the relationships between what can be designed/managed and what emerges and evolves. Creating this kind of actionable knowledge depends on understanding the internal logic of evolving educational ecosystems – knowing how to evaluate, what data to collect, how to connect sources of evidence in a robust explanatory framework, and so on. Chapter 8 draws upon the work of a number of authors who have explored ecological ideas in educational contexts. It lays out some foundations for a new branch of applied research whose outputs can help university leaders achieve a better understanding of how educational ecosystems actually function, and how they can be strengthened.

Chapter 9 builds on these foundations by identifying a number of practical, inclusive, approaches to doing educational ecology. It describes four such approaches, taken from a much larger set: soft systems methodology, realist formative evaluation, formative interventions and participatory design-based research. Chapter 9 also discusses, and makes some practical suggestions about, ways of organising research–practice relations to avoid some of the well-known but obstinate problems in this area. It has become clear that linear models of knowledge flow, in which research insights and evidence 'trickle down' to the spaces, organisations and people capable of acting upon them, are neither accurate descriptions of the world, nor productive methods for managing innovation and quality enhancement. Recent experience in the health sector, in particular, has demonstrated the value of having specialist staff and agencies charged with proactively enabling and strengthening knowledge exchange, translation and application. So in Chapter 9 we talk about applied research processes and structures: about the roles, activities and methods used by people engaged in translational design, boundary work and research–practice partnerships – reinterpreting experiences from the health and the school sector for application in university systems.

At the end of the book, we offer some concluding thoughts about leadership and educational ecology, linking once more the problems raised in Part I of the book to the conceptual and methodological toolkits suggested in Part II.

References

Archer, M. (2003). *Structure, agency and the internal conversation*. Cambridge: Cambridge University Press.

Ashwin, P. (2012). *Analysing teaching–learning interactions in higher education: accounting for structure and agency*. London: Continuum.

Bailey, D. E., & Barley, S. R. (2011). Teaching–learning ecologies: mapping the environment to structure through action. *Organization Science, 22*(1), 262–285. doi:10.2307/20868858

Bain, A., & Zundans-Fraser, L. (2017). *The self-organizing university: designing the higher education organization for quality learning and teaching*. Singapore: Springer Nature.

Barad, K. (2007). Meeting the universe halfway: quantum physics and the entanglement of matter and meaning. Durham, NC: Duke University Press.

Barker, R. G., & Wright, H. F. (1949). Psychological Ecology and the Problem of Psychosocial Development. *Child Development, 20*(3), 131–143. doi:10.2307/1125869

Barnett, R. (2018). The ecological university: a feasible utopia. London: Routledge.

Barnett, R., & Jackson, N. (eds). (forthcoming). *Learning ecologies*. Abingdon: Routledge.

Biggs, J., & Tang, C. (2007). *Teaching for quality learning at university: what the student does* (3rd edn). Buckingham: Open University Press.

Bligh, B. (2014). Examining new processes for learning space design. In P. Temple (ed.), *The physical university: contours of space and place in higher education* (pp. 34–57). Abingdon: Routledge.

Bligh, B., & Flood, M. (2017). Activity theory in empirical higher education research: choices, uses and values. *Tertiary Education and Management, 23*(2), 125–152.

Bronfenbrenner, U. (1979). *The ecology of human development: experiments by nature and design*. Cambridge, MA: Harvard University Press.

Carvalho, L., & Goodyear, P. (2018). Design, learning and service innovation. *Design Studies, 55*, 27–53. doi:10.1016/j.destud.2017.09.003

Clark, A. (2011). *Supersizing the mind: embodiment, action, and cognitive extension*. Oxford: Oxford University Press.

Cope, B., & Kalantzis, M. (eds). (2017). *e-Learning Ecologies: Principles for New Learning* and Assessment. New York: Routledge.

Damsa, C. I., & Jornet, A. (2016). Revisiting learning in higher education—Framing notions redefined through an ecological perspective. *Frontline Learning Research, 4*(4), 39–47.

de Corte, E., Linn, M., Mandl, H., & Verschaffel, L. (eds). (1992). *Computer-based learning environments and problem solving*. Berlin: Springer Verlag.

Dewey, J. (1938). *Democracy and education*. Whitefish, MT: Kessinger.

Ellis, R., & Goodyear, P. (2010). *Students' experiences of e-learning in higher education: the ecology of sustainable innovation*. New York: RoutledgeFalmer.

Entwistle, N., Meyer, J., & Tait, H. (1991). Student failure: disintegrated patterns of study strategies and perceptions of the learning environment. *Higher Education, 21*(2), 249–261.

EY. (2018). *Can the universities of today lead learning for tomorrow? The university of the future*. Retrieved from www.ey.com/au/en/industries/government---public-sector/ey-university-of-the-future-2030

Fenwick, T., Edwards, R., & Sawchuk, P. (2011). *Emerging approaches to educational research: tracing the sociomaterial*. Abingdon: Routledge.

Ford, P., Goodyear, P., Heseltine, R., Lewis, R., Darby, J., Graves, J., . . . King, T. (1996). *Managing change in higher education: a learning environment architecture.* Buckingham: SRHE/Open University Press.

Gibson, J. (1979/1986). *The ecological approach to visual perception.* Hillsdale, NJ: Lawrence Erlbaum Associates.

Goodyear, P. (2002). Psychological foundations for networked learning. In C. Steeples & C. Jones (eds), *Networked learning: perspectives and issues* (pp. 49–75). London: Springer Verlag.

Goodyear, P., & Carvalho, L. (2014). Framing the analysis of learning network architectures. In L. Carvalho & P. Goodyear (eds), *The architecture of productive learning networks.* New York: Routledge.

Goodyear, P., & Dimitriadis, Y. (2013). *In medias res:* reframing design for learning. *Research in Learning Technology, 21.* doi:http://dx.doi.org/10.3402/rlt.v21i0.19909

Goodyear, P., & Jones, C. (2002). Implicit theories of learning and change: their role in the development of eLearning environments for higher education. In S. Naidu (ed.), *eLearning: technology and the development of teaching and learning.* London: Kogan Page.

Hannafin, K., & Hannafin, M. (1996). The ecology of distance learning environments. *Training Research Journal, 1,* 49–70.

Heft, H. (2005). *Ecological psychology in context: James Gibson, Roger Barker, and the legacy of William James.* Hove: Psychology Press.

Imms, W., Cleveland, B., & Fisher, K. (eds). (2016). *Evaluating learning environments: snapshots of emerging issues, methods and knowledge.* Rotterdam: Sense.

Ingold, T. (2000). *The perception of the environment: essays in livelihood, dwelling and skill.* Abingdon: Routledge.

Jacobson, M., & Reimann, P. (eds). (2010). Designs for learning environments of the future: international perspectives from the learning sciences. New York: Springer.

Kaptelinin, V., & Nardi, B. (2006). *Acting with technology: activity theory and interaction design.* Cambridge, MA: MIT Press.

Knight, P., & Trowler, P. (2001). *Departmental leadership in higher education.* Buckingham: SRHE/Open University Press.

Krippendorff, K. (2006). *The semantic turn: a new foundation for design.* Boca Raton FL: CRC Press.

Lewin, K. (1952). *Field theory in social science.* New York: Harper & Bros.

Littlejohn, A., & Hood, N. (2018). *Reconceptualising learning in the digital age: the [un]democratising potential of MOOCs.* Singapore: Springer.

Luckin, R. (2010). *Re-designing learning contexts: technology-rich, learner-centred ecologies.* New York: Routledge.

Markauskaite, L., & Goodyear, P. (2017). *Epistemic fluency and professional education: innovation, knowledgeable action a actionable knowledge.* Dordrecht: Springer.

Mintrom, M., & Gunn, A. (2018). Governing Australia's post compulsory education ecosystem. Paper presented at the Monash Commission's Designing the Future Seminar Melbourne. www.monash.edu/__data/assets/pdf_file/0007/1476142/Mintrom-and-Gunn-August-2018.pdf

Nardi, B., & O'Day, V. (1999). *Information ecologies: using technology with heart.* Cambridge, MA: MIT Press.

Orlikowski, W. J. (2010). The sociomateriality of organisational life: considering technology in management research. *Cambridge Journal of Economics, 34,* 125–141.

Parker, S., Dempster, A., & Warburton, M. (2018). *Reimagining tertiary education: from binary system to ecosystem*. KPMG. https://home.kpmg.com/content/dam/kpmg/au/pdf/2018/reimagining-tertiary-education.pdf

Patterson, L., & Holladay, R. (2017). *Deep learning ecologies: an invitation to complex teaching and learning*. Circle Pines, MN: Human Systems Dynamics Institute.

Rogoff, B. (2014). Learning by observing and pitching in to family and community endeavors: an orientation. *Human Development*, *57*(2–3), 69–81.

Secomandi, F., & Snelders, D. (2011). The object of service design. *Design Issues*, *27*(3), 20–34.

Sfard, A. (1998). On two metaphors for learning and the dangers of just choosing one. *Educational Researcher*, *27*(2), 4–12.

Shuell, T. (1986). Cognitive conceptions of learning. *Review of Educational Research*, *56*(4), 411–436.

Sterelny, K. (2012). *The evolved apprentice: how evolution made humans unique*. Cambridge, MA: MIT Press.

Walberg, H. (1976). Psychology of learning environments: behavioral, structural or perceptual? In L. Shulman (ed.), *Review of Research in Education* (Vol. 4). Itaska, IL: FE Peacock.

Wilson, B. (ed.) (1996). *Constructivist learning environments*. Englewood Cliffs, NJ: Educational Technology Press.

Part I

Universities in a changing environment

Situating our research

There are dangers in generalising about 'the university'. Around the world, some 200 million students are involved in tertiary education. This number has more than doubled since the start of the century and is likely to double again by 2030. Over 6 million people teach in tertiary education – a number which is also rising (Altbach, 2016). Estimates vary, but there are somewhere between 18,500 and 26,500 universities in the world (Barnett, 2018, 59; IAU, 2018).

Within these large and growing numbers, there are, of course, some patterns – universities take on 'family resemblances', especially within national borders. Some of these universities share characteristics that are common in the richer countries of the world and in systems that reflect British, German and/or American models. But very many do not (Mihut et al., 2017). Anglophone scholarship in higher education is still quite restricted in its knowledge and gaze. Recent developments in, and fascination with, global and national ranking systems, for all their ills, have opened the space of interest somewhat. But apart from an important seam of work in comparative higher education, much of what is visible in the Anglophone literature of higher education is still restricted to the characteristics and functioning of an elite grouping of 500 or so universities. Moreover, much of the Anglophone literature on teaching and learning, educational technology and learning spaces is from and about experiences in relatively well-resourced universities in North America, Northern Europe, Australasia and East Asia. To speak of 'the university' obscures these facts and distracts attention from the variety of arrangements and experiences.

We have spent most of our professional lives working in universities in the UK and Australia. These are the systems we know best, and they share a number of common characteristics. Universities in these countries, and the staff working in them, have been dealing with multiple concurrent changes and challenges: massification, with its attendant diversification of students needs and expectations; volatile funding regimes; neo-liberal governments experimenting with regulated quasi-markets; increasingly complicated and costly accountability requirements; intensification and fragmentation of academic work; growing competition from private-sector tertiary providers, including fully online providers; a growing need to partner with, and purchase from, third-party companies in areas of core business (e.g. with learning management systems); changes in course, curriculum and credential design and shifts in conceptions of good pedagogy and 'good learning'. Moreover, all of this is taking place in a wider world where new technological developments are enabling the disruption of whole economic sectors, jobs are disappearing or being redistributed across skillsets and global spaces, certainties about workforce needs are evaporating, economic crises and austerity measures have impoverished public services and deep concerns about social justice and discrimination are rightly regaining traction in national and university affairs. Of course, these circumstances are not unique to Australia and the UK, though they combine and manifest themselves somewhat differently in other countries.

The research that we share in Chapters 3 to 5 of this book was undertaken in 2016 and 2017 in Australian universities. We believe it paints a reasonably representative picture of issues being raised by education, technology and facilities leaders in the Australian system. We were able to interview about half of the most senior leaders in each of these three groups, and our interviews come from 39 of the 42 Australian universities. Our interviews did not dwell on the forces at work in the broader environment. The dynamics of the leaders' work are closely connected to the shaping forces of the external environment, as registered in the internal characteristics of their universities: existing structures and processes, expectations and practices and capacities for resistance and change. So we focused on how these senior leaders conceive of their work and of the main challenges confronting them in relation to new course, curriculum and credential designs, and in relation to better integration of IT and physical spaces and learning. Ecological metaphors sprang up almost unbidden in trying to make sense of what the leaders told us. It may be that the Australian university system, and some of the universities, are at a tipping point: that major irreversible transformations are taking place, because incremental adjustments are no longer effective. It may be that they are moving to a new kind of balance. It may be that counter-currents will grow in strength and effects: that the predictions of technological and free-market determinists will prove erroneous. We will see. We hope.

Although our research is located in Australia, we want the broader arguments that we present in this book, especially in its second part, to be of interest to scholars and leaders of higher education wherever they are situated. Many universities, perhaps all, are subjected to pressures that can seriously distort their mission and sap their vitality. Perhaps 'pressure' is the wrong metaphor. Our main concerns are about forces of fragmentation, rather than those that might compress, shrink or collapse a university. Responding to competing demands, visions and interpretations threatens to pull some universities apart, and those forces are sometimes felt very badly by junior members of university staff who are least able to modify the system. When research, teaching and service obligations are in competition for time, energy and attention, leaving junior staff to resolve the tensions is morally wrong. Part of our argument arises from a desire to find better ways to reconnect these areas of academic work.

The disruptive ambitions of Silicon Valley start-up culture have caused many commentators to speak about how universities might be 'unbundled': whether to widen access or create opportunities for profit. We do not think universities should be protected from such scrutiny. Nor do we think of them as incapable of reform or improvement. Far from it. But this book is motivated by two deeply held beliefs: that society, indeed the planet, needs a healthy population of universities and that intellectual work needs to be done to assist universities in explaining and strengthening the coherence of what they do (Macfarlane, 2017; Barnett, 2018). We want to test the proposition that an applied ecological science of higher education can help with that.

The next part of this chapter provides some basic information about the Australian higher-education system. Among other things, it may help readers from outside Australia better understand the context. In the three sections after that, we provide brief reviews of some developments that are shaping the fields in which education, technology and facilities leaders operate. Some of the topics on which we touch – like quality assurance, innovation, employability and student retention – straddle two or more of these fields. An understanding of the direction and strength of some of these developments is, we believe, helpful in understanding current priorities and sources of tension. Finding new ways of resolving some of those tensions, by redesigning structures and functions, is – we argue – part of the way forward. The penultimate section of the chapter considers some staffing issues, for the massification of higher education in Australia, under conditions of volatile and uncertain public expenditure, has also put enormous pressures on staff and has created a casualised academic and professional 'precariat'.

In each of these brief sections on education, technology, spaces and staffing, we draw on a mix of literature and data sources; mostly from Australia, but with some supplementary material from the US and UK. We are not aiming to provide a proper comparative analysis; rather, we are using recently published data and research from each of these sources to anchor, extend and illustrate the core account.

There is much to be celebrated in higher education – extraordinary achievements in difficult circumstances – but there is also a growing sense that universities, in particular, are squaring up to take on bigger challenges, of global significance. So the final section of this chapter summarises a number of the issues and how they are presenting to university leaders, especially in the spaces where education and technology converge.

Higher education in Australia

Australia's size conceals some important facts that are relevant to understanding its higher education system. The land mass is 7.7 million square kilometres (about 20 times the size of Germany) or 3 million square miles (about four-fifths the size of the USA). Its most northerly and southerly state capitals – Darwin and Hobart – are 3,700 kilometres apart, as are its most easterly and westerly (Brisbane and Perth). These are bigger distances than Madrid to Moscow, or Washington, DC to Los Angeles.

But the population of this enormous country is small and highly urbanised: two-thirds of the 23.4 million people recorded in the 2016 national census live in one of the state/territory capitals. Indeed, 9.3 million (40% of the total population) live in either Greater Sydney (4.8M) or Greater Melbourne (4.5M). Moreover, 90% of the population live in urban areas: similar to the Netherlands (91%), higher than the UK (83%), the USA (82%), Canada (82%), France (80%) and Germany (76%) (World Bank, 2018).

There are currently 42 universities, of which one is a specialist university of divinity and another is internationally owned. There are also approximately 127 'non-university higher-education providers' of which 105 (mostly very small and specialised) are in the private sector. In this book, we are primarily concerned with the 40 'mainstream' universities, which dominate enrolments. There are around 1.5 million students, of whom nearly 400,000 are from overseas. While some universities operate branch campuses, the majority have their main campus in one of the eight capital cities. The vast majority of domestic students study at a university in their home city. For financial reasons, many domestic students continue to live with their parents and work part-time. The experience of university for many Australian students is more 'commuter' than 'campus resident'. It is rare for students to relocate between states to study. Some universities make an excellent job of catering for the needs of Australian students in rural areas. Australia's prominence as an innovator in distance education is partly rooted in this mission. But the overall picture is of a highly urbanised system, reflecting Australia's highly urbanised demography.

Australia's oldest universities date back to the 1850s. However, the system has taken its current shape over the last 30 years. Many of its features reflect the 'Dawkins Reforms' of the late 1980s. 'Dawkins ... turned colleges into universities, free education into HECS, elite education into mass education, local focuses into international outlooks, vice-chancellors into corporate leaders, teachers into teachers and researchers ...He remodelled higher education and how it was funded' (Croucher et al., 2013). Actions by another Labor government, following the Bradley Review in 2008 (Commonwealth of Australia, 2008), uncapped student places and released a surge in demand. In 2014, domestic student enrolments reached 1 million for the first time (Norton & Cakitaki, 2016). Higher-education policy and funding have been subject to some uncertainties since then (James et al., 2017) and, at the time of writing, changes to the funding of places and demographic factors are likely to pause the growth of domestic undergraduate enrolments (Norton et al., 2018).

On many counts, Australia has a very successful system of higher education: some things are working very well. In crude economic terms, the system has grown healthily at 5% per annum over the last 15 years. Recent estimates show that the 'Group of Eight' research intensive universities contribute $66B AUD annually to the Australian economy (London Economics, 2018). Success in attracting overseas students partly reflects the quality of the system and makes the education of international students Australia's third largest export earner, contributing $31B AUD to the economy (Universities Australia, 2018) and strengthening other aspects of Australia's overseas trade (Min & Falvey, 2018). There are understandable concerns about over-dependence on too few source countries (China, South-East Asia, India) and subject areas (Business Studies). Moreover, many universities are now very financially dependent on overseas student fees and it is far from clear that any of the universities is making a good job of integrating overseas and domestic students (Arkoudis et al., 2018).

Domestic student numbers have expanded much faster than population growth. Over 40% of 19-year-olds are enrolled in higher education, compared with 27% in 2000 and 18% in 1989 (Norton et al., 2018). The proportion of people aged 25–34 with at least a bachelor degree has risen steadily from 27% to 39% since 2004 (Universities Australia, 2018). Today, 58% of domestic students are female – and they have formed the majority since the late 1980s (Norton et al., 2018). Enrolments of domestic students with a disability increased by more than 100% between 2008 and 2016. In the same period, enrolments of indigenous students increased 89%, students from low SES (socio-economic status) backgrounds by 55%, and students from regional and remote areas by 48% (Universities Australia, 2018).

Some of these improvements come off a low base, meaning that much remains to be done before the system can be regarded as equitable (Zacharias & Brett, 2018). For example, 45% of people aged 25–34 living in the major cities have at least a bachelor degree. The equivalent proportions in regional, remote and very remote areas are between 20 and 23% (Universities Australia, 2018). The proportion of low SES students going to university is still well below the proportions of middle and high SES students. Indigenous students are also under-represented. Student retention and graduate employability are areas attracting significant attention (see below).

Australian universities do well in the international higher education rankings: 20–25% of its public universities regularly place in the top 100 universities globally. But this says more about elite, research-intensive, universities than the system as a whole. Making this same argument, a recent study by Universitas21 (U21) has attempted to rank entire national systems of higher education (Williams & Leahy, 2018). The U21 study uses aggregate national data drawn mainly from the Organisation for Economic Co-operation and Development (OECD), the United Nations Educational, Scientific and Cultural Organization (UNESCO) and Web of Science sources to rate university 'systems' on 25 attributes, grouped into two 'input' and two 'output' modules. The input modules tap into resource provision and the operating environment. The output modules tap achievements in education and research as well as connections with industry and internationally.

Table 1.1 Rankings on U21 analysis of higher education systems

	Resources	Environment	Connectivity	Output	Overall
1	Switzerland	USA	Switzerland	USA	USA
2	Sweden	*Australia*	Austria	UK	Switzerland
3	Singapore	New Zealand	UK	*Australia*	UK
4	Denmark	Singapore	Netherlands	Switzerland	Sweden
5	Canada	Finland	Denmark	Denmark	Denmark
6	USA	Hong Kong	New Zealand	Sweden	Finland
7	Norway	UK	Sweden	Canada	Netherlands
8	Austria	Taiwan	Finland	Netherlands	Canada
9	Finland	Netherlands	Belgium	Finland	Singapore
10	Saudi Arabia	Belgium	Singapore	Israel	*Australia*
11	Netherlands	Switzerland	USA	Germany	Austria
12	Malaysia	Sweden	Canada	Belgium	Norway
13	Hong Kong	Canada	Germany	France	Belgium
14	*Australia*	Poland	*Australia*	Norway	New Zealand
15	Belgium	Malaysia	Ireland	Singapore	Germany

Source: compiled from Williams and Leahy (2018, 6–16).

Australia ranks tenth overall in the U21 dataset but, as Table 1.1 shows, it ranks third on Output measures (behind the US and the UK). It comes 14th on Resources input, just ahead of Belgium, the UK, France and Germany, which indicates that Australia has a very *efficient* HE system. Part of the explanation for this – in very broad terms – appears in Australia's positioning as second on the 'Environment' measures: capturing autonomy and diversity. In this regard, Williams & Leahy argue: 'A consensus is emerging that for a quality higher education system, institutions need considerable financial autonomy, but there also needs to be appropriate diversity, competition between institutions and external monitoring of performance' (2018, 12).

In summary, by international standards, Australia has an efficient and very successful system of higher education, within which there is scope for greater diversity in mission and greater innovation in broadening the range of ways in which student learning can be supported and accredited. There is also an urgent need to work with other providers of tertiary education, especially in the sub-degree area, to provide a more integrated, flexible and navigable architecture for post-compulsory education provision. Funding needs further reform, to allow longer-term planning, make the use of education revenues more transparent and provide adequate resources for research. Community and industry engagement are patchy and underfunded: it is a difficult area in which to provide appropriate policy settings and incentives, given that large swathes of Australian industry are ambivalent about innovation (Australian Government Office of the Chief Economist, 2017). These characteristics of the operating environment are shaping the work of the university leaders we interviewed, and also making their work more vital.

it is a truism that effective institutional leadership is vital to the success of Australia's future tertiary system regardless of the policy settings. The challenges associated with leading large academic organisations, especially universities, have long been acknowledged. In Australia, universities have largely operated as autonomous institutions with complex but stable governance structures modelled on traditional Western universities established centuries ago in Europe. Yet, higher education leaders now face very different challenges than their 20th century predecessors ... The imperative for leaders to make decisions that will ensure their institutions are responsive, agile and innovative for financial viability and relevance into the 21st century is in contrast with often bureaucratic and slow-moving governance arrangements. How universities and other tertiary institutions reconcile increasingly corporate organisational models with the traditional educational roles of leaders to align with the fast-moving and competitive nature of tertiary education may define the market position of institutions into the future.

(French et al., 2017)

In each of the next three sections of this chapter, we drill down a little more to identify some of the main developments that are creating the context for, and shaping the work of, education, technology and facilities leaders. Within this account, we also identify a number of conundrums that complicate the work of these leaders. They might indeed be considered 'wicked problems' – where there are active disputes and/or deep uncertainties about what should be done (Watson, 2000; Marshall, 2018).

Because there is some overlap in concerns, and since technology and space are enablers of education, we have placed a number of these overlapping issues into the education section, which appears first.

Education

In this section we cover five areas that bear heavily upon the leadership work of Australian deputy vice-chancellors (education) (DVCEs) and their teams: students' experiences of higher education; retention and attrition; graduate employability; course, curriculum and assessment reform, and quality management.

Quality of educational experience

At first glance, feedback from Australian university students suggests they feel they are getting a very good education. In the most recent national survey, 79% of them gave a positive overall rating for the quality of their higher-education experience (QILT, 2018a). The figure was higher for commencing students (81%) than for later year students (75%).

The Quality Indicators for Learning and Teaching (QILT) Student Experience Survey has been designed in a way that makes comparison with US and UK data easier, though some caution needs to be exercised. In general, a higher proportion of US and UK students give a positive overall evaluation of their experience: 85% of final-year students responding to the US NSSE (National Survey of Student Engagement) rated their overall education experience positively; and UK students completing the National Student Survey (NSS) posted a 6% margin over Australian students (QILT, 2018a, 23–25).

One might say that, against these international benchmarks, the Australian data paints a positive picture, but with significant room for improvement. It could be that the somewhat lower figures are due to some characteristics that distinguish Australian universities from those in the UK, and from a number of the high-performing universities in the US. For example, there are well-established correlations between student ratings and size of institution: in general, smaller universities enjoy higher ratings and many Australian universities are very large by British and Ivy League standards.

However, there are substantial variations *within* the Australian survey data – significant differences between universities in the feedback they receive – and such warning signals are being treated seriously by many university leaders.

For example, looking at data on a university-by-university basis, students' evaluations of the quality of the teaching they have received, and the help they have had with skills development, both vary from a high of 93% to a low of 74% (expressing positive views). Evaluations of student support – covering administrative systems and the availability of advice and other support services – vary between 91% and 58% positive (QILT, 2018a, 17–18).

Aspects of teaching quality have also received critical feedback (QILT, 2018a, 90). For example, only 52% of students responded positively to the statement 'Teachers commented on your work in ways that help you learn' (54% in 2016) and only 59% responded positively to 'Teachers demonstrated concern for student learning' (61% in 2016). While overall assessments of teaching quality were reasonably high (79%), there are clearly some areas of weakness that matter deeply to significant numbers of students.

Burgess et al. (2018, 10) have analysed trends in ten years of UK NSS data. They have identified that the best thematic predictors of overall satisfaction are (1) teaching quality and (2) organisation and management. Their best single item predictor is the statement: 'The course was *well designed* and running smoothly' (emphasis added). In a similar vein, numerous analyses of US student data have shown that 'clear and organised instruction' strongly predicts student satisfaction and Grade Point Average outcomes (Roksa et al., 2017). Clear and coherent design for learning is key – and we return to this in Chapters 6 and 7.

There is one other issue, arising from the QILT data, on which we need to comment: the sense of disconnection many Australian students appear to feel from their university (QILT, 2018a, 89). In the most recent survey, only 51% of students responded that they felt a sense of belonging with their university

(53% in 2016). Only 44% reported that they had interacted with other students outside of study requirements (46% in 2016), and only 51% of students said that they had interacted with students 'very different from them' (52% in 2016). Another strand in the arguments we present in the second part of this book concerns the importance of building and benefitting from closer working relationships, helping students take on an identity as a member of a university community, and creating more convivial learning environments. The QILT data suggest that there may be a long way to go.

The big conundrum in this area arises from uncertainties about how well-placed students are to give informed feedback on the educational opportunities made available to them (Uttl et al., 2017). For example, it is well known that many students are averse to unfamiliar methods, seeing them as a source of risk to their grades, and some educators will argue that students should not be regarded as expert judges of pedagogy or curriculum design. On the other hand, students need to learn to become better at learning, which also includes knowing how to assemble the learning resources they need to tackle problems after graduation. Also, students can be said to be 'experts on their own lives' and a number of loosely related higher education initiatives are giving them a more central place in organising their own learning and defining their own needs (Davidson, 2017). In short, teaching staff and DVCEs can neither ignore, nor be driven by, student feedback scores; work needs to be done to enable all participants to play more informed and effective parts in understanding and improving educational provision.

Retention

The QILT, NSS (UK) and NSSE (US) data presented above reflect the views of students while they are still enrolled. But significant numbers of students leave university without completing their studies. There are a number of ways of measuring non-completion of an undergraduate degree. By the OECD method, some 30% of Australian students fail to complete their degrees, which is fractionally better than the OECD average. First-year attrition rates (the proportion of students who do not come back for their second year of study) have been steady at between 14 and 16% over the last ten years. However, retention and attrition rates have become a very significant issue in Australian higher education and policy circles because the *absolute* numbers of students have increased substantially. Consequently, so have the numbers who do not complete their degrees.

Cherastidtham et al. (2018) have analysed some of the risk factors associated with non-completion among Australian university students. They report an analysis of students who first enrolled in 2006, 2007 or 2008. It turns out that more than 50% of online students, part-time students and indigenous students did not complete their degrees. Around 40% of students aged over 25 at the start of their degree, and 40% of students from remote areas, also did not complete. Closer examination shows that part-time study, and especially low-intensity part-time study, is a very strong risk factor, and some of the risk associated with online study may actually be caught up in this factor. In other words, there are significant numbers of older people giving university a try, on a less than half-time basis, who turn out not to be well placed to complete. Family, work and other responsibilities are implicated in decisions not to continue.

(The conundrum here is that making entry and/or mode of attendance and/ or academic progress requirements much more demanding, to improve retention rates, would probably exclude many such students from the benefits of higher education. It is important to note that many discontinuing students say that they have benefited from their studies, even if they did not complete them (Cherastidtham et al., 2018). The latent demand for bite-sized higher education revealed by the massive open online courses (MOOCs) adventure has caused some fresh thinking among university leaders, including in areas like micro-credentialing.)

There are significant variations between disciplines in retention rates, some of which are explained by variations in the composition of student cohorts. But some appear to be closely linked with complaints about teaching quality – placing them firmly on the agenda for DVCEs.

Since the data on off-campus vs on-campus study have implications for some of the core concerns in this book, including the roles of digital and physical educational infrastructure, it is important to be as clear as possible about this issue:

> High drop-out rates for off-campus students seem to largely reflect characteristics other than their mode of study. … Compared to on-campus students, off-campus students are much less likely to say that they work or socialise with other students, and moderately less likely to say they have online or face-to-face discussions with other students. However, the differences between on- and off-campus students disappear for questions about their teachers. Off- and on-campus students are equally likely to agree that teaching staff are approachable and helpful, and that teaching staff actively engage students. These results suggest that universities are working to overcome, as far as possible, the apparent pedagogical limitations of online study.
> (Cherastidtham et al., 2018, 16–17)

Australian DVCEs and others have been very active in working on the quality of the first-year experience, in part because improvements in student experience in the first year can make a substantial difference to retention for students from low SES and indigenous backgrounds. A number of approaches have been applied, generally to good effect, though sometimes initiatives have been niche and co-curricular, rather than comprehensive and systemic (Jamelske, 2009; Kift, 2009; Bowman & Holmes, 2018). A striking feature of work in this important area is the weakness of causal explanations. A substantial body of empirical research has built up over the years, particularly in the US, establishing correlations between demographic variables and retention. But there is still a gap in explanations of how student background *results* in drop-out. Recourse is sometimes made to proxy variables like 'involvement' or 'engagement' but not much is really known about the actual events and activities that are implicated in drop-out, retention and success (Astin, 1984; Tinto, 1987; Kahu & Nelson, 2018).

Graduate attributes and employability

The return that Australian students get on their investment in higher education is substantial, though estimates vary and the extent of the advantage also varies from time to time and between groups. Overall, graduates are more likely than non-graduates to secure a job and the jobs they secure tend to be better paid. That said, there are variations in benefits between men and women, between socio-economic groups and between disciplines/professions (Kassenboehmer et al., 2018; Norton et al., 2018).

Public returns to investment in higher education are also significant here: government policy in many countries implicitly or explicitly looks to the higher-education sector to equip people with the skills that will be needed in a rapidly changing global economic system, even though the exact nature of future workplace, practices and skills is impossible to pin down (Tomlinson, 2012; Goodyear & Markauskaite, forthcoming).

The significance of both private and public benefits means that governments, universities, students, parents and others are conscious of levels of graduate (un)employment and the match or mismatch between what capabilities employers say they need and what universities are focusing upon. The arguments here are clouded somewhat by vested interests, and there is some evidence of discrepancies between the claims of senior industry representatives and what the direct supervisors of new graduates have to say. In general, the latter report higher levels of satisfaction with new graduates (QILT, 2018b).

Against this background, Australian universities – like many around the world – have become more focussed on graduate employability issues, on the capabilities that employers say they are looking for, and on the development of valued graduate attributes (Tomlinson, 2012; Sarkar et al., 2016; Clarke, 2017). This is a problematic area, for a number of reasons, and not just those that resolve into a clichéd dispute between academic and vocational conceptions of the purposes of higher education. Even when all participants are in agreement that improving graduate employability is a desirable goal, there are conceptual and terminological difficulties in pinning down exactly what it is that workplace capabilities entail, how so-called 'graduate attributes' map to these capabilities, and how they can be defined, assessed and developed (Smith & Bath, 2006; Vogler et al., 2018; Markauskaite & Goodyear, 2017; Goodyear & Markauskaite, forthcoming).

Tables 1.2 and 1.3 provide a glimpse of the capabilities Australian employers have been articulating in relation to graduate recruitment. Table 1.2 is from a survey of Australian employers, asking them to nominate selection criteria they use regularly when hiring graduates, the qualities they find least desirable among graduates and their levels of satisfaction with attributes of recently hired graduates.

Table 1.2 Employers' selection criteria

Most important selection criteria	% of employers listing this among top three criteria
Interpersonal and communication skills	58.3
Cultural alignment/values fit	34.3
Emotional intelligence	26.2
Reasoning and problem-solving skills	22.6
Academic results	19.6
Work experience	19.1
Technical skills	14.4
Demonstrated leadership	13.1
Extracurricular involvement	7.4
Community/volunteer service	1.6

Least desirable characteristics in graduates	% of employers mentioning
Arrogance	24.8
Poor oral communication	24.5
Poor communication skills	21.5
Poor cultural fit	20.7
Unwillingness to learn	20.7

Attributes of recently hired graduates	% of employers saying the attributes were good or very good
Academic results	90.8
Professionalism	81.1
Participation in extra-curricular activities	79.9
Communication skills – verbal	79.9
Communication skills – written	78.0
Presentation skills	76.6
Knowledge of your organisation	65.5
Prior work experience	61.1

Source: GCA (2016, 19–21).

Table 1.3 summarises headline data from a large (n = 4000) survey of Australian supervisors of recently hired graduates. It shows that those who are best placed to make judgements about the fit between recent graduates' skills and the skills needed for effective working in the organisations hiring them are very satisfied with the match.

In sum, many Australian supervisors of recently hired graduates would say that universities are doing a good job in helping their students develop attributes that enhance their employability. Performance on some of the indicators could be improved, and outcomes are unlikely to be equal across all students, universities, disciplines and professional fields. Moreover, projections about future

Table 1.3 Employer satisfaction with recent graduate hires

Skills area	% of direct supervisors reporting satisfaction with graduates' skills
Foundation skills (general literacy, numeracy and communication skills and the ability to investigate and integrate knowledge)	93
Adaptive skills (the ability to adapt and apply skills/knowledge and work independently)	90
Collaborative skills (teamwork and interpersonal skills)	86
Technical skills (application of professional and technical knowledge and standards)	93
Employability skills (the ability to perform and innovate in the workplace)	85
Overall	84

Source: QILT (2018b).

workplace needs suggest that education for employability is likely to be a very volatile area, demanding greater agility in the design and roll-out of new educational offerings. We turn to this next.

Course, curriculum and assessment reform

There are a number of drivers for the extensive work that universities are doing on course, curriculum and assessment reform. These include growing diversification of the student intake, concerns about graduate employability, pressures to contain costs through simplifying programs and courses, as well as a recognition of the need to provide better support for a wider range of student learning activities, including making significant improvements to the efficacy of feedback.

At the heart of much of this work is careful consideration of what university education is actually *for*. When a university develops a new education strategy, the process is usually accompanied by some rehearsal of core beliefs – about the distinctive nature of the education to be offered and its underpinning rationale. There is scope for endless debate on such foundational issues, but resolutions typically come from a balancing of traditional academic, vocational and critical interests. Within Australia, Davis (2017), Forsyth (2014) and others have argued that the vocational has deep roots: that an understanding of university as a place to prepare to work in a profession has outweighed (say) the American conception of liberal education, the passing on of culture and the shaping of mind and character.

Actually, it is not hard to argue that there are remarkable degrees of overlap in the educational outcomes of these apparently competing conceptions of university education: many of the skills and dispositions involved in the application of a critical imagination to complex demands of contemporary knowledge work can be fostered through academic apprenticeship (Sullivan & Rosin, 2008; Fung, 2017; Markauskaite & Goodyear, 2017). In consequence, there is a strengthening interest in course and curriculum reform that reinforces connections between research and education, rather than pushing them in separate directions. Among other approaches, we might mention engaged enquiry, connected curriculum, epistemic resourcefulness and evaluative judgement (Fung, 2017; Markauskaite & Goodyear, 2017; Boud et al., 2018; Davies & Pachler, 2018).

In Australian universities, many course, curriculum and assessment reform activities involve new combinations of disciplinary, interdisciplinary, community and workplace-oriented experiences, including various forms of work-integrated learning (WIL) but also opportunities to develop high-order capabilities for participating with others in demanding forms of academic, workplace and community praxis (Cooper et al., 2010; Bowen & Drysdale, 2017; Dohn, 2018).

At the level of pedagogy, universities are also finding ways of using large-scale educational reform to widen the use of 'high-impact practices' of various kinds (Kuh, 2008).

Quality management: assurance, enhancement and innovation

> it's time to stop thickening the rule book, reorganising the boxes on the organisation chart, and introducing more key performance indicators – and to do something more sophisticated.
>
> (Braithwaite, 2018, 3)

As will become clear in Chapter 3, issues of quality assurance and educational innovation are front and centre for DVCEs. A preliminary sketch here may help provide some context and reveal another 'wicked problem' for DVCEs and others: that it is hard to resolve tensions between the needs of innovation and quality assurance.

Analysing international developments in quality assurance and quality management systems, Martin & Parikh (2017) identify two main kinds of drivers, depending on whether or not the national higher-education system is primarily market based:

> In many higher education systems, governance reforms have led to the creation of external Quality Assurance (QA) schemes and national qualifications frameworks. Both reforms have triggered the development of QM [quality management] mechanisms by HEIs [higher education institutions], to put

them in a position to respond to the requirements of external QA. In other contexts, HEIs were simply asked by government to create structures and processes of internal quality assurance (IQA) as part of a national governance reform. ... In administrative contexts where HEIs are operating closer to the market, the enhancement of external image or an aspiration for international visibility are important drivers of efforts to strengthen the market position of an HEI.

(Martin & Parikh, 2017, 71)

Senior educational leaders in Australian universities have been heavily involved in several strands of work that weave together as quality assurance, quality enhancement and quality management systems. Surveying developments over the previous 30 years, Krause argued that concerns for quality assurance have heavily overshadowed work on quality enhancement in Australian higher education: 'the policy spotlight has focused more intensely on quality assurance and accountability, while responsibility for quality enhancement has remained within the purview of universities' (2013, 129).

For an all-too-brief period, the Australian Learning and Teaching Council (ALTC) was able to act as a catalyst for sector-wide quality enhancement and innovation initiatives, allowing individual universities to share risks and benefits. (Table 1.4 gives a flavour of its outputs and a sense of scope and priorities. The government's Office for Learning and Teaching temporarily managed legacy activities and outputs, until it too was closed.)

But with the demise of the ALTC in 2011, the policy emphasis of the Australian government returned to narrower issues of assurance and accountability. At the time of writing, the Tertiary Education Quality and Standards Agency (TEQSA) is charged with a primarily regulatory role, guided by a set of 100 standards that comprise the Higher Education Standards Framework.

> While the federal government's umbrella strategy of 'advancing quality' is an admirable one, there will be little progress on the quality enhancement front unless there are clearly articulated policy directions to this effect, combined with practical support for institutions as they seek to transform their approaches to quality enhancement ... national policy needs to include commitments of funds and resources to enable enhancement initiatives across the sector.
>
> (Krause, 2013, 135)

This privileging of quality assurance and accountability over quality enhancement and innovation is associated with another phenomenon, which turns out to be fundamental: a concern for *outcome measures* at the expense of *process models*. In other words, a consequence of the focus on demonstrating high-quality outcomes – on measures like student satisfaction or graduate employment – has been a relative neglect of questions about how such outcomes are achieved.

Table 1.4 Major reports from ALTC projects

Student experience	*2011*	*Gale and Parker*	*Student transition into higher education*
	2014	Arkoudis and Doughney	English-language proficiency
	2011	Rice	Assessment of Science, Technology, Engineering and Mathematics (STEM) students
	2011	Oliver	Assuring graduate outcomes
	2013	Freeman and Ewan	Assuring learning outcomes and standards
Curriculum	*2011*	*Narayan and Edwards*	*Curriculum renewal*
	2013	Hamilton et al.	Postgraduate research and coursework degrees
Learning and Teaching	*2012*	*Southwell*	*Revitalising the academic workforce*
	2011	Leask	Learning and teaching across cultures
	2013	White et al.	Innovative indigenous teaching and learning
	2011	Nash	Clinical practice
	2011	Orrell	Work-integrated learning
	2011	Partridge	Blended learning
	2011	Keppell et al.	Technology-enhanced learning and teaching
Learning space	2010	Mitchell et al.	Retrofitting university learning spaces
	2011	Lee and Tan	A comprehensive learning space evaluation model

Source: copies of reports available from: www.olt.gov.au.

Obtaining and sharing a better understanding of how different teaching and learning arrangements actually function has not been a high priority among senior educational leaders, it seems. As Shah & Richardson (2016) have helped demonstrate, from an analysis of Australian universities' strategic plans, it is much easier for leaders to make aspirational statements about the student learning experience (and what outcome data will be used to measure success) than it is to design and justify processes to engender those experiences.

Pattison (2017) summarises Australian, US and UK experience with respect to quality enhancement and quality improvement in university education and comes to the view that there is much more consensus on identifying the core issues of assessing quality than there is on strategies for advancing quality improvement, whether at national or institutional levels. In our view, she rightly identifies the meso-level of programmes and discipline teams, rather than individual academics or whole-of-institution, as the most appropriate locus of action on quality enhancement. However, her treatment of the issues focuses strongly on outcome indicators and ways of enabling and encouraging academic teams to use them. She has little to say about the need to understand the mechanisms through which actual learning and teaching systems generate outcomes. The same can be said about Probert's otherwise masterly conspectus of quality assurance and enhancement in Australian higher education (Probert, 2015).

Aspects of this outcome vs process issue turn out to be very salient in our interviews with university leaders. Indeed, the challenges of understanding how complex learning and teaching systems work, and how to provide better resources for them, motivate much of what we have assembled in the second half of the book.

Technology

Chief information officers (CIOs) and directors of IT in Australian universities participate annually in a national survey of the main issues confronting them. Their current and recent priorities include: information security, data management and governance, business transformation, change leadership and sustainability (CAUDIT, 2018). That is, they have a number of concerns that are common across CIOs in large organisations, outside as well as inside education. University CIOs also have to support university research needs: an increasingly demanding and complex area. All of that is in addition to a focus on the university's educational mission.

In the CAUDIT surveys, a number of education-facing issues come at or near the top of the CIOs' priority list: bundled together under 'supporting student success'. Within this area, there is a strong focus on system-wide use of learning analytics data.

> Substantive contributions to student success flow from integrating delivery of and access to support across learning and teaching, library services, academic advising, career and other student services. ... Staff and students need seamless access to integrated, accessible student success technologies. They serve retention and timely progress by acknowledging each student's path to completion. Proactively using student data across different systems enables academics to pre-emptively address issues that may impede student success. Seamless access implies a student-centred approach. The technical challenge includes balancing migration to cloud-based access with privacy and security considerations. It encompasses designing delivery platforms that foster attributes which influence student success – engagement, building students' confidence in taking responsibility for their learning, collaboration, knowing when to seek assistance and feeling welcomed when they do. ICT leaders and their staff meet these challenges through structured interactions with academic and professional staff, and with students. Achieving purposeful integration rests on a willingness across the institution to endorse ongoing, iterative adaptations to technologies that respond to course design parameters and students' personal circumstances.
>
> (CAUDIT, 2018, 11)

Buried within this statement is another of the conundrums complicating the work of university leaders, encapsulated in competing views about students. On the one hand, there is a view that students are 'customers to be managed', and that the capture and use of extensive learning analytics data is justifiable as a way of identifying risks to their progress and completion. On the other hand, there is a view that students deserve more privacy, autonomy and respect, and should be treated as novice members of the academy, not customers to be spied upon and nudged. Of course, there are not just two views and what makes this a wicked problem is that there is no consensus over how to resolve matters. This leaves CIOs in a very exposed position.

To provide some further context on the challenges faced by CIOs and their teams, in the education-facing aspects of their work, we describe recent developments in two areas: (1) the shift to near-ubiquitous ownership of laptops and smartphones; and (2) blended learning, hybrid learning spaces and the integration of IT and facilities planning.

The growing use of personal technologies

Use of and access to digital technologies of various kinds has changed dramatically in the last 10–15 years, mainly through growth in ownership of laptops and smartphones and other personal technologies. Over the last decade or so, university students' use of digital technology has grown very considerably. In 2017, 95% of Australians aged 12–24 owned a smartphone. Much of the best data available on this is from the US and UK, but personal devices have also been making inroads, and changing study practices, in far less affluent economies. Of course, it is the combination of higher levels of personal device ownership coupled with increasing access to ever-richer online information sources that has been enabling and prompting changes in the usage of digital technologies, for study and for other areas of life.

In Ellis & Goodyear (2010) we drew on US data collected by Educause to sketch the landscape of IT usage among university students. Ten years ago, most of the students surveyed had a computer of some kind, though only 74% had a laptop and only 12% a smartphone. Only half of the laptop owners regularly brought their laptops to university, because of their weight and fear of theft. The most recent Educause data (Brooks & Pomerantz, 2017), based on a survey of 35,760 students from 110 institutions, shows that 95% own a laptop and 97% own a smartphone – nearly all students own both and value the combination of the two devices as important in successfully dealing with their academic work (see also Luo et al., 2018). In addition, 78% of students rate their smartphone as being at least moderately important for academic work.

> That both of these devices are used and viewed as important by students may be a product of their functionality; that is, laptops handle the heavy lifting of student work (e.g., composition, statistical analysis, graphics), while smartphones

are conducive to more agile tasks (e.g., communication, easy information access, photography). Tablets, which lie somewhere in between—not as powerful as laptops, not as agile as smartphones—appear to be falling from favor.

(Brooks & Pomerantz, 2017, 13)

Near ubiquitous ownership of laptops and smartphones could enable much wider and smarter use of technology to enhance educational practices. (After all, poor access to technology was held up as a major blocker for technology-assisted learning over the last half century.)

However, there is deepening uncertainty about the value of personal technologies in the classroom. A few studies reporting negative correlations between device use and academic grades have received widespread publicity, especially in the higher education press (e.g. Patterson & Patterson, 2017). This, plus incidents in their own teaching experiences, has prompted some teaching staff to ban the use of smartphones and/or laptops in lecture classes (Pomerantz & Brooks, 2017). There is very little research on this point in Australian universities, but US data suggests that the teaching staff ('faculty') most likely to have an outright ban on personal devices are typically younger and more risk-averse.

faculty policies regarding laptops and tablets are associated with the faculty member's age, though not in the direction one might expect: Older faculty members are more likely to encourage or require students to use a laptop or a tablet in the classroom.

(Pomerantz & Brooks, 2017, 29)

The problematic issue arising here is that Australian CIOs have been under pressure, for some years now, to provide 'bring your own device' (BYOD) infrastructure that allows students to make use of networked personal devices during classes. Now that students have 24/7 ubiquitous access to the Internet, doubts are emerging about the educational benefits – to the point where some teaching staff are banning their use in lectures. From the point of view of educational technologists, it is clear that it is not the devices themselves that are the problem, it is how students are using them (distracting themselves by checking Facebook during lectures, for example). Significant numbers of teaching staff are not providing guidance or appropriate scaffolding about the best ways of using IT in class. Moreover, very little use is being made of the more advanced IT-based epistemic tools; instead, students are mainly using generic applications software. These uncertainties complicate the lives of CIOs and make strategic, education-led planning for student IT extremely difficult.

'Blended' learning

This second area is on the agenda of university CIOs for at least two reasons. Over the last five years or so, many university leaders have exhibited uncertainty about the degree of disruption to their institutions and business models likely to be brought about by fully online education. This is not a new question: it arose 20 years ago, just before the 'dotcom' bubble burst. It arose again, as if anew, with MOOCs. We will not attempt to summarise the history of that particularly panicky period (2012–2014) but rather will move on to make the point that the vast majority of enrolled university students in the US, UK and Australia express a clear preference for courses that are neither fully online nor fully face-to-face (Baik et al., 2015; Newman et al., 2018; Pomerantz et al., 2018). So CIOs have to find ways of providing appropriate leadership on (a) infrastructure that allows students to carry out as much of their work as possible, wherever they are (e.g. remote access to digital library collections, access to course materials on a learning management system – LMS); and (b) proper integration of physical learning spaces and IT, to support increasingly sophisticated requirements, particularly from more demanding and innovative teachers.

The term 'blended learning' is widely used to cover educational approaches that mix face-to-face and online activities, though the diversity of arrangements hidden under the label makes it risky to use in planning, research or design (Oliver & Trigwell, 2005; Bliuc et al., 2007; Means et al., 2013; Smith & Hill, 2018). In the US-dominated Educause/ECAR data, university instructors also express a preference for teaching in a 'blended' way. Students and their teachers differ somewhat in the activities they prefer to undertake in face-to-face and online environments (Table 1.5), but there are some strong overlaps, pointing to areas where there is both educational consensus and some backing from research about the educational effectiveness of well-organised activities.

In short, high value is placed on face-to-face activities that involve interactions between staff and students and among the students themselves. Students say they value the opportunity to hear staff explain and enthuse about their subject and answer students' questions (in lectures). Staff said they valued the opportunity to provide light supervision for face-to-face discussions and other kinds of student group-work activities. Students were unconvinced about the educational value of online discussions, preferring face-to-face discussions (as do the Australian students in the survey data analysed by Baik et al., 2015; see also Guest et al., 2018). Both students and faculty placed a high value on the capacity of online quizzes, and so on, to provide low-stakes, timely, formative evaluation and feedback.

A strong implication drawn by Pomerantz et al. (2018) is that future evolutions to university LMSs will (need to) reflect such preferences about the distribution of educational activities across physical (face-to-face) and virtual (online) learning spaces. Rather than seeing the LMS as just a platform for online work, it may be valuable to integrate tools that help with the orchestration of face-to-face activities as well.

Table 1.5 Student and faculty preferences for face-to-face and online activities

	Face-to-face		Online	
Rank	Students	Faculty	Students	Faculty
1	Lecture	Discussion	Exams/quizzes/tests	Exams/quizzes/tests
2	Discussion	Collaboration	Homework	Discussion
3	Exams/quizzes/tests	Lecture	Writing essays	Reading
4		In-class activities		Video
5		Exams/quizzes/tests		Homework
6		Instruction		Research

Source: compiled from Pomerantz et al. (2018).

Notes: Students' preferences for face-to-face lectures were double those of face-to-face discussion; faculty preferences for discussion were double those of collaboration and lectures; exams/quizzes/tests was the overwhelming number one choice for online, among both students and faculty.

From user-oriented to activity-oriented design thinking

Priorities for Australian CIOs are reflected in the annual CAUDIT surveys. The most recent of these emphasises the need for CIOs and their teams to liaise closely with users in order to increase the chances that IT will deliver what is needed, in a timely and affordable fashion.

> ICT leaders need to consult widely to understand how information technologies align with teaching and research practice across disciplines. They need to support change in diverse contexts – architecture studios, intelligent classrooms, and other specialised environments, and to understand user needs that accompany both pedagogical advances, and new research areas and methodologies. ... Defining purpose and intended practice is dependent on structured iterative collaboration between ICT specialists and every institution's system users and data consumers.
>
> (CAUDIT, 2018, 17–18)

This is no easy task. More than half the Australian universities have over 30,000 enrolled students; four universities have over 60,000. In addition, 125,000 staff are employed across the higher-education sector. It is no surprise if, in practice, user-centred systems design amounts to little more than working with averages and stereotypes.

Norman (2005), one of the early proponents of user-centred design, has been arguing for a shift from a necessarily cumbersome and conservative paradigm of user-centredness to one centred on activity. As we go on to explain in Chapters 6 and 7, CIOs have a way forward here in helping reform approaches to eliciting and meeting user requirements. Current practices depend on a mixture of user stereotypes, aggregate preference data and technology-driven speculation. An activity-centred approach can cut through this by having IT staff work with other stakeholders to identify ways in which IT can support a manageable number of (educational) activity systems, including 'traditional' lectures and more innovative group-based collaborative learning arrangements. The key is to construct a portfolio of supported arrangements – not so few that IT provides a straitjacket on educational activities, and not so many that the options are impossible to read, navigate or manage. In other words, what is needed is a legible architecture of supported activity systems.

Learning spaces

How then can we move beyond this endless oppositional swing between stereotypes of money-minded estates managers who do not understand what teaching and learning involves, and academics who are entirely self-centred and self-interested?

(Boys, 2011, 54)

Like CIOs, facilities managers have a very broad remit, covering much more than provision of education-oriented spaces. For example, facilities managers are responsible for linking estates and corporate strategy, emergency preparedness and business continuity, environmental footprint and sustainability, responding to changing patterns of user demand and incorporating new technology into buildings (Kamarazaly, 2014). They carry out this work in institutional cultures that tend to see physical infrastructure as a source of costs to be minimised rather than value to be maximised (Boys, 2011). They have oversight of an area in which existential questions are being asked – about the need for a 'bricks and mortar' campus (at all); about the role of lecture theatres and other spaces geared to didactic teaching of large groups – and in which demands for new kinds of learning spaces come unaccompanied by evidence or precise specifications.

In Australia, as in the UK and the US, the early to mid-2000s witnessed a burst of interest in (physical) learning spaces in higher education. Lead bodies in each country – Carrick/ALTC, JISC and Educause – sponsored studies, meetings and publications on this neglected topic. As Temple (2008) has noted, the initiative was almost stopped in its tracks by the global financial crisis, though the better economic fortunes enjoyed by Australia meant that both university building and renovation programmes and research on the topic continued to grow. It is hard to work out what precipitated this interest, across three or more continents, though some of the factors include:

1. a response to the growth of online learning in the late 1990s, with some serious thought being paid to the value of (provision for) on-campus learning experiences;
2. growing criticism of the lecture as the default teaching method – with associated questions being raised about the need for lecture theatres;
3. a concomitant growth of interest in collaborative learning – and the provision of spaces equipped for both supervised and unsupervised group work;
4. questions about the need for undergraduate science students to experience learning in traditional 'physical' labs and proposals to replace them with virtual labs;
5. discussions about the future of the university library, with the growing availability of digital holdings and the scope for repurposing spaces as 'learning commons'.

Temple's review of the literature on learning spaces, and his subsequent book, make it clear that the envisaged changes 'on the ground' in universities had very little research or theory on which to draw (Temple, 2008, 2014). Moreover, changes in the availability and role of technologies complicated planning and design considerably, particularly for people trying to work systematically on the integration of physical space provision and technology (Boys, 2015). Much of the research connecting pedagogy, space and technology is still rather poorly conceived and good methods for carrying out empirical studies that can produce useful knowledge for designers and planners are few and far between (Goodyear et al., 2018; Thomas et al., 2018).

Table 1.6 emphasises this point: that within the practices of learning space architects, facilities managers and their staff, educational technologists and others, there is no consensus on how best to think about relations between space and learning.

Jos Boys puts it like this:

> we do not yet have effective tools for accurately mapping the dynamic intersections of pedagogies, spaces, access, ownership, timetabling, and cost in our existing or planned campuses; are not effectively integrating an understanding of pedagogic and scholarly activities with space and technology in university strategies and implementation processes; and have not yet developed sophisticated planning methods that can make value decisions across learning space performance and other demands such as sustainability, business and community partnerships, and so on.
>
> (Boys, 2015, 102)

Table 1.6 Theorising relations between space and learning

	Space as ...	
0	Insignificant	Much of the work within education (including educational technology) simply ignores the spatial
1	Impeding	Space conceived as a set of generalised obstacles to be overcome
2	Containing	Spaces as having particular properties and contents; properties and missing resources constrain activity
3	Stimulating	Spaces as stimulating thinking, providing for certain kinds of action; space as affording
4	Associative	Foregrounds relations between abstract space and experienced place; focus on place-making; congenial and convivial places
5	Constitutive	Mind, body and world are entangled/mutually constitutive; since cognition is distributed, space extends the mind
6	Socially constitutive	Foregrounds spaces as socially produced; community rather than the individual as focus for analysis and design

Source: after Bligh and Crook (2017).

And yet, experimentation with new configurations of physical space and digital technologies is proceeding apace, in Australian universities and elsewhere (Harrison & Hutton, 2014; Boys, 2015). For example, there are promising examples in areas such as digitally augmented laboratory teaching, collaborative learning across digital and physical spaces and real-time tracking of student activity in informal learning spaces (e.g. Bower et al., 2017; Auer et al., 2018; Schneider et al., 2018). The challenge for university leaders and their teams is to distil lessons learned from such experiments and determine what they mean for future visions and strategies.

Staffing

We have commented already on the *efficiency* of the Australian university system, as measured for example through comparing resource inputs and educational and research outputs (Williams & Leahy, 2018). This is achieved through the passion and commitment of university staff. In this section, we mention two areas of concern: the growing use of casual and part-time teaching staff – an 'academic precariat' – and the pressures on all categories of staff that are leading to burnout and exhaustion.

Some scholars of higher education refuse to see the 'precariat' as part of the academic workforce 'proper' and effectively ignore them in research on the academic workforce (Hermanowicz, 2018). Fortunately, their situation is now becoming better documented. A reliance on casual staff is not a new phenomenon in Australia. In the mid- to late 1990s, almost half the undergraduate teaching was being carried by an 'underclass' of casual and part-time staff: casual staff numbers rose from 4759 FTE in 1990 to 12670 in 2000 (Kimber, 2003). Kimber associates this growth with an 'unbundling' of the academic role, with increasing separation between research and teaching and a greater use of casuals for both teaching and research assistance. She labels this trend in terms of a growing divide between a 'tenured core' and a 'tenuous periphery'. By 2012, the higher education sector had the third highest proportion of casualised workers in Australia (after health care and retail), and it was estimated that 80% of the teaching of first-year undergraduates was being done by casual staff. Because most casual academic jobs are part-time, the proportion of full-time equivalent staff on academic contracts is around 20–25%. But this disguises the absolute size of the academic precariat – in 2017, 94,500 people working casually, compared to 123,000 on fixed-term or permanent contracts (Norton & Cakitaki, 2016; Kniest, 2016). As Ryan et al (2013) demonstrate, casual teaching staff are often excluded from opportunities to participate in course and curriculum planning meetings and from professional development opportunities. This has significant implications for the staff themselves and also for processes of quality enhancement and innovation.

Increasing workloads, role conflict and role ambiguity are well-known precursors of burnout and emotional exhaustion in university staff (Sabagh et al., 2018). In a systematic review of the literature on academic burnout, covering sources that included the UK and Australia, Watts & Robertson noted university staff reporting higher levels of stress than those found in comparable areas of employment. This is associated with reduced autonomy, poor communication and impaired working relationships, as well as increased workloads and the need to excel in research as well as teaching.

> national surveys of university staff have concluded that academia is no longer a comparatively low-stress working environment, identifying both mounting workload and an increasing pressure both to publish and acquire external research funding as significant contributory factors to academic distress
> (Watts & Robertson, 2011, 34)

As we will see in the interview material in Chapters 3 and 4, many of the problems and initiatives on the agendas of education, technology and facilities leaders depend upon buy-in from academic and/or administrative staff. They depend upon the time and energy of staff, not just to help implement new ways of working, but to learn how to work in new environments and arrangements. A highly casualised, over-stretched workforce is not well placed to do this.

Rising to face emerging challenges

In this final section of the chapter we add some further (but necessary) complexity to the already considerable challenges facing Australian university leaders – acknowledging that much more will be expected of universities in the future. Universities have vital roles to play in democratic societies that are searching for sustainable solutions to the wicked problems generated by neo-liberalism over the last 50 years (Sullivan & Rosin, 2008; Barnett, 2018; Peters et al., 2018). 'A democracy cannot exist without informed citizens and public spheres and educational apparatuses that uphold standards of truth, honesty, evidence, facts and justice' (Giroux, 2018, 198). After sketching some of the implications of these emerging challenges, we draw out some of the key elements identified in the chapter and relate these to sections in the rest of the book.

Global challenges

The landscape sketched in this chapter is one marked by significant change: what universities are aiming to achieve – through overhauling their education, IT and estates strategies – can be understood as a response to projections about the changing skillsets needed for future graduate employment as well as increasing global competition in the tertiary education market. As we noted earlier in the chapter, some of these projections need careful scrutiny, based as they are on speculation and the interests of giant consulting firms. There is a good deal of hubris in the air. (As a corrective, we might observe that none of us know much about what challenges the twenty-first century will bring. Predictions from 1919 about 'twentieth-century skills' are likely to be more accurate than their equivalents today, given the accelerating pace of technological change and the concomitant fact that we know less about the future every year.)

As a further corrective, we also suggest that some of the analysis about the role of higher education coming from *within* the academy deserves more attention. Universities are a distinctive and potentially very valuable genus of social institution. A growing number of knowledgeable commentators, albeit sympathetic insiders, are arguing for a clearer affirmation of this distinctive mission. For example, Sydney Deputy Vice-Chancellor (Research) Duncan Ivison (2018) identifies a 'triple challenge'. Universities need to:

- become genuine engines of social mobility and equality of opportunity;
- harness their research strengths in new, multidisciplinary ways, and help address problems that neither governments nor firms can tackle on their own (wicked problems and complex systems);
- make their boundaries more porous and their research more visible and transparent, in order to build trust with the communities they serve.

Australian National University Vice-Chancellor Brian Schmidt puts it more starkly:

> But despite their visibility, university leaders cannot be slaves to the rankings and their evolving methodologies. Rather, we must have the confidence to

do the best we can at our missions and hope the rankings sensibly reflect our successes and failures – noting each of our idiosyncrasies. More than anything, universities must place themselves at the epicentre of society, and guide the transformations that must occur if humanity is to achieve a globally sustainable future. The alternative is not worth contemplating.

(Schmidt, 2018, n.p.)

These strategic challenges will mean nothing if they remain as mere rhetorical flourishes in mission statements. Translating their implications into educational reforms and more ambitious curricula will prove difficult, but ultimately rewarding. At heart, they must involve helping students acquire the 'moral know-how' needed to understand complex problems and work with others to do something about them. 'Universities ought to be important centers of critical conscience and students should be important actors in challenging the status quo and campaigning for a more just and equal society' (Macfarlane, 2017, xii).

Summarising the main issues

We now need to recap the biggest issues populating the landscape(s) in which education, technology and facilities leaders are working. From the 'education' section, above, we take the following key messages.

First, most students in Australian, US and UK universities rate their overall experience positively. But in the US and UK, 15% of students rate their experience negatively, as do 20% of Australian first-year students and 25% of Australian final-year students. That is a very sizeable number of disappointed people.

Second, Australian students identify a number of areas that are particularly weak. Half of them report that they do not feel a sense of belonging with their university. A similar proportion say they are not interacting with other students unless their course requires it; nor are they interacting with students 'very different from' themselves. Around half of students say they do not feel they are getting useful feedback on their work.

Third, graduates still enjoy a labour-market advantage and their immediate supervisors are satisfied with their capabilities. Huge efforts are going into course, curriculum and assessment reform, with employability as a strong driver. However, it is still not clear that there is a sharp enough understanding of workplace capabilities, and how to develop them, to be confident that the sizeable changes underway will lead to proportionate benefits.

Finally, the analysis of retention needs to inform two lines of thinking and action: one aimed at minimising risk factors for those who want to stay the whole course, the other aimed at more flexibly and proactively meeting the needs of older students who have work, family, community and/or caring commitments. Bite-sized courses, micro-credentials and peripheral engagement in ongoing learning communities may prove to be a good combination here.

The key points we take from the technology and facilities sections, above, are as follows. First, the great majority of students in Australian universities, like their peers in the UK and US, are now well equipped with personal digital technologies. For now, a combination of laptop and smartphone meets many of their more obvious IT and communicative needs. In most universities, technology leaders and their teams have responded well to the challenges of providing the infrastructure necessary for very large numbers of students and staff to use heterogeneous devices in their educational work. Wireless connectivity, extensive digital library 'holdings', an LMS and integration of IT and audio-visual services in teaching and learning spaces are all notable achievements that could not be taken for granted ten years ago. The focus now shifts from ownership levels, access and equity to *best use*. This second point can be thought of in terms of better integration between technology and educational activities, wherever those activities may be located. There is an emerging consensus about the value of 'blended learning' course designs, and about what educational activities are best carried out face-to-face and online. Good provision for face-to-face learning activities that involve collaborative work and discussion, with light to moderate supervision by teaching staff, entails planning appropriately furnished physical learning spaces, with digital tools and infrastructure that support the students and the teacher(s) in their work. We return to this theme of designing for complex group work and workflows in Chapters 6 and 7. More specifically, we argue that leaders should be bold in tackling the 'flexibility monster' and commit to designs that provide students and staff with *enabling structures*. This raises the third point, concerning the place of pedagogy in designing physical and digital learning spaces and tools – in particular, how pedagogical knowledge and reasoning can best play a role in design. In the literature on university learning spaces, 'pedagogy' rapidly dissolves into 'kinds of teaching and learning activity'. In Chapter 7, we provide a tighter definition of what pedagogy can offer, and how IT and facilities specialists can accommodate it in their approaches to design and management of digital systems and learning spaces.

Summary of Chapter 1

In this chapter, we have provided a survey of some of the main issues shaping the environment in which university leaders are working. We have paid particularly attention to developments and data in the areas of education, IT and facilities, since these are the areas led by the people we interviewed and the leadership work that gets done across these three areas is important in shaping possibilities for learning and teaching. We also sketched the Australian university system, and hope thereby to have made the data we share in the next part of the book easier to interpret and translate by those readers who are more familiar with other systems. In the next chapter, we explain how we approached our empirical research.

References

Altbach, P. (2016). *Global perspectives on higher education*. Baltimore, MD: Johns Hopkins University Press.

Arkoudis, S., Dollinger, M., Baik, C., & Patiences, A. (2018). International students' experience in Australian higher education: can we do better? *Higher Education*. doi:10.1007/s10734-018-0302-x

Astin, A. W. (1984). Student involvement: a developmental theory for higher education. *Journal of College Student Personnel, 25*(4), 297–308.

Auer, M., Azad, A., Edwards, A., & de Jong, T. (eds). (2018). *Cyber-physical laboratories in engineering and science education*. Cham: Springer.

Australian Government Office of the Chief Economist. (2017). *Australian Innovation System Report 2017*. Canberra: Department of Industry, Innovation and Science.

Baik, C., Naylor, R., & Arkoudis, S. (2015). *The first year experience in Australian universities: findings from two decades, 1994–2014*. Melbourne: Melbourne Centre for the Study of Higher Education, University of Melbourne.

Barnett, R. (2018). The ecological university: a feasible utopia. London: Routledge.

Bligh, B., & Crook, C. (2017). Learning spaces. In E. Duval, M. Sharples & R. Sutherland (eds), *Technology enhanced learning: research themes* (pp. 69–88). Cham: Springer.

Bliuc, A.-M., Ellis, R., & Goodyear, P. (2007). Research focus and methodological choices in studies into students' experiences of blended learning in higher education. *The Internet and Higher Education, 10*, 231–244.

Boud, D., Ajjawi, R., Dawson, P., & Tai, J. (eds). (2018). *Developing evaluative judgement in higher education: assessment for knowing and producing quality work*. London: Routledge.

Bowen, T., & Drysdale, M. (eds). (2017). *Work-integrated Learning in the 21st century: global perspectives on the future*. Bingley: Emerald Publishing Limited.

Bower, M., Lee, M., & Dalgarno, B. (2017). Collaborative learning across physical and virtual worlds: factors supporting and constraining learners in a blended reality environment. *British Journal of Educational Technology, 48*(2), 407–430.

Bowman, N. A., & Holmes, J. M. (2018). Getting off to a good start? First-year undergraduate research experiences and student outcomes. *Higher Education, 76*(1), 17–33.

Boys, J. (2011). *Towards creative learning spaces: re-thinking the architecture of post-compulsory education*. New York: Routledge.

Boys, J. (2015). *Building better universities: strategies, spaces, technologies*. New York: Routledge.

Braithwaite, J. (2018). Changing how we think about healthcare improvement. *British Medical Journal, 361*, 1–4.

Brooks, D. C., & Pomerantz, J. (2017). *ECAR Study of Undergraduate Students and Information Technology, 2017*. Louisville, CO: ECAR

Burgess, A., Senior, C., & Moores, E. (2018). A 10-year case study on the changing determinants of university student satisfaction in the UK. *PLOS ONE, 13*(2). doi:10.1371/journal.pone.0192976

CAUDIT. (2018). *CAUDIT 2018 Top ten report*. Retrieved from www.caudit.edu.au

Cherastidtham, I., Norton, A., & Mackey, W. (2018). University attrition: what helps and what hinders university completion? Grattan Institute.

Clarke, M. (2017). Rethinking graduate employability: the role of capital, individual attributes and context. *Studies in Higher Education*, 1–15. doi:10.1080/03075079.2 017.1294152

Commonwealth of Australia. (2008). Review of Australian Higher Education: discussion paper. Retrieved from: www.dest.gov.au/sectors/higher_education/policy_issues_ reviews/reviews/highered_review/#Review_of_Australian_Higher_Education_Discus sion_Paper_June_2008

Cooper, L., Orrell, J., & Bowden, M. (2010). *Work integrated learning: a guide to effective practice*. New York: Routledge.

Croucher, G., Marginson, S., Norton, A., & Wells, J. (eds). (2013). *The Dawkins revolution: 25 years on*. Melbourne: Melbourne University Press.

Davidson, C. N. (2017). *The new education: how to revolutionize the university to prepare students for a world in flux*. New York: Basic Books.

Davies, J., & Pachler, N. (eds). (2018). *Teaching and learning in higher education: perspectives from UCL*. London: UCL Institute of Education Press.

Davis, G. (2017). *The Australian idea of a university*. Melbourne: Melbourne University Press.

Dohn, N. (ed.) (2018). *Designing for learning in a networked world*. Abingdon: Routledge.

Ellis, R. A. & Goodyear, P. (2010) *Students' experiences of e-learning in higher education: the ecology of sustainable innovation*. London: Routledge.

Forsyth, H. (2014) *A history of the modern Australian university*. Sydney: University of New South Wales Press.

French, S., Kelly, P., & James, R. (2017). Futures for Australian tertiary education: developing an integrated, coherent policy vision. In R. James, S. French, & P. Kelly (eds), *Visions for Australian tertiary education* (pp. 1–6). Melbourne: Melbourne Centre for the Study of Higher Education.

Fung, D. (2017). *A connected curriculum for higher education*. London: University College.

Giroux, H. (2018). What is the role of higher education in the age of fake news? In M. A. Peters, S. Rider, M. Hyvönen & T. Besley (eds), *Post-truth, fake news: viral modernity & higher education* (pp. 197–215). Singapore: Springer Nature.

Goodyear, P., Ellis, R., & Marmot, A. (2018). Learning spaces research: framing actionable knowledge. In R. Ellis & P. Goodyear (eds), *Spaces of teaching and learning: integrating perspectives on research and practice* (pp. 221–238). Singapore: Springer Nature.

Goodyear, P., & Markauskaite, L. (forthcoming). The impact on work and practice of wicked problems and unpredictable futures In J. Higgs, D. Horsfall, S. Cork, & A. Jones (eds), *Practice Futures for the Common Good*. Leiden: Koninklijke Brill NV.

Graduate Careers Australia (2016) *Graduate outlook 2015*. Melbourne: GCA.

Guest, R., Rohde, N., Selvanathan, S., & Soesmanto, T. (2018). Student satisfaction and online teaching. *Assessment & Evaluation in Higher Education*, 1–10. doi:10.1080/0 2602938.2018.1433815

Harrison, A., & Hutton, L. (2014). *Design for the changing educational landscape: space, place and the future of learning*. London: Routledge.

Hermanowicz, J. (2018). The professoriate in international perspective. In M. B. Paulsen (ed.), *Higher education: handbook of theory and research* (pp. 239–294): Springer.

IAU (2018). World higher education database, www.whed.net/home.php (accessed 18 May 2018).

Ivison, D. (2018). Learning to be human: universities in a world of rising inequality and technological change. Retrieved from www.oecd-forum.org/users/107302-duncan-ivison/posts/32733-learning-to-be-human-universities-in-a-world-of-rising-inequality-and-technological-change (accessed 17 May 2018).

James, R., French, S. & Kelly, P. (eds). (2017). *Visions for Australian tertiary education*. Melbourne: Melbourne Centre for the Study of Higher Education.

Jamelske, E. (2009). Measuring the impact of a university first-year experience program on student GPA and retention. *Higher Education, 57*(3), 373–391.

Kahu, E. R., & Nelson, K. (2018). Student engagement in the educational interface: understanding the mechanisms of student success. *Higher Education Research & Development, 37*(1), 58–71. doi:10.1080/07294360.2017.1344197

Kamarazarly, M. (2014). *Challenges in strategic facilities management: analysis of problems faced by university facilities managers in New Zealand and Australia* (PhD thesis), Massey University.

Kassenboehmer, S. C., Leung, F., & Schurer, S. (2018). University education and non-cognitive skill development. *Oxford Economic Papers, 70*(2), 538–562.

Kift, S. (2009). *Articulating a transition pedagogy to scaffold and to enhance the first year student learning experience in Australian higher education*. Sydney: Australian Learning and Teaching Council.

Kimber, M. (2003). The tenured 'core' and the tenuous 'periphery': the casualisation of academic work in Australian Universities. *Journal of Higher Education Policy and Management, 25*(1), 41–50. doi:www.tandfonline.com/loi/cjhe20

Kniest, P. (2016). The rising tide of insecure employment at Australian universities. National Tertiary Education Union

Krause, K.-L. (2013). Quality enhancement: the Australian scene. In R. Land & G. Gordon (eds), *Enhancing quality in higher education: international perspectives* (pp. 129–140). Abingdon: Routledge.

London Economics (2018). *The economic impact of Group of Eight universities*. Retrieved from: https://londoneconomics.co.uk/wp-content/uploads/2018/08/Go8_London-Economics-Report.pdf

Luo, L., Kiewra, K. A., Flanigan, A. E., & Peteranetz, M. S. (2018). Laptop versus longhand note taking: effects on lecture notes and achievement. *Instructional Science.* doi:10.1007/s11251-018-9458-0

Macfarlane, B. (2017). *Freedom to learn: the threat to student academic freedom and why it needs to be reclaimed*. London: Routledge.

Markauskaite, L., & Goodyear, P. (2017). *Epistemic fluency and professional education: innovation, knowledgeable action and actionable knowledge*. Dordrecht: Springer.

Marshall, S. J. (2018). *Shaping the university of the future: using technology to catalyse change in university learning and teaching*. Singapore: Springer Nature.

Means, B., Toyama, Y., Murphy, R. F., & Baki, M. (2013). The effectiveness of online and blended learning: a meta-analysis of the empirical literature. *Teachers College Record, 115*, 1–47.

Mihut, G., Altbach, P., & de Wit, H. (eds). (2017). *Understanding global higher education*. Rotterdam: Sense publishers.

Min, B. S., & Falvey, R. (2018). International student flows for university education and the bilateral market integration of Australia. *Higher Education, 75*(5), 871–889. doi:10.1007/s10734-017-0175-4

Newman, T., Beetham, H., & Knight, S. (2018). *Digital experience insights survey 2018: findings from students in UK further and higher education*. Bristol: JISC.

Norman, D. A. (2005). Human-centered design considered harmful. *Interactions* (July–August), 14–19.

Norton, A., & Cakitaki, B. (2016). *Mapping Australian higher education 2016*. Melbourne: Grattan Institute

Norton, A., Cherastidtham, I., & Mackey, W. (2018). *Mapping Australian higher education 2018*. Melbourne: Grattan Institute

Oliver, M., & Trigwell, K. (2005). Can 'blended learning' be redeemed? *E-learning*, 2(1), 17–26.

Patterson, R. W., & Patterson, R. M. (2017). Computers and productivity: evidence from laptop use in the college classroom. *Economics of Education Review, 57,* 66–79.

Pattison, P. (2017). Standards and quality in Australian higher education. In R. James, S. French, & P. Kelly (eds), *Visions for Australian tertiary education* (pp. 101–110). Melbourne: Melbourne Centre for the Study of Higher Education.

Pomerantz, J., & Brooks, D. C. (2017). *ECAR Study of Faculty and Information Technology, 2017.* Louisville, CO: ECAR.

Pomerantz, J., Brown, M., & Brooks, D. C. (2018). *Foundations for a next generation digital learning environment: faculty, students, and the LMS*. Louisville, CO: ECAR.

Probert, B. (2015). *The quality of Australia's higher education system: how it might be defined, improved and assured*. Canberra: Office for Learning & Teaching.

QILT (2018a). *2017 Student experience survey: national report*. Canberra: QILT.

QILT (2018b). *2017 Employer Satisfaction Survey National Report*. Canberra: QILT.

Roksa, J., Trolian, T., Blaich, C., & Wise, K. (2017). Facilitating academic performance in college: understanding the role of clear and organized instruction. *Higher Education, 74*(2), 283–300.

Ryan, S., Burgess, J., Connell, J., & Groen, E. (2013). Casual Academic Staff in an Australian University: Marginalised and excluded. *Tertiary Education and Management, 19*(2), 161–175. doi:10.1080/13583883.2013.783617

Sabagh, Z., Hall, N. C., & Saroyan, A. (2018). Antecedents, correlates and consequences of faculty burnout. *Educational Research*, 1–26. doi:10.1080/00131881.2018.1461573

Sarkar, M., Overton, T., Thompson, C., & Rayner, G. (2016). Graduate employability: views of recent science graduates and employers. *International Journal of Innovation in Science and Mathematics Education, 24*(3) 31–48

Schmidt, B. (2018) Keynote address to The Times Higher Education World Academic Summit, Singapore, 26 September. www.anu.edu.au/news/all-news/vice-chancellor-speech-to-the-world-academic-summit

Schneider, B., Sharma, K., Cuendet, S., Zufferey, G., Dillenbourg, P., & Pea, R. (2018). Leveraging mobile eye-trackers to capture joint visual attention in co-located collaborative learning groups. *International Journal of Computer Supported Collaborative Learning, 13*(3), 241–261.

Shah, M., & Richardson, J. (2016). Is the enhancement of student experience a strategic priority in Australian universities? *Higher Education Research & Development, 35*(2), 352–364.

Smith, C., & Bath, D. (2006). The role of the learning community in the development of discipline knowledge and generic graduate outcomes. *Higher Education, 51*(2), 259–286.

Smith, K., & Hill, J. (2018). Defining the nature of blended learning through its depiction in current research. *Higher Education Research & Development*. doi:10.1080/07 294360.2018.1517732

Sullivan, W. S., & Rosin, M. S. (2008). *A new agenda for higher education: shaping the life of the mind for practice*. San Francisco, CA: Jossey Bass.

Temple, P. (2008). Learning spaces in higher education: an under-researched topic. *London Review of Education*, 6(3), 229–241.

Temple, P. (ed.) (2014). *The physical university: contours of space and place in higher education*. Abingdon: Routledge.

Thomas, C. L., Pavlechko, G. M., & Cassady, J. C. (2018). An examination of the mediating role of learning space design on the relation between instructor effectiveness and student engagement. *Learning Environments Research*. doi:10.1007/ s10984-018-9270-4

Tinto, V. (1987). *Leaving college: rethinking the causes and cures of student attrition*. Chicago: University of Chicago Press.

Tomlinson, M. (2012). Graduate employability: a review of conceptual and empirical themes. *Higher Education Policy*, 25(4), 407–431.

Universities Australia (2018). *Data snapshot 2018*. Canberra: UA.

Uttl, B., White, C. A., & Gonzalez, D. W. (2017). Meta-analysis of faculty's teaching effectiveness: student evaluation of teaching ratings and student learning are not related. *Studies in Educational Evaluation*, 54, 22–42.

Vogler, J. S., Thompson, P., Davis, D. W., Mayfield, B. E., Finley, P. M., & Yasseri, D. (2018). The hard work of soft skills: augmenting the project-based learning experience with interdisciplinary teamwork. *Instructional Science*, 46(3), 457–488.

Watson, D. (2000). Managing in higher education: the 'wicked' issues. *Higher Education Quarterly*, 54(1), 5–21.

Watts, J., & Robertson, N. (2011). Burnout in university teaching staff: a systematic literature review. *Educational Research*, 53(1), 33–50. doi:10.1080/00131881.2011. 552235

Williams, R., & Leahy, A. (2018). *U21 ranking of national higher education systems*. Melbourne: Melbourne University.

World Bank (2018). *Urban population*. https://data.worldbank.org/indicator/SP.URB. TOTL.IN.ZS

Zacharias, N., & Brett, M. (2018). *Student Equity 2030: a long-term strategic vision for student equity in higher education*. Bentley, WA: National Centre for Student Equity in Higher Education.

Research approach

The next part of the book – Chapters 3 to 5 inclusive – presents an analysis of issues arising for university leaders whose portfolios include education, IT and physical campus infrastructure. These senior members of academic and professional staff have leadership responsibilities that are highly relevant to the effective integration of educational activity, IT and learning spaces. To succeed in their roles, they need to pay close attention to current challenges and also help position their universities for the future. Given the complexity of contemporary universities, the rate of technological, social and economic change, and the difficulties of seeing far into a very uncertain future, these leaders have extremely difficult roles.

To find out more about how they do their work, how major issues are understood and how ideas and action are brought together within their organisations, we conducted a series of in-depth, semi-structured interviews. Interviewing senior university staff is not always straightforward. We felt it would be helpful to approach this in collaboration with some research partners who have got deep experience in the areas concerned. In carrying out the interviews themselves, and for some of the subsequent analytic work, we were joined by:

Nicholas Klomp: at the time of the interviews, Deputy Vice-Chancellor Academic at the University of Wollongong; now Vice-Chancellor at Central Queensland University.
Bruce Meikle: formerly Chief Information Officer at the University of Sydney, where he worked for over a decade.
Kenn Fisher: architect and University of Melbourne academic specialising in physical learning spaces who has extensive experience as a consultant on major university educational infrastructure projects.

We collectively undertook research that aimed at gaining a *second-order* perspective on issues pertaining to education, IT and learning spaces. In other words, our focus was and is on how the senior staff leading these areas understand the world(s) in which they work and the phenomena and forces involved. We did not set out to independently verify what they told us. We treat their understandings of the matters as real and important: their beliefs have consequences.

Chapters 3 and 4 summarise the main themes that emerged from our analysis of the interviews with the education leaders and the IT/facilities leaders respectively. We present these results in some detail, because there is still very little literature that reports on such matters (Smith & Adams, 2008; Floyd & Preston, 2018; Kenedi & Mountford-Zimdars, 2018). But in addition to their intrinsic interest, we also use the insights gained in order to make an important step in the core argument of the book: that the complexity of the challenges being faced by university leaders, and indeed by the whole university community, requires some additional ways of conceptualising the main issues. To help with this argument, Chapter 5 presents a capability and alignment assessment – a portrait that reveals how difficult it can be to align the processes needed to deal coherently with new educational challenges, educational technologies and learning spaces. The rest of this chapter explains how we went about this piece of the research.

Research aims

The high level aims of the research can be expressed through the following questions:

1. What organisational elements are required for effective university learning and teaching systems?
2. How are these elements related to innovation and quality assurance, especially when these concern new course designs, student learning and teaching experiences and well-integrated learning spaces?
3. How are these elements related to each other and thereby to the success of a university's education mission?

Behind these questions sits an idea that a focus on new programme and course designs, created through innovative practice, reveals how the student and teaching experience is changing, the challenges for quality assurance that this creates and how universities need to design, configure and provide physical and virtual learning space in order for programmes and courses to achieve their outcomes. In short, we suspect that all of these aspects are interrelated in ways which are not yet fully understand, and that by conceiving of their relationships in ecological terms, we are more likely to understand their subtle and complex interdependencies.

Interviewing the university leaders

We interviewed 54 senior leaders working in 39 Australian universities (see Table 2.1 below). Universities vary considerably, even within one national system, in the job titles given to senior staff. The three categories of leaders we interviewed included people with the following titles:

Educational leaders: deputy vice-chancellors (education); deputy vice-chancellors (academic); pro vice-chancellors (teaching and learning).
Technology leaders: chief information officers; directors of ICT.
Facilities leaders: directors of property, facilities or estates; university architects.

Prior to conducting each interview, members of the research team consulted the published educational strategies and related documentation available on the websites of the participating universities.

This documentation also provided some additional framing for each of the interviews.

Interviewing the education leaders

The education leaders can be defined as the most senior university leaders responsible for the learning and teaching or education strategy. (In one case, the deputy vice-chancellor nominated a director of teaching and learning to take her place.) The interviews were semi-structured with a standard set of guiding questions used for each interview. For the education leaders, the guiding interview questions were as follows:

1. What university-wide frameworks guide course design at your university? [Note: In the interview discussions 'course design' was interpreted broadly, to include programme, course and credential design.]
2. What do the changes and challenges arising in this area mean for university teachers and students?
3. What strategies exist in your institution to address these challenges?
4. What institutional impediments need to be overcome for an effective university teaching and learning system that supports innovative course design?
5. How are effective relations made between new course designs and integrated learning spaces? [Note: In discussion, 'integrated learning spaces' was used to connote integrations of physical and digital spaces, tools, resources, etc., with the aim of supporting more 'seamless' learning and teaching.]

Interviewing the technology and facilities leaders

The technology leaders are those responsible for how the digital strategy, or equivalent, supports their university's mission, including its education strategy. The participants were predominantly chief information officers or directors of IT. The facilities leaders are those who are responsible for how the estates strategy supports the university mission, including its education strategy. The participants were predominantly directors of facilities, property or estates, with an associate director sometimes being nominated instead. In two cases, we interviewed pro vice-chancellors who had responsibility in this area.

Table 2.1 Distribution of interviews across the universities

No.	University	Education leader interviews	Technology leader interviews	Facilities leader interviews	Total interviews
1.	University GG	✓			1
2.	University B		✓	✓	2
3.	University I	✓	✓		2
4.	University Q	✓			1
5.	University L		✓		1
6.	University G		✓		1
7.	University J		✓	✓	2
8.	University H		✓		1
9.	University D		✓		1
10.	University F		✓	✓	2
11.	University A		✓	✓	2
12.	University C		✓	✓✓	3
13.	University R		✓		1
14.	University L		✓	✓	2
15.	University M	✓	✓	✓	3
16.	University K			✓	1
17.	University N	✓		✓	2
18.	University X	✓		✓	2
19.	University T		✓		1
20.	University MM		✓		1
21.	University V		✓		1
22.	University FF			✓	1
23.	University U			✓	1
24.	University O			✓	1
25.	University KK	✓		✓	2
26.	University Z	✓			1
27.	University S	✓		✓	2
28.	University AA	✓			1
29.	University E		✓		1
30.	University CC		✓		1
31.	University DD	✓			1
32.	University JJ	✓			1
33.	University HH	✓			1
34.	University P	✓			1
35.	University W	✓			1
36.	University Y	✓			1
37.	University BB	✓			1
38.	University II	✓			1
39.	University EE	✓		✓	2
Total		19	18	17	54

Since we have a strong interest in whether and how thinking about the physical (facilities) and the digital (IT) come together, we focused the interviews around the idea of 'learning space'. For the technology and facilities leaders, the guiding interview questions were as follows:

1. How would you define 'learning space'? To what extent is that definition understood across your institution?
2. What strategies does your institution adopt to plan and develop learning space?
3. What can impede the effective development of learning space?
4. What things would you resolve to improve effective learning space innovation and planning?

Analysing the interview transcripts

All the interviews were recorded and fully transcribed. The questions opened up wide-ranging discussions on the links between university missions, course designs, student learning and teaching experiences, physical and virtual learning space, and innovation and quality.

Identifying major themes: key organisational elements

The interview transcripts were analysed by the broader researcher team using a thematic analysis approach (Marton and Booth, 1997; Bryman, 2015). This involved reading, discussing and re-reading the interviews, and identifying sub-themes which, through further review and synthesis, merged to become larger themes.

Five major thematic areas emerged from this stage in the analysis. These can be thought of as the main *organisational elements* featuring in the work of university leadership, namely: strategy, governance, policy, management and funding. We discovered that categorising the transcripts in terms of the insight they offered into the strategy, governance, policy, management and funding of learning and teaching systems helped to illuminate the quality and innovation issues raised by the interviewees, with respect to: courses, learning and teaching, the student experience and integrated learning space. All three sets of leaders talked about issues that were categorised as strategy, governance or management. The education leaders also reported concerns about policy and the professional leaders reported concerns about funding. These five organisational elements can be understood as follows. Bear in mind that the background to discussing each of these was consideration of new course designs and integrated learning spaces.

Strategy

Education strategy is the means by which a university community decides on key priorities for courses, curricula, learning and teaching, learning spaces, learning resources, and so on over the next time period (typically three, five or ten years). Education strategy is normally intended to complement other institution level strategies, such as research and international. Each such strategic area typically has a senior leader – typically a deputy vice-chancellor (education) (DVCE) for education strategy – and local versions of the strategy are created, implemented and monitored at lower levels in the university (e.g. faculties and departments).

Governance

Governance is the mechanism by which the university implements strategy: how decisions are made, how progress is measured, how priorities are determined, how processes need to adapt and change in order to make strategy work. Ensuring that decisions are made at the right level, by the right set of people, are key challenges for leadership in education, IT and facilities.

Policy

In the Australian context, policy frameworks tend to combine both statements of intent and procedural guidance (specifying mandated, desirable and/or prohibited actions). They provide means of connecting higher-level goals and values with specific actions 'on the ground'. Universities tend to accumulate policies; maintaining coherence can be challenging. It is primarily through policy frameworks that external agencies, such as Tertiary Education Quality and Standards Agency (TEQSA), have effects on local practices.

Management

Management connotes the processes involved in controlling and guiding the activities of the people (teaching staff, providers of infrastructure, etc.) whose work directly shapes learning opportunities and learning environments for students. Management emerged in our interviews as the most problematic aspect of leaders' work. It is in day-to-day management activities that tensions, contradictions, 'wicked problems' and other complexities of organisational life present themselves, demanding timely resolution.

Funding

Funding offers the means by which the university provides resources that enable strategy to be shaped by governance and implemented through management processes. Overall quantities of funding are important here, but so too are decisions that shape the integration, alignment and interdependence of budgets. For example, IT and facilities leaders frequently mentioned that budgets for new IT and physical space initiatives rarely acknowledged concomitant needs for funding professional development, curriculum redesign or ongoing maintenance.

A detailed account of these themes and their sub-themes is presented in Chapter 3, where we focus on the DVCE interviews. Chapter 4 offers a similar treatment of issues arising from the interviews with technology and facilities leaders.

Evaluating capability and alignment

In addition to identifying the main themes and sub-themes in the interview data, members of the broader research team also scored the transcripts and associated university documents on what they revealed about *capability* (with respect to each of the five organisational elements) and *alignment* between the organisational elements (see Table 2.2).

The top row in Table 2.2 shows the five organisational elements pertaining to university learning and teaching, IT and learning spaces. The second row shows the criteria the team used to describe how capable each element was in performing its role, and the third row highlights how the individual element needs to align to the other elements in order for the whole system to operate effectively. These capability and alignment criteria were developed from the transcripts by the researchers in an iterative process. The constructs depicted in the table are explained in more detail in Chapter 5.

For example, the capability criteria for assessing an effective university teaching and learning *strategy* include: that it is sufficiently comprehensive to guide relevant activities for new program and course designs in integrated physical and virtual learning space; that the strategy has the student at the centre of its design; that it is sufficiently teaching-informed to support teachers effectively and inform those supporting teaching; that it is clear and unambiguous in its goals; and that all relevant stakeholders feel they own the strategy.

The capability criteria for effective *governance* of the university teaching and learning system include that it represents all appropriate stakeholders, that it is sufficiently integrated into the university governance structure; that the governance structure is effective in implementing the strategy; and that it encourages a collaborative approach to strategy implementation.

The capability criteria for assessing effective *policy* for the university teaching and learning system include that it is practical, that it is informed by best practice, that it adopts a student perspective in its formulation, and that it focuses on outcomes and is externally aligned.

The capability criteria for effective *management* of the university teaching and learning system includes that it is agile, engages all stakeholders appropriately, ensures the quality of processes and outcomes, it is integrated and that it is delivered effectively.

The capability criteria for effective *funding* of the university teaching and learning system include that it is structured across operational and capital budgets appropriately, it is well balanced across the areas requiring funding, that it is prioritised through a shared sense of purpose by all stakeholders and that it is risk-managed.

Table 2.2 Capability and alignment criteria

Elements and criteria	Strategy	Governance	Policy	Management	Funding
Capability criteria	Comprehensive Student-centred Teaching-informed Clear Shared ownership	Representative Integrated Effective Collaborative	Student-centred Outcomes-focused Practical Best practice Externally-aligned	Agile Engaged Quality assured Integrated Effective delivery	Well-structured Balanced Prioritised Risk-managed
Alignment criteria	Strategy effectively informs governance, management of its implementation within funding envelopes.	Governance directs strategy and oversees its effective management and funding.	Policy reflects strategy achieved through good governance in ways that can be effectively managed within funding envelope.	Management implements strategy, directed by governance, aligned with policy within funding envelopes.	Funding effectively realises the strategy, directed by governance, aligned with policy and implemented by management.

Table 2.3 Rating schedule

Rating Description	Very poor = 1	Poor = 2	Average = 3	Very good = 4	Excellent = 5
Description of capability rating	The element does not meet capability criteria	The element meets a few capability criteria	The element meets some capability criteria	The element meets most capability criteria	The element meets all capability criteria
Description of alignment rating	The element is not aligned with the other elements	The element is partially aligned with some of the elements	The element is partially aligned with all the elements	The element is mostly aligned with all the elements	The element is completely aligned with all the elements

Note: 'Average' should be understood as a neutral midpoint – neither good nor bad. It is not an arithmetic average of the observations made.

Table 2.4 Levels of agreement amongst the researcher classifications

	Strategy		Governance		Policy		Management		Funding	
	I	C	I	C	I	C	I	C	I	C
Researcher 2	75%	90%	70%	90%	85%	100%	80%	95%	75%	90%
Researcher 3	80%	95%	75%	95%	75%	90%	85%	90%	90%	95%
Researcher 4	85%	100%	70%	90%	85%	95%	75%	90%	85%	100%

These criteria for the capability of the organisational elements of strategy, governance, policy, management and funding are discussed in more detail in Chapter 5 where we describe a maturity model emerging from our findings.

When categorising the interview extracts, the researchers also rated the interviews and associated university documents according to how *aligned* the organisational elements seemed to be in supporting learning and teaching. The researchers rated the capability and alignment of each of the elements on a scale of 1 to 5 using the above criteria. The rating schedule for capability and alignment is shown in Table 2.3.

Using the criteria described in Table 2.2 and the ratings described in Table 2.3, the researchers achieved the levels of agreement shown in Table 2.4. Column I shows the percentage agreement after an initial round of scoring. Column C shows the percentage agreement after consultations between the researchers.

Table 2.4 identifies the levels of agreement between researcher 1 and researchers 2, 3 and 4. Researcher 1 participated in classifying all the interview transcripts and related university documentation on websites. Each of researchers 2–4 classified the transcripts relating to the areas in which they had specialised understanding and experience. Researcher 2 classified the transcripts from the interviews with the educational leaders; Researcher 3 and 4 respectively classified the transcripts from the interviews with the IT and facilities leaders. The overall process was scrutinised by a fifth researcher, for content validity and internal coherence.

It is important to note that the responses in the interviews were the perceptions of the university leaders at the time of the interviews, without any opportunity for them to confirm the scope and completeness of their answers. Our purpose in classifying the transcripts and related documents was not to provide a categorical assessment of any individual institution; this would require a very different process, involving triangulation against other sources of data.

Rather, the purpose of the classification of the interview transcripts was to contribute to the development of a conceptual model of the maturity of university-level teaching and learning systems. This is discussed in more detail in Chapter 5.

Summary of Chapter 2

Chapter 2 describes the approach taken to the investigation that comprises the first part of the book. University leaders were interviewed to better understand the challenges, difficulties and successes associated with leading in the areas of education, IT and facilities. In total, 54 leaders from 39 Australian universities were interviewed, and their interview transcripts were analysed, by specialists in the areas of education, IT and facilities. After extensive iteration amongst the researchers, five high-level themes identifying key organisational elements of university leadership emerged from a classification of the transcripts: strategy, governance, policy, management and funding. Using the criteria of 'capability and alignment' the transcripts and associated university materials were rated by the researchers for completeness and integration of the organisational elements. The next two chapters present the findings from the interviews. Outcomes are synthesised in Chapter 5.

References

Bryman, A. (2015). *Social research methods*. Oxford: Oxford University Press.

Floyd, A., & Preston, D. (2018). The role of the associate dean in UK universities: distributed leadership in action? *Higher Education, 75*, 925–943.

Kenedi, G., & Mountford-Zimdars, A. (2018). Does educational expertise matter for PVCs education? A UK study of PVCs' educational background and skills. *Journal of Higher Education Policy and Management, 40*(3), 193–207.

Marton, F., & Booth, S. (1997). *Learning and awareness*. Mahwah, NJ: Lawrence Erlbaum Associates.

Smith, D., & Adams, J. (2008). Academics or executives? Continuity and change in the roles of pro-vice-chancellors. *Higher Education Quarterly, 62*(4), 340–357.

3

The views of university educational leaders

With Nicholas Klomp

As we explained in Chapter 2, analysis of the full set of transcripts from the interviews with the educational, technology and facilities leaders revealed five thematic areas. We labelled these as 'organisational elements' – strategy, governance, policy, management and funding. Of these, the education leaders did not say much about funding and the chief information officers and facilities leaders did not say much about policy. In this chapter, we share the education leaders' perspectives on the other four of these organisational elements, addressing each in turn. The major themes embrace a number of cross-cutting sub-themes. Summarising these and providing illustrative quotations from the interviews makes up the bulk of this chapter. In the last part of the chapter we also visit the topic of 'learning space' and start to make connections to themes and issues covered in Chapters 4 and 5. Many of the education leaders we interviewed held the rank of deputy vice-chancellor (education) – see Chapter 2 for further information on this. In this chapter, to keep the explanation concise, we refer to this set of interviewees as either the 'education leaders' or the 'DVCEs'. Also, to keep things focused, much of the discussion with them was framed around the challenges arising in designing new programmes, courses, curricula and credentials. For brevity, we do not always use all of these words in describing what the DVCEs had to say about their work.

Education leaders' views on effective strategy

Within a university, the *purpose of an education strategy* is to focus attention, harness activity and resources, galvanise people and processes into action, align internal systems and raise awareness of external pressures, all in order to achieve the education mission. Although much of the work done within the university is focused inward, education strategy also has to look outward. As far as possible, it needs to anticipate changes in the external environment and better position the university relative to the changing environment, including to competitor institutions. As we investigate the successes and challenges of strategy development in this chapter, it becomes evident that strategy needs to be well structured, sufficiently detailed and clear about its role in university advancement. It also becomes clear that education strategy needs to interact, integrate and align with other organisational elements (e.g. governance, policy) and with other areas of strategy (e.g. IT, facilities) in order for the whole to work effectively.

The education leaders' views on effective strategy touched on the following five sub-themes:

1. quality and innovation frameworks;
2. teaching and learning outcomes;
3. the professional development of staff;
4. change across the sector;
5. third-party strategies.

I Quality and innovation frameworks

The interviewees spoke about the fraught nature of education leadership in Australian universities. There are usually multiple education goals; sometimes these are in conflict (if only for time, attention and resources) and sometimes the tension between them threatens to generate mutually incompatible strategies. For example, putting quality assurance and innovation together in strategy development is sometimes difficult because of the different requirements and approaches they demand.

> I've often described the DVC (Education) role as a sort of uneasy blend of being an enabler and a policeman and I think that's a bit of an art form really. On the one hand you *do* have to drive innovation. You're charged with managing the organisation to ensure that you push the boundaries, know where the boundaries are and understand the educational and opportunities that arise. On the other hand, you need to know the environment in which you're working and make judgements around what you can do and what you can't do and what you have to do different ways. I think that's the art form of being a DVCE really.
>
> (University Q)

> It's the classic tension, and a healthy one, between quality assurance and quality enhancement. There's a compliance element to these roles and then at the other end there is a need to innovate … actually you need to create space to think outside the box and to think entrepreneurially as well.
>
> (University KK)

To address these different aspects of their role, the DVCEs discussed the importance of implementing quality and innovation frameworks which help guide and structure activities in these areas.

Our quality and standards framework has been really useful for saying that there are threshold expectations in terms of what we will deliver and assure our students when they come in to study 'X course' and that is a requirement across the board. So I should be able to talk to any academic staff member and ask them about how they are monitoring and assuring standards in terms of assessment in their units.

(University KK)

We're actually in the process of rebuilding our quality assurance framework around review cycles, et cetera. We're also developing a bunch of quality indicators which will inform the work of everyone in the teaching and learning space. They'll be aligned with the external indicators.

(University I)

In designing internal quality and innovation frameworks, the DVCEs referred to international and national frameworks as a point of reference. Across the Australian university sector, a few are designing their formal programmes for professional development in relation to international teaching and learning standards.

So what we did is we went for the option of the Higher Education Academy in the United Kingdom. Now the reason we went for that was partly because there was a framework there that we were familiar with. It is quite prestigious and it really focuses on individual teaching capabilities and trying to scaffold through in a more sort of formative approach, rather than trying to do workshops and sessions, which of course we do as well.

(University Z)

As mentioned in Chapter 1, since 1995 the Australian Qualifications Framework (AQF) has laid out the relationships between awards across all levels of Australian education, to improve transparency to stakeholders and better enable recognition of prior learning. It does so by describing the types of outcomes that should be achieved at each level and the associated 'volume of learning' which typically accompanies such an award. Some education leaders do not find that the framework limits innovation.

My personal view is that nothing in the Australian Qualification Framework is totally prescriptive. The AQF has certain boundaries, boundaries around volume of learning and expected learning outcomes requirements. With the exception of the entry requirements, which I think will break down over the period of time simply because it's unmanageable in a more granular atomised approach to building up learning, there's nothing in volume of learning and learning outcomes that are totally prescriptive really ... there are plenty of opportunities to be innovative.

(University Q)

But not all education leaders agreed that the national framework was sufficiently flexible for new credential and course designs.

> I mean some of the issues are about public policy, public funding and that overall architecture ... That the AQF allocates funding according to workforce needs is an inherently limiting set of issues and as long as we keep telling the world that there's something magical about three years of learning, irrespective of what career you're going into, three years is somehow the 'magical' number. And if we keep on insisting that public funding will only go into certain types of degree courses with certain volumes of learning, then we're only ever going to be able to make so much change. So there's a public policy set of issues that need to change
>
> (University BB)

With some variation in views on the flexibility of the national quality framework, and a general recognition that innovation in course design and management to improve student experiences and outcomes is needed, a common strategy across the sector over the last few years has been to simplify programme structures and pathways through degrees. Many of the education leaders talked about the benefits of removing blockages in the structure of undergraduate degrees. They seek to make it easier for students to choose the elements of their own programme, to improve student engagement through clear pathways and improve access to courses from other disciplines, to increase students' exposure to different ways of thinking.

> We've done a major revamp of undergraduate programmes in terms of the course structure and examining how they work. So that occurred in last year whereby, like at most universities, we looked at cutting down the range of 'obscure options' and getting a core set of degrees that had much clearer ways forward in terms of the design ... getting probably more clarity for students in many ways about what they can do and how they can actually work through their courses and what choices they have.
>
> (University X)

The redesign of undergraduate programmes across many universities in the sector is aimed at providing a more coherent, rational and flexible curriculum architecture. Common aspects include core components focused on disciplinary knowledge, extension courses for interdisciplinary experience and capstone units to emphasise graduate attributes and 'job-readiness'.

> We've devised the structure of the three-year degree into courses with minimum and maximum requirements for three kinds of units. So every major has a minimum requirement for what we're calling 'Disciplinary Major units'. We've also created a thing called 'Degree Core Knowledge units',

which are something like a Capstone ... Then there's a third type of unit which we're calling 'Extension and Engagement units' and these are breadth units. These are multi-disciplinary, real-world problem units that can't be delivered by a single faculty. They're funded additionally and funded as cross-faculty offerings. And the students have to do two breadth units across their three years of study in every degree. It's also where we're putting the work experience, where we can make the opportunity for degree-credited service community engagement, volunteering or degree-credited travel or study abroad.

(University W)

Even though the DVCEs recognised that overseeing quality and guiding innovation were two key areas of responsibility, there was some variation in opinion on how these two areas related. Some DVCEs found managing the tensions between quality and innovation frameworks a challenge.

I don't think that quality is going to lead to innovation. I think innovation is a different sort of head space. I think it's a cultural thing for me. It's about engendering a bit more experimentation for teachers and allowing students to come into the design process a bit more and opening up a little bit how we look at things. So I think to put quality and innovation too close together at this stage, I don't know if it would be that beneficial. Because it feels to me that it's a different set of drivers behind them. One is sectoral improvement of quality and the other is about creating a way you can actually support innovation across the piece.

(University Z)

Part of the challenge is how you manage that duality of the core business; the threshold quality expectation and those who are working outside of that more innovatively. And in the blended learning space, we're seeing that, people who are being encouraged to experiment and allowed to 'sail' if you like ... one of the main things that we try and address are these challenges of managing both sides of the organisation; the innovation and the ubiquitous standards that we expect of everyone.

(University KK)

Many of the education leaders felt that strategic development of quality and innovation should not *necessarily* be in tension with each other, even though this may occur.

I think there shouldn't be tension between quality and innovation in some ways, but I know there is. Quality frameworks, I think, need to set minimum standards for what we want. So for instance do we want everyone to be using ten assessment items in every unit that they teach? Probably not.

But we want to have a reasonable number of assessments. And so a quality framework needs to specify that and allow some consistency across the university.

(University X)

I don't see quality and innovation as a tension so much as a necessity. I mean, we need to have quality frameworks and we need to have innovation. We just need to find a way for it to work. Certainly I don't think they're mutually exclusive. You can absolutely have innovation and quality ... you need some innovation to inform quality processes if you know what I mean? Certainly a culture of stasis does not lead to quality outcomes. So you'd be encouraging innovation through the quality indicators as well.

(University I)

To actively link the two areas, many of the DVCEs took the outcomes of innovation into the area of quality oversight. Once transferable innovations in course design that are working are recognised, the DVCEs discussed how to transfer them as minimum thresholds across programmes, through a principled approach of some kind. In many cases, the DVCEs adopted a pragmatic approach to new standards for activity design across the curriculum.

It all comes down to thinking about making sure that we have the appropriate learning outcomes and that we constructively align those through to the assessment and then build the appropriate learning activities in place. We do have some principles of the curriculum change. The principles are that we: develop pre-class activity for our students and post-class activity, that we have active in-class learning, and that we also make sure that assessment is threaded through both summative and formative elements of assessment. We then allow faculties to very much flavour that to their particular areas of discipline, etc.

(University P)

Summarising the main ideas about quality and innovation, the education leaders emphasised that, in the current higher-education climate, focusing on both quality and innovation is essential to their role, but considerable work needs to be undertaken to make it clear how quality and innovation can integrate strategically and effectively. From the interviews undertaken, there seems to be a better grasp of what a quality framework involves for course development and the student experience, but there is some uncertainty about how an accompanying innovation framework is best structured and integrated. The challenge for an integrated innovation framework lies somewhere in the space between encouraging creativity and risk-taking, while at the same time not undermining a systemic approach to standards.

2 Teaching and learning outcomes

We explained in Chapter 1, drawing particularly on the work of Krause (2013), that the 'quality agenda' in Australia has been dominated by concerns for quality assurance rather than quality enhancement and that thinking about quality is strongly shaped by *outcomes-based* approaches. Some university leaders strongly espouse the belief that universities 'know what they're doing', and that they only need to know how their outcomes relate to the outcomes of other institutions (Matchett, 2011). Later in the book, we will advance an argument for paying closer attention to educational processes, not just outcomes, particularly if leaders are to play a positive role in enabling 'grassroots' developments that are inspired by innovations in other universities. (Many educational innovations travel 'horizontally' through academic fields and disciplines, rather than 'vertically' within any one university.) Understanding more about how the educational leaders thought about, and worked with information on, student outcomes is an important source of ideas for moving forward.

In pursuing their quality agendas, the education leaders reported that they have focused on a *variety* of outcomes. However, the range of outcomes sought, each providing a lens through which assessment needs to be framed, can create great complexity, which needs to be addressed through both process and outcomes-based approaches. This is often reported as being very difficult.

> Well, we have the usual assessment requirements and we have a requirement that everybody develops graduate attributes. We have employability skills embedded in them, innovation and entrepreneurship, global citizenship and sustainability thinking. We have the discipline knowledge and we have the usual rules and regulations around progression. But a layer on top of that is the strategic plan requiring around 60 per cent of students being enrolled in subjects that are taught in a blended mode ... so it's too complex. So what that's led to is a lot of kind of box-ticking... any choice becomes very complex and very difficult.
>
> (University AA)

In thinking about quality of outcomes for students, leaders referred to combinations of deep disciplinary understanding, relational understanding of interdisciplinary topics and a range of graduate attributes that are often conceived of as transferable or generic skills. Commonly used umbrella phrases included 'employability' and 'workplace readiness' skills or attributes. Activities aimed at fostering employability included various forms of 'work-integrated learning' or WIL.

> Let's start with strategy. So at the top there's the university strategy and that has some particular things that says around the types of graduates that the university wants to produce. There were big drives towards embedding

attributes within courses and programmes, so that's the big case; so a big, big push in including things around entrepreneurship, global perspective, global ability and interdisciplinarity. There was a clear space in the strategy that this was not about developing a few separate programmes that would cater for a sub-set of students. This was about embedding these in all programmes.

(University Q)

It gets back to what is the strategy of what we're looking at. It's about looking at employability and getting students into the workforce. To do that, we believe we have to put in place different placements in terms of the work-integrated learning, industry-based learning in which students can participate during their programmes. And again there's a variety of those that they can work on and that's a central feature of our university experience, work-integrated learning, to participate in those areas.

(University X)

While there was a general consensus on the *outcomes* required from work-integrated learning, there was much less general agreement on the *processes* that would ensure quality outcomes in this area. Only a few of the leaders interviewed reported a principled approach.

There are placements of some sort for the most part, so internships, short-term placements, work experiences. But we also have companies coming onto campus and setting problems for students. The key thing is it involves an external partner so that students actually have to engage with a real environment and it requires that students do something that's relevant to their programme of study. So we have that as a mandate for every undergraduate programme.

(University I)

Many of the education leaders emphasised the importance of work-integrated learning, but few felt that they had got the process exactly right. Some universities offered paid internships for three months, some offered year-long placements that counted as credit towards a degree, some offered industry-based projects that were designed and assessed in partnership with the industry sponsor, and some offered combinations of these. The message from the education leaders, about this example of change occurring in course and programme design, was that to ensure students' work-integrated learning experiences were effective and satisfactory for all stakeholders, a focus on the quality of the process was necessary to achieve outcomes which were deemed acceptable.

An intention to understand the underlying processes of strategy in more detail was a noticeable theme throughout the interviews; and it was accompanied by a lament that there was not more sector-level agreement and sustained attention on principled processes that were assessed in relation to the likelihood of achieving quality outcomes. As a consequence, strategy development without detailed operational plans accompanying them were often little more than lists of objectives, with little detail of how to go about achieving them. This is not true for all aspects of teaching and learning strategy across the sector, but for many aspects of strategy development, a sector-level understanding of processes required to achieve the necessary outcomes is embryonic, at best.

3 Professional development of staff

The education leaders were clear that strategy for new programme, course and credential design that does not address the related professional development needs of university staff would not succeed. The variety and combinations of change at present are just too great to be realised effectively and coherently in degree programmes in an unsupported environment. Consequently, effective strategy requires a clear framing and purpose for professional development that enables teaching staff to innovate in ways that also take account of quality concerns.

> I mean having a really good rigorous, supportive, academic development framework that's supported by a very effective promotions and probations area I think is critical and that's an area that we still need more work. Connecting up the PDRs, Performance Development Reviews, and having a consistency of the performance reviews, the way they're undertaken ... I think some people have been scared to go to a classroom and to use technologies more because they haven't had the right skills to do that. So for me it's building up the skills base that is critical.
>
> (University Z)

> When I first arrived we had a suite of initiatives which were specifically designed to rejuvenate excitement in teaching. So we had things like flagship programmes which got a little bit of extra money to do some of the course build and this sort of thing... Interestingly, staff picked up fairly early that there wasn't a lot of language in the strategic plan about the drivers around teaching or what that actually meant. Now there are statements around what teaching of the future looks like and the sorts of things we're going to need to do to be able to engage with learners of the future.
>
> (University Q)

The education leaders pointed out that effective professional development for teachers should aim for the types of skill sets that will promote innovative approaches to course design, including creativity.

For me it's sort of trying to bring more creativity into what we do and I think that's what innovation needs. And that's why I think of innovation is more of a cultural change I think, because it's not so much that we can just tick a box and say: 'Okay that's done!' You've got to create a context where innovation is supported and where it's actually advocated and where it's seen as a good thing, not where it's not really more of a compliance culture where we have to just do the things we did before and just make sure we just do them a bit better.

(University Z)

A number of the education leaders recommended that professional development aspirations should be tempered and developmental. On this view, there is nothing more ineffective than chopping and changing across strategic themes without the disciplinary areas in universities and their teachers being able to develop depth to their approaches.

I think probably we don't think about incrementalism enough. We try to think about the changes being these big steps. But I don't think change has to be big steps. I think it can be incremental improvements. For me the innovation piece is really around how do we shift the culture ... you've got to create an environment where people want to change and where they want to move forward and if you don't bring everyone on-board you're not going to have effective change agendas.

(University Z)

The changes and challenges facing professional development frameworks were indicative of wider changes to the role of the teacher as well as course designs.

4 Change across the sector

'Change' was a recurrent theme raised by the education leaders in the interviews. For example, there is a widespread recognition of the changing roles of the teaching profession in the higher-education context.

So I *do* think the role of the university teacher is changing substantially, whether it's the capacity to be able to teach classes digitally online or to be able to create different learning experiences for assessment and exercises within the context of spaces like clinical environments, laboratory environments. What that means is in fact it's coming, in some sort of strange way it's coming back to that's what academics do better ... The trouble is I think we've created a cohort of academics who are focused on teaching efficiency and there's a different type of design efficiency that's needed now.

(University Q)

The big changes are that teachers need to move away from didactic approaches to co-design. And they need to have skills in blended and online learning and doing it effectively to teach in that environment, through to knowledge of assessment that doesn't just include exams and multiple choice. They need to know about the use of scholarship in their learning and teaching. They need to have the digital literacy skills so that they can cope with the changing way that we're teaching.

(University X)

However, if universities are seeking change and curriculum innovation, they need to create a context in which course leaders are not penalised for experimentation.

I think the institutional requirements that we have around career progression for academic staff can be an impediment. Academic work on a typical career progression route relies heavily on the security of the status quo in terms of offering a tried and true course, getting your student evaluations and making your progression through the normal academic promotion pathway. We're not very good at making allowance for outliers and people who don't necessarily follow the typical path and fear of failure and especially in the form of student feedback as that's the only way in which we assess staff success; and they're all impediments I think to innovation.

(University KK)

Without a way to enable positive growth and change to find its place, the system as a whole suffers. In the quotation above, the point being made is that an overemphasis on quality can dampen innovation. At present in the Australian sector, quality frameworks are reflected in promotion processes but they can be ambivalent about rewarding teacher creativity. Promotion processes that encourage creativity and protect the teacher from student dissatisfaction when *some* things do not work are vital if innovation in course design and teaching is to be sustained. A key point raised by the education leaders was that changes occurring in the professional practice of teaching staff need to be properly recognised and rewarded, otherwise efforts to improve both quality and innovation are unlikely to succeed.

I think we haven't quite got our incentivisation of all of this right. So at the teaching level we have, up until quite recently, rewarded teachers who have high levels of student satisfaction. And to some extent that's been mitigating against innovation, because people who move into some of these flexible directions feel that it might hit their satisfaction bottom line and compromise their promotion performance reviews. One staff member stopped teaching online because a) he was taking a hit in his student satisfaction surveys because of innovation and b) the faculty didn't have any workload model to accommodate it.

(University N)

We've had a series of grants where academics can redesign their courses and subjects. It's been put into the promotion criteria. We have an annual teaching and learning awards where that's one of the particular categories. We've got learning and teaching fellows. But we recently had a group of academics together and I said, 'Of all the things that we've done, which has been the most important in helping you to change?' and I thought they were going to say 'grants' because that's really been the way in which they can employ people to help them make the change. But surprisingly they said it was 'recognition and reward'.

(University S)

Instead of developing integrated innovation frameworks that work as a nested part of quality frameworks, some universities are looking at other strategies to promote an innovative approach to course development. One strategy is to create a new category of teaching staff that is allotted more time for course development. Some Australian universities are making greater use of 'education-focused' staff who specialise in teaching and are allocated workload to develop new task designs and teaching approaches that better meet the needs of students.

Well, it actually means that we're looking closely at our academic workforce ... about putting education-focused staff to work innovatively with students who are under-prepared, who need additional time in small groups. That means looking at the workloads of staff and quite clearly saying to them 'we need education-focused staff who are spending more allocated time on teaching' and that means 'we will expect less of you in terms of research hours and we will give you a career path and will recognise your contribution and we will provide you with professional development'.

(University KK)

Even with a more strategic distribution of incentives across research and teaching, other key issues remain to be tackled, if innovation is to prosper in a quality-assured setting. Moreover, such issues can restrict both local innovation and its wider take-up, across each university and beyond. In some universities, the changes required to engage in supporting educational innovation may:

- be culturally at odds with prevailing practice and very slow to change;
- be hampered by existing industrial relations agreements;
- involve knowledge and/or services which are not part of a university's experience;
- seek to 'hothouse' certain innovations before they become part of mainstream activity;
- require particular technology systems that provide access to new student markets and/or educational affordances.

In such cases, universities sometimes turn to a use of third parties in teaching and learning activity.

5 Third-party strategies for teaching and learning

The growing prevalence of third-party components and partnerships across the Australian higher-education sector signals a potential tipping point for the system as a whole. While the growth in third-party strategies is significant, the experience of third-party relationships reported in the interviews was mixed.

When analysing third-party relationships with universities, it is helpful to consider them from two perspectives. The first perspective is one of relationships in which universities have an active partnership with a third party that involves profit-sharing in some way, for example from joint course delivery. The second perspective is where universities use third-party components in course design and delivery. These carry very different levels of risk, and so place different requirements on leaders and strategies.

All of the universities involved in our interviews had third-party products distributed throughout their educational provision, including components such as learning management systems and disciplinary content from publishers which they purchased through some type of annual licence and made available to faculties and their staff for course and curriculum development and delivery. Of the 39 universities involved in our interviews, only about a third said they actively pursued and managed partnerships in which there was some type of profit-sharing relationship with a third-party. The following extracts are typical of the various approaches adopted.

> We don't engage much with third parties, with the exception of the learning management system. We use tools as we need them. I've always been disappointed at the lack of interest that vendors show in trying to understand what our business is and how they can help.
>
> (University S)

> We've a significant body of international students taught through on-shore partnerships. We do the offshore as well but it's the onshore that's interesting. And so these are partners that basically deliver our degrees for us under our control and we've been doing that probably since the mid-1990s. And so over that time one of the most important questions is, 'How do you ensure the quality of the teaching that the students are getting, the quality of the assessment and the quality of the student experience and the quality of the overall qualification when they graduate?' So we've had to spend a lot of time thinking about this and putting into place a pretty all-embracing quality-control process. We actually have in the university a group that essentially mediates the relationship between our academic faculties on the

one hand, who provide the programmes and our partners on the other who do the delivery for our international students.

(University JJ)

The growth of third parties is creating new challenges for Australian education leaders: How should the risks of using or not using third parties be assessed? What markets offered by third parties are unique to their arrangement? Why couldn't my university play directly in those student markets bypassing the third party?

To sum up: the education leaders reported a number of major areas of concern, with respect to education strategy, and some others could be inferred from what they volunteered. The main issues included combining quality assurance and innovation within a single coherent strategy; providing incentives and time for teaching staff to lead and adapt to innovations; managing risks and opportunities associated with third-party providers. To this we have added: creating circumstances in which a shared understanding of the processes that lead to (or block) valued outcomes can be developed within the university. We now turn to what they said about governance and decision-making arrangements.

Education leaders' views on effective governance

The national body responsible for quality in the Australian higher-education system (the Tertiary Education Quality and Standards Agency – TEQSA) defines academic governance as follows:

Academic governance is the framework of policies, structures, relationships, systems and processes that collectively provide leadership to and oversight of a higher-education provider's academic activities (teaching, learning and scholarship, and research and research training if applicable) at an institutional level. The collective oversight of the academic community is usually exercised through a single body (e.g. an academic board, with or without sub-committees) and/or a variety of other structures (e.g. faculty boards, teaching and learning committees or course advisory committees).

(TEQSA, 2017)

The education leaders we interviewed spoke about the importance for governance of the executive teaching and learning committee, which most of them chaired and which reported to the most senior executive committee of the university, itself chaired by the vice-chancellor. They also emphasised the importance of a partnership with the highest academic authority in the university: typically an academic board composed of representatives from across the institution, reporting to a university senate or council.

In the past, when material dimensions of the learning environment – for example, digital technology – did not play such a strategic role in teaching and learning activity, a division between strategic direction, academic standards and resource allocation could be sustained. Issues could often be decided upon in a sequential fashion: a strategy was devised, it was tested to meet academic integrity and other standards, and then resources were allocated.

However, with technology becoming inextricably entwined in contemporary processes of teaching and learning, a decision to engage in a particular strategy may commit an institution to a particular position on resource allocation, or equity or privacy. It may create an ongoing funding requirement which is above the ordinary and it may also require a particular policy framework that needs to be in place before the practice of teaching and learning commences within the new strategy. In other words, these days, it is problematic if educational and resourcing decisions are decoupled. Better integration across the key organisational functions and services is necessary.

University governance arrangements are there to ensure that processes are in place to achieve outcomes. So without an ability to focus on the associations between process and outcome, governance will fail to achieve one of its key purposes. The questions the education leaders concerned themselves with included the following: Does governance have the tools in place to achieve the processes that will lead to desired outcomes? Does it have the necessary policy development, risk management and funding management tools? Governance needs to understand cultural change and what things can be measured to identify the changes required to achieve the outcomes sought.

That said, there was significant variation across the DVCE interviews about the challenges faced in the area of governance. The sub-themes that were raised included:

1. modernising governance;
2. engaging the institution;
3. student-centredness;
4. risk management.

The education leaders emphasised that poorly thought-through arrangements for governance membership and purpose meant that faculties, teaching staff and students did not get the sense that the leaders of the university were of one mind or were coordinated in their strategic approach. This further multiplies the difficulties of governance.

I Modernising governance

Many of the education leaders recognised that changes in teaching and learning strategy and practice were requiring renewed approaches to governance. They noted that if governance itself is not configured to implement strategy effectively, it can fail before it begins.

> What I would do firstly is modern governance and membership. Often the conversations that we have in the highest university committee and all the subsidiary committees, including at the faculty committees, have to be re-hashed to the inexperienced, who really are in fairly alien territory and who have come out of a long chalk-and-talk tradition. The second thing I'd do is invest an awful lot more in support structures. So, support for online development, support for work-integrated learning development, support for student engagement, and whilst we've got quite a lot, we're never quite where we want to be in the sense of being able to be deploy strategy and govern simultaneously across all parts of the university.
>
> (University W)

Modernising governance in the Australian university sector includes a move to-wards simplification. If governance processes are too bureaucratic, too restrictive and not aware of the cultural change issues involved, they can hamper ongoing development.

> Institutions, I think, sometimes form their own impediments. I suspect that over time we've become so bureaucratised in institutions, particu-larly in the learning and teaching programme accreditation. The staff have kind of adopted an approach 'we can't do this because we won't get accredited' or 'we won't be able to get through our internal course registration process'. So I think it's very much a cultural thing of trying to get people to first of all think that it can be done and licensed to do it. Academics are like, you know, got to be some of the most creative and imaginative people around. You give the space, the reward, the time to be able to do it.
>
> (University Q)

> I would say the bureaucracy that seems to proliferate around course ap-proval is an impediment. I'm all for making sure that we meet requirements and assure standards, but the process of course design and course approval seems to take on a life of its own and we seem to do very well at creating more and more bureaucracy. So I think figuring out how we are streamlined and be as nimble as we can be in terms of encouraging new course designs that don't take a year to get through the system is essential.
>
> (University KK)

Bureaucratic impediments to effective governance can come not only from in-ternal complexities, but also from external pressures. In a context of innovation and the modularisation of courses using technology, the professional bodies responsible for accrediting many of the programmes in universities can show themselves as risk-averse.

> The professional bodies would have to massively loosen up their idea around the accreditation structures. They're very locked in to volumes of learning and subjects of learning for their particular need and the modularised approach to learning will really butt up against the transferability of modules of learning, not just within Australia ... we're wasting our time if we only think about within Australia, it has to work internationally ... modularised learning is going to be difficult to sell internationally unless there's a global conversation about it.
>
> (University BB)

These external regulation and accreditation arrangements will need to adapt to the changing context of course provision if they want the education experiences of students to embrace any benefits that arise from current innovation.

In universities, much innovation in course design, learning and teaching starts in the faculties. If governance arrangements do not reflect awareness of the knowledge and capacity in faculties, then governance is likely to fail in engaging staff.

2 Engaging the institution

The education leaders emphasised that part of modernising governance was ensuring the whole institution was engaged effectively. A renewed approach to governance needed to spell out how faculties were expected to engage with the demands of changes in teaching and learning strategies. While the education leaders were in agreement about the importance of effective engagement, they were not all of the same mind about the best way to tackle it.

> Indicators of faculty engagement in university strategy are things like ensuring there's appropriate committee structures and appropriate reward mechanisms in place for teaching, so faculty teaching awards align, so there is engagement with the whole cycle. Ensuring the faculties commit sufficiently to professional development and resources. So those kind of baseline things that we need to know but we need to make sure that faculties are actually walking the walk. And ultimately we need to boil down a number of KPIs [key performance indicators] for key faculty leaders to make them accountable.
>
> (University I)

> I think academic leadership is about being able to understand the disciplinary culture of each area and somehow connect that with the student expectations, government expectations, funding and the regulations. And

> I think that impediments are about people's mindsets, about what is their job, what a course looks like, what teaching looks like and how to measure learning. All of those things are thrown up in the air. You can set the general direction to where we need to be going, but I think the implications for leadership are that you have to be very clear about your key messages, you need to check that they're being heard.
>
> (University AA)

The two quotations above present different views on engagement. In the first, the leader rests the approach on getting faculty leaders to achieve KPIs. In the second, the responsibility is allocated more to the leader who needs to be clear about the messages being sent and what is heard. To implement the intent of the less prescriptive approach (illustrated in the second quotation above), some of the education leaders engaged directly with staff in an effort to get them on board with strategy development.

> We talked to over 500 people and then asked them a couple of questions. They said, 'What's the one thing our university can do to be educationally interesting?' and 'Are you on-board with the digital agenda? What would get you on-board?' And we thought the answers would be all around technology and of course they weren't. Everyone said, 'Look! The one thing that would make the difference is if everyone were enthusiastic about teaching. That would make the biggest difference.' They said 'I'm at wherever the vice-chancellor's at'.
>
> (University M)

In many universities, unambiguous messages from the senior executive about the importance of innovating in teaching and learning were seen as fundamental for staff to engage in meaningful ways. Too often, for example, the rewards for research were higher than those for teaching, which does not encourage many staff to spend time on educational innovation.

A complementary issue raised by many of the education leaders was the difficulty of engaging across the institution successfully if the implications of strategic decisions were not properly thought through in the governance process.

> A lot of strategies at the university, particularly in learning and teaching, disappoint staff because we might do something on this and that without recognising the knock-on effects. So a simple example of that is if we're telling educators to make this transformation, but we have not thought about how to train and support our educators; or how are we then recognising them through reward, et cetera.? So there's all these different elements and we want to make sure that all came together appropriately.
>
> (University P)

To get sustained engagement across the majority of staff, the strategy and governance supporting it need to be as clear and unambiguous as possible, not least to help staff identify, and the institution avoid, unintended consequences of strategic decisions. Governance needs to inform, and be informed about, how processes achieve intended outcomes.

3 Student-centredness

Amongst all the philosophical positions adopted by the education leaders in the interviews, one of the few common themes shared by them was the importance of the student perspective. 'Student-centredness' was held up as a value that all stakeholders could recognise as being an appropriate shared objective for governance.

The education leaders stressed the importance of governance adopting a student perspective on all issues. Without considering things from the point of view of students, the quality and innovation frameworks being put in place could lead to significant student dissatisfaction or, worse, learning failure. A salient example of this foregrounding of the student relates to arrangements for the 'first-year experience'. These arrangements need to ensure there is sufficient support to enable students from all backgrounds to transition into, and thrive in, their first year of study.

> It means, for example, that we look at the core curriculum in our first year of accounting, for example, and we look at the first assessment and we look at where students often fail. And then we look at what the tertiary preparation programme has to offer and adapt that so that students are getting additional support to help them with their study and develop the skills in situ, if you like. So that's a work in progress and it's a good example of how a university has to be pretty innovative and creative in looking at the augmentation of course design beyond the core curriculum to make sure that students develop those skills early on in their first year. It means a bit more time on scheduled study time for students in class, 'seat time' if you like, whether it's online or on campus.
>
> (University KK)

Then, at the end of a course, adopting a student perspective on the quality of the experience and the relevance of the outcomes was an essential focus for both internal and external reasons.

> Quality, that's what indicated from student surveys, sort of a quantitative approach. We use a number of factors as a quantitative indicator which includes things like student satisfaction, good teaching: the sort of measurables that you get externally as well as our internal survey results. But we'd also include factors such as 'employability' and all of those sorts of things.

The data was brought together and ... success rate was another that was
included. The success rate, particularly above or below the national average,
which you can calculate. So we had a whole range of broad 'field of education' indicators that had been accrued by various programmes.

(University Q)

The student perspective was often conceived in terms of a 'life cycle'. This allowed the education leaders to identify common issues facing students at different stages of their candidature, such as those described above.

4 Risk management

In a context characterised by multiple innovation drivers, coupled with responses by some institutions to partner up with third parties in profit-sharing
arrangements, the education leaders stressed that concern for the student experience had never been so important. As some of the education leaders put it,
partnering with third parties who were more interested in increasing revenues
than in the quality of students' learning created distinct risks. Finding a way
to prioritise the quality of student learning, but also find a balance with the
interests of third-party partners, is a growing role for education governance in
universities.

Well when you partner with a for-profit corporate entity, you've got to design your quality-assurance mechanisms to ensure that there is a balance
between growth for the purposes of profit on their part and quality and
reputation ... So yes, it's often around how we balance the quality assurance
against growth.

(University GG)

I think if you allowed third parties to do their own thing, you're going
to have a concern. I think the way I look at the partnerships is I've set up
the learning and teaching framework and I have to find partners who will
work in that framework. If they can't do that, then they're not one of our
partners.

(University X)

Changes in course design, particularly changes that are dependent on technological infrastructure subject to contracts with third-party providers, create a new raft of risks that need to be managed by governance. Some of the
changes a university wants to make, for good educational reasons, turn out
to be constrained and reshaped by the contractual conditions and technology
frameworks provided by the vendors of learning systems. These also create
important governance issues for education leaders: for both current and new
arrangements.

We see through that, right? So when I was previously at a large metropolitan Australian university, we moved off a particular proprietary learning management system because we didn't want analytics to be around just one piece of software. We wanted analytics to be across the suite of what we were doing. It was all about proprietorial control of what they thought 'at risk' was and we didn't like that one bit … I had people write to me and say 'we've got this brilliant retention software. It'll improve your retention to 85 per cent!' And I write back and say, 'My retention is 94 per cent, thank you very much!' So we're deeply suspicious of proprietorial relationships with software vendors.

(University M)

The education leaders noted that academic governance needed to pay particular attention to the quality tensions that could arise when designs for courses, assessments, credentials and/or intended outcomes were partly shaped by third-party partnerships.

Most people in the sector, I think, are talking to third-party entities to help them with their course designs and there's not many I know of that are not … So I think they need to be managed very carefully, to make sure they don't go off on their own tangent and keep doing what they've done before.

(University X)

I think it's a substantial risk to be managed when credentialing relies on third-party organisations as you modularise at lower level. It's easy for that to just proliferate. For a person in my role, that just sends shivers down my spine. The governance over processes like that is absolutely critical. We need to be very clear about what are the principles around our academic governance, what do we need to sign off on, who is the team with oversight for this and as more things come into play, being very clear about who has accountability. And I'm all for being innovative and looking at different ways of constructing courses, but there has to be a strong academic governance around that. Not to choke it, but to make sure that it is enabled and sustainable, otherwise the risk is just too great.

(University KK)

Risks created by new course and credential designs in the sector have far-reaching implications for teaching, which go beyond issues to do with third parties. Governing substantial change in design that requires role changes for teaching staff can raise significant industrial relations challenges.

The industrial framework, in terms of workload allocation for example, and that includes terms and conditions, can become incredibly bureaucratic. So there is absolutely a very important place for workload agreements and enterprise agreements. But when they become so rigid as to stifle any possibility of innovation and creativity and atypical academic pathways, then I think that isn't in anyone's interest. I think there's a real balance to be struck there and flexibility is the key.

(University KK)

To address the challenges for new course delivery, Australian universities are doing more than just using third-party components. They are also recognising the importance of new types and quantities of services and support that teachers require in order to make innovative practice a part of everyday academic enterprise. The education leaders argued that governance should address all the challenges being raised by changing course designs.

More education project management support is required! Rather than trying to fit course design and subject design around the life of a busy academic who might only have two hours to spare this week and three hours next week and then something pops up, so they cancel the three hours next week. Some better type of project-supported, project-management systems and processes to design courses and subjects and to put together teaching and delivery teams ... I think part of the cultural resistance comes back to the fact that these days, we're asking too much of our academics.

(University GG)

The more the education leaders talked about the complexity of their leadership role, the clearer it became that a joined-up view of the educational context was required in order to understand which elements were most important to alter in order to achieve particular outcomes in particular areas. A holistic approach to educational leadership is needed: moving away from thinking that a single component of the learning ecology is the thing that needs to change. Instead, a focus on understanding multiple elements, their direct and indirect associations and accompanying processes, are required in order to effect change.

In summary, the education leaders argued that governance needs to be aligned to the needs of strategy in order to be effective, which involves having the right membership – people who understand teaching and learning outcomes and the changing processes involved. Engaging the institution effectively requires a holistic understanding of how processes relate to outcomes, otherwise unintended knock-on effects and/or taking the wrong pathway can thwart even the best intentions to engage staff and improve outcomes. Adopting a strongly student-centred perspective – informed by student needs and experience across all stages of their candidature – can help give focus to governance arrangements and processes. This can also give an integrity to governance that enable it to work appropriately with profit-orientated third parties and other emerging players.

Education leaders' views on effective policy

Once strategy is in place and being governed effectively, the teaching and learning policy framework comes into focus for education leaders. After introducing a new strategy, the alignment of the policy framework typically begins with a review of the extent to which existing policy will support strategy and governance, and what additions and amendments might be necessary to align the relevant policies to the rest of the system. The themes raised by the education leaders in this area included:

1. policy renewal;
2. policy-led approaches;
3. policy effectiveness.

I Policy renewal

About half of all the DVCEs we interviewed reported that their universities had undergone significant policy change over the last five years, supporting curriculum renewal and for the purposes of improving teaching and learning practice.

> We have a new curriculum white paper which contains all the priorities and policies for, and the guidance for course writing teams and that includes how we categorise every type of unit within the undergraduate and the postgraduate degrees, coursework degrees, as well as the ways in which we're providing new forms of awards within the AQF and flexibility to drop in and drop out of the programmes. We did an environmental scan of all of the pressures on universities global, national, local and that was a big part of the justification for the change. But the most important part was we tried to anticipate what . . . the students five years and ten years hence –based on what the current students are telling us – what the needs of those students are. So the fundamental premise was less a supply-based curriculum and much more a student needs-based curriculum. So it was a fundamental re-think rather than a tinkering with academic structure.
>
> (University W)

One of the key roles of policy development for curriculum renewal is quality assurance. Effective policy involves systematic review of programmes at different intervals of time.

> We have annual programme review documents which are highly quantitative, lots of detail, as well as focus-group information in them and that would inform any outcomes that took place in programmes such as Capstone courses for sure. What we developed as part of the Australian Qualification Framework compliance piece was a series of schedules which clarified

for faculties what was core to the programme (what was directed) and what was elective in terms of the structure. But beyond that there was a fair degree of flexibility for the programme convenors or course coordinators to deliver the sorts of outcomes that were required for the programme.

(University Q)

Much of the curriculum renewal over the last five years in Australian universities has involved simplifying the curriculum architecture. Policy approaches tend towards being more flexible rather than being more restrictive. The education leaders reported that such an approach is essential if a university is to encourage innovation in course design across disciplines.

Staff have to build for flexibility... We have very strict rules about our degrees being quite modular ... degrees just hook on like Lego blocks basically. But also the courses themselves should be able to be taken as options by any student ... there are a certain number of free electives that students can do anything so they should be able to access those ... the students often know sensibly about what they want put together more than we do, right ... So we have a basic rule to say the course should be available everywhere, unless it's a designated medical course or a priestly law course for which there's restricted enrolment.

(University M)

We've reduced the named degrees a lot. We had a lot of courses. So we've tried to reduce them so there's more clarity for students. But we still have a lot of flexibility and a lot of range of what they can do. It is a major undertaking. I wouldn't recommend it unless you really are very committed and you've got a very committed senior team because there's a lot of hard work and bringing everybody on-board is not straightforward. We had four-point units so we've reduced to three-point units and we've reduced assessment, we've reduced student workload, we've reduced contact time. It's a big programme of work that we went through.

(University Z)

A common approach has been to standardise curriculum structures across disciplines. Providing guidelines for the development and structure of undergraduate degrees is common. This is particularly helpful where university leaders need to be able to talk about comparability in students' experiences and to demonstrate alignment with external frameworks, university registration standards, and so on.

So the principles, the idea behind the new curriculum is really to bring inter-disciplinarity, to bring research into the curriculum and to support better transition and to be work-focused through the Capstone offerings.

And then the breadth is about group disciplinarity, learning about how to apply your knowledge in different context. So basically doing units that will support inter-disciplinarity and breadth. And then the transition unit is really about taking them through and making sure they have the right base levels of skills when they come from school and transitioning into the university experience.

(University Z)

I suspect we're going to get a great deal more sophistication around the way in which we assess outcomes. I think in time what will happen is we're going to take for granted certain of the learning outcomes we've historically had to test then acquire and spend much more time on the Capstone group work. The 'project type' of experiences for students that allow us to build in assessment, more creative ways within the context of actual hands-on learning activity. I suspect that's the way inevitably the universities will find that they can add value by creating that environment, whether it's virtually or on-campus or workplaces or however you deliver. But the assessment is going to become more sophisticated because the learning analytics are providing so much more of the immediate feedback on outcomes for students with lower-level learning outcomes.

(University Q)

External quality frameworks influence policy development. The national quality framework for university registration in Australia changed from the beginning of 2017. One of the main changes is a move to assuring learning at the level of degree programmes, rather than just at the level of individual courses.

In terms of the policy environment right now, we've made some significant policy shifts. The quality-assurance frameworks are much more up to date. We have a wholly different course-approval process and we have a wholly different course policy, which we actually just approved this year with a set of procedures underneath it that redefine the way in which we think about courses. Those design principles put the focus on degree-level learning outcomes ... thinking of degree design as an end-to-end student experience. 'What are the combination of ... flexible learning experiences we provide to students to get them to that degree-level learning outcome?'

(University N)

2 Policy-led approaches

All of the education leaders regarded policy development as an essential element in successful leadership. This is not just a matter of aligning policy to strategy. Policy is regarded as a key tool in the implementation of strategies to effect institutional change. They described a policy-led approach as necessary to promote new and renewed elements in curriculum design – as in the case of describing graduate qualities, the timely review of degrees and pathways to recognising prior learning.

> The qualities we want from our graduates are articulated in university policy, a statement of the graduate identity. So the graduate identity is the sort of next stage along from identifying what we used to call graduate attributes or something. They're all in programmes and all of those things embedded in the AQF that you have to do. So there was a focus on the curriculum to ensure currency of the professionally accredited disciplinary content but also a strong focus on those student features.
>
> (University Q)

A policy-led approach included providing principled statements about what the university wanted to achieve from its teaching and learning enterprise, in terms that could inform the practice of course designers and teachers.

> So the policy framework is really supporting new curriculum development, obviously updating our assessment policies and other sort of attached policies to the curriculum. We try to basically be principle-driven, but really trying to pick up that quality piece as well and to make sure that all of our graduates get certain sorts of skills and exposures to certain sorts of experiences.
>
> (University Z)

3 Policy effectiveness

Effective policy development includes the capacity to be able to deal with new challenges in teaching and learning activity, such as mainstreaming innovations or managing the issue of micro-credentials.

> Two years ago we initiated our blended learning initiative. That was an attempt to get us into the kind of online delivery area because the university has not been a traditional provider of distance education. And so online and blended delivery was fairly undeveloped here up until about two or three years ago. Now we have basically a learning and teaching policy which essentially drives a much more blended delivery for new programmes and that's been pushed pretty hard. So probably 40 per cent to 50 per cent of our content is now online as well as being delivered face to face.
>
> (University JJ)

Everyone's looking at these micro-credentials, the flexible pathways that may provide some different ways through degrees. So the micro is probably one several universities are looking at… You've got micro-units, you've got micro-credentialing. And if you look at a unit or a subject twelve weeks, a micro-unit is a third of a unit and so you can actually then put them together to create an entire unit or subject.

(University X)

Effective policy was recognised as being able to deal with changes to the teaching and learning enterprise as they are occurring. For example, increasing the ability of universities to assess and accredit prior learning was recognised as a growing policy challenge for many universities.

Ultimately the higher-education market won't give universities a choice. It will be the student or the customers' choice about how they obtain certain things. The educational free market means that if somebody comes to you with ten MOOCs [massive open online courses] and some completion of things like that from third parties, it's up to us to recognise and determine whether or not the evidence they've got adequately covers something that we're going to give credit for.

(University Q)

Effective policy needs to take into account changes occurring in the teaching and learning enterprise and needs to influence those changes, through recognising and promoting activity that increases the likelihood of desired outcomes being achieved.

In summary, in Australian universities, policy development is moving towards supporting more flexible degree designs, with simpler end-to-end pathways through programmes. Degrees are being redesigned to increase flexibility, to improve student choice and to strengthen interdisciplinary perspectives. They are also consolidating a core component, and focussing on programme-level learning outcomes. When new strategies are being implemented, strategic policy development requires existing policy to be realigned, so as not to blunt the cutting edge of new educational developments. But the relationship is not one way. It is synergistic, because policy can be used as a tool to effect institutional change, rather than just being reactive to new strategic directions. To have effective policy development, universities need to adapt to changes in the broader environment, such as the growing trend towards modular course design, lifelong learning and micro-credentialing. Renewed policies are only likely to have an impact if they take account of such developments in the context of the university strategy and are as unambiguous as possible, easy to understand and enforce.

Education leaders' views on effective management

Generally summarising, the area of managing new course and curriculum design processes was the most fraught of all the organisational elements discussed by the education leaders. Contributing factors were the speed of change occurring across the sector: new pedagogies, new technologies, new student markets and changing expectations about what a university experience should involve. Strengthening the impact of these factors was a lack of understanding of: the processes involved in course development that would most likely lead to desired outcomes; how the processes involved aggregated at the level of institutions to create systemic opportunities and impediments, and how activities at the chalkface – traditional and digital – should be supported.

As a group, the education leaders recognised that the way universities manage course designs, and the accompanying student and teaching experiences, needed to change in order to cope with a range of simultaneous challenges. Issues shaping effective management included:

1. managing cultural change;
2. managing quality;
3. managing innovation;
4. managing the future.

I Managing cultural change

Managing staff opinion on, and attitudes to, the changes required for new course design was recognised as one of the most difficult "challenges" by all of the education leaders.

> Change in teaching practice is profoundly emotional. If a person has a sense of identity and worth and history that are tied around notions of teaching in a particular way, you go out there and say 'sorry the sky's just fallen down', you actually challenge that person's identity. That's a hurtful thing to do ... Just imagine it from this position. You've got a class of 800, you're a professor, you've got PhD students tutoring for you and then this tutor comes along and says your students are not coming to your lectures after Week 2. That can be very threatening and upsetting for some.
>
> (University M)

> I think academics are conservative by nature and they tend to teach the way they were taught, if they haven't gone through certain new ways of teaching. I think the impediment is the change in mindset of teachers to look at things in a different way. Getting them to move away from 'Content is king!' to 'the student!' Recognising that we're teaching 'students' and realising that as soon as we teach content, by the time they graduate, some of that could be obsolete. So we have to teach students to continue to learn.
>
> (University X)

The cultural change for staff involved in innovative course design is one of the main impediments to ongoing improvement.

> The cultural change has been enormous ... there's been lots of things for academics to grapple with. Some of them feel disempowered, some of them might feel that their academic freedom is being impinged on.
>
> (University GG)

> So there's a lot of changes. I mean this is not new stuff, but I think we're at a point in time in higher education where this is just what we've got to do. Because blended learning is the new norm and teaching online for some parts of what you do could be just a 'given' in your degree programme. So that's what's going to change for teachers... The teaching side will be the major change management aspect, but it will be a necessary aspect of what we all have to do in the universities.
>
> (University X)

To help address the challenges of cultural change appropriately, a number of universities have established teaching academies, to articulate and disseminate strategies that work by those actually involved in the work. The most successful of these academies appear to be those that have faculty representatives running the academy.

> I launched a teaching academy and the important thing there was to ensure that it was not owned by the centre of the university, but making sure it was run by the faculties. So it's run by an executive with representation of one member from each faculty. They elect their own chair, they are given a healthy budget, they're given a team of administrative staff to help them and they have to make sure that they're providing opportunities that support better teaching and learning.
>
> (University P)

The education leaders recognised that new course designs often require the involvement of teams of people. However, the adjustments required by staff to fit into teams mean the interaction is not always easy.

> So there's all of the typical resistances around academics' understanding of their own discipline. We have had some pushback from teachers who kind of said, 'I don't want a learning design person telling me that assessment item's not up to scratch'. So there were all of the struggles about trying to be multi-disciplinary teams where an academic is a member of a team designing a course.
>
> (University GG)

Teachers having digital literacy skills of a certain nature that will allow them to teach and keep learning. Being savvy with the major tools that are needed in teaching now and into the future. These are becoming the norm or they should be the norm, but our teachers, a certain percentage of them I think, are still conservative and still struggling with even 'Why should we do blended learning?', you know 'I think the only way I can teach is face-to-face with a four-hour lecture'. 'I can't get through all my content in that time'. So I think we've got to move away from teaching content to teaching students.

(University X)

One common strategy which the education leaders thought was necessary was the provision of education designers who could work with teaching academics to help shape and disseminate blended activity designs that might work across the institution.

To implement strategy, we have provided full-time educational designers to faculties. All we ask in return is 10 per cent of their time back into community practice project to share good practice with each other. The single most important factor for deans is having educational designers with know-how that work with them. At least five of our faculties have then gone out and employed more educational designers themselves and educational technologists, so they now have teams sitting within each of their faculties. We work with the associate deans education on developing a roadmap of the units that those educational designers and their educators will work towards. It's been a real enabling element to have the education designers there. We've also put in six micro-studios across our campuses for people to go in and record and we've got a significant number of nano-studios as well. So it's about putting in appropriate resources, again just to enable our academics.

(University P)

One of the things that we have tried to address the fears of teachers is to have a team of developers. Actually they started with our MOOC team so people could actually design content for online people that could write on-line materials, web developers, copyright people, et cetera. And that team, we've separated them from the faculty because we're now using them as a kind of swat team to go into every area and build capacity in each of the faculties. So they next went into Arts. And when they've finished in Arts, we've got a trained up team in Arts. And then we're moving that team into another area … But there's no doubt that the need for support to academic staff is the biggest constraint on the ambitions of what we're trying to do.

(University W)

Cultural change is inevitable in the current context in which there is ongoing development and a desire for improvement. The growth of team-based approaches to course design and teaching is exacerbating the cultural challenges faced by some teaching staff. While a team-based approach is becoming increasingly common across the sector, a shared understanding of what this means for quality, innovation and procedural change is yet to be developed or properly embedded in quality and innovation frameworks across the sector.

2 Managing quality

While there was a recognition of the necessity of allowing quality frameworks to enable innovation, there are few examples of how to deal with this properly across the sector. To give one example, when innovation changes the internal structure of a programme to include elements of much smaller grain-size, then issues of quality management as well as alignment to outcomes become more complex.

> Our most recent innovative course design, which at this stage nobody else will replicate in the university, relates to a discipline which has more than 300 modules in it, each with 'X' number of hours. And the students work their own way through those modules after a bit of a standard first twelve month curriculum. It has a strong entrepreneurial bit and the students spend the last two years in four different workplaces.
>
> (University GG)

> Increasingly I think the stacking of courses, particularly in postgraduate to start with, but increasingly at undergraduate level. I think we can see across the country, at least in Australia for domestic students, a decline in interest in quite a range of postgraduate programmes. And I suspect that's because the quality is what people get with just-in-time learning from other sources now is quite good. So universities now have to play catch-up a bit in terms of being able to deliver programmes in shorter chunks, a little bit digital. But even I think executive-style and corporate-style education are a much more granular approach to assembling courses and programmes, which means that we have to think much more carefully about the framework in which we measure learning outcomes, particularly the higher order of learning outcomes.
>
> (University Q)

In such cases, and particularly in the context of the new Australian university registration standards, some leaders are considering decoupling quality assurance of outcomes at the course level and are reconstituting them at the level of whole-degree programmes.

I think it comes through a misconception really, because it suggests that there's a prescribed level of granularity to a learning outcome. I think there's an active debate to be had, as to whether our assessment framework needs to be so tightly linked to our course and programme framework? And it's an open question because I think faculties will challenge it when we come to credentials. Do you need to check-box learning outcomes at the granular level? Or do you have, at some point in time, a sufficiently robust 'exercise', 'capstone' or 'core unit', whatever you like, that lets you determine the assessment ... I do think that there's a different model where the assessment framework is not tied as close to the educational experience.

(University Q)

You could look at it from the point of view of moving away from course-based learning outcomes to programme-based learning outcomes and working the assessments so that they have to achieve those. And that's the way you would do it if you were structuring in modules. There are some universities around the globe that are doing that. So they're forgetting about the course outcomes which become too complicated in a module-based scenario as long as the student by the end of the entire degree programme has achieved five to eight big programme outcomes.

(University X)

Another significant challenge in managing quality with new course designs is student identification and authentication. For example, if students are studying off-site much of the time, and need to be examined off-site too, this can create risks.

The elephant in the room remains the delivery of credential upon identity ... authentication and verification remains ... and it is actually an issue with traditional exams as well. So how do you know the person is who they say they are when they send back the work? That's the biggest issue that people are aware of and we're really pushing to see if we can get some solutions to that.

(University M)

3 Managing innovation

Management of innovation in large courses often involves multiple stakeholders coming together to agree on numerous issues, including the infrastructure needed; for example, the virtual learning space and associated digital resources required. This can include how to manage third-party solutions.

So we did have serious disagreement about which software system would enable the atomisation of the degree into hundreds of modules successfully.

But the IT unit, the division of Learning and Teaching and the Faculty representatives sat down and resolved that ... the tensions were about the team, the learning and about the software. So we certainly took a long time to pick our system.

(University GG)

I think that technology is a given. I think we all see that as the norm these days, that we have a multitude of technologies in an eco-system for the university that needs to be structured and that is fit for purpose for the institution. So I think we're all going through that, whether it's learning management systems, or plagiarism systems, or different aspects that we're examining. I think we're getting better at that. I think it needs a lot of thought from really the central learning and teaching units and the university information technology services to come up with that infrastructure that's going to be fit for purpose for learning and teaching ... you've got to identify the technologies that prove their worth in the eco-system.

(University X)

Within Australian universities it seems clear there is a need for a better understanding of the educational affordances of new technologies and learning spaces: how these can help, influence and/or change student and teacher activities and experiences. Without a robust understanding of this kind, debates about prospective technology acquisitions are quickly reduced to haggling over features.

4 Managing the future

In looking to the future, the education leaders offered some ideas about where they thought difficulties in managing strategy implementation for learning and teaching were likely to occur.

Number one would have to be increasing the quality and extent and type of digital engagement. Digital learning I think is becoming a priority and that's not only the innovation piece. It's just really all the types of ways in which programmes are structured to enable learners to pace themselves, to get things back quickly, to use the learning analytics and those sorts of things. I think that's racked up considerably in the past couple of years and I think it's going to rack up a lot more in the future.

(University Q)

The issue around space which generally universities tend to provide and I think we are going to see a split in universities. Over the next ten years we'll see those universities that have a very clear view that the campus environment, the connection with research and knowledge creation, the innovation activities in a precinct, is something that they will retain as part of their reputation. And I suspect that the other model is much more of a virtual provision, with students typically getting together in a variety of different places from time to time that may or may not be the university's space at all. So I think that that does shape a little bit about how that sort of innovation will play out.

(University Q)

When considering the organisational elements of strategy, governance, policy and management, the education leaders recognised that improvements needed to be made to each element, and particularly in how they were used together to steer the teaching and learning enterprise.

Discussions with the educational leaders also underscored the need for a more coherent understanding of the material aspects of learning and teaching. For example, we found no evidence of a shared conceptual or terminological framework for discussing learning spaces. We turn to this in the final section of the chapter.

Education leaders' views on learning space for new course designs

A number of the education leaders talked about learning spaces using a student-centred perspective.

> Learning space is wherever the student is. It has to be seamless … all those spaces just blend.
>
> (University AA)

> I mean for me, learning space is the real learning environment that our students sit within, and that can be both physical and online and their ability to interact and collaborate with others to get the best learning experience they can.
>
> (University P)

> Learning space is anywhere really that learning occurs, same time/same place and it's also the asynchronous, different times. So all of those different configurations really offer opportunities for learning, and we just need to have the technologies to support that, but also a good pedagogical understanding of the course that underpins and facilitates learning within those spaces
>
> (University II)

> Learning space is that combination of physical spaces and of course the virtual workspace, the learning space that you have with our online element of our delivery. So there's quite a few learning spaces there really.
>
> (University JJ)

While there was general consensus that the student experience across physical and virtual learning space had to be seamless, what that *meant* was less clear. However, an absence of well-designed and integrated physical and virtual learning space was considered a real impediment to learning and teaching development. A number of the education leaders reported that many of their aspirations for new course designs were inhibited by the configurations of existing physical and virtual learning space.

> So that comes back to learning space being an integrated element. One impediment from the staff they said was, 'Well you're telling us to do all this great active learning stuff, but you're giving us no spaces to do that within'. Therefore tackling our on-campus space, both formal and informal, and saying, 'How do you bring the online elements into those spaces appropriately?' 'How do we connect best to our international campuses?', 'How do we make our online learning a social learning environment?', rather than saying, 'You're an isolated learner here and not connecting with others'. And so that made us really think about our learning spaces differently and our learning environments particularly on-campus but also all those other elements, and how did they interconnect with each other? And so what we recognised quite clearly was that unless we enable our learning environments, we can't do any of those other elements successfully and our students will not be able to achieve their learning outcomes.
>
> (University P)

> The virtual learning spaces where the students are coming online, getting materials, maybe watching video of captured lectures and tutorials and interacting in forums, I think we're not as good perhaps at integrating that with our other learning spaces as perhaps we could be and that's probably an area where we need to improve in.
>
> (University JJ)

It was in the combination of the learning activities of the discipline, interactions between students and teachers, and the integration of physical and virtual learning space that the education leaders thought most progress in teaching and learning improvements needed to be made. Many of the education leaders talked about the necessary alignment of the learning environment – the different spaces in which students and teachers find themselves – to achieve the sorts of goals and aspirations that new course designs introduced.

> The fact is we've got a campus environment that needs to be fit for purpose for the students who go there. Both undergraduate and postgraduate. But our online spaces and offshore campuses or multiple campuses have to have that same sort of look and feel as well. So space becomes probably

the unifying nature of working across the curriculum. Because it has to be aligned with what we're doing. If I want better assessment, I need better informal spaces around the campus so that students can do their group projects. Everything has to be aligned much more carefully I think. Space, technology, curriculum, the course and programme have to be all aligned. The teachers I think will need to become much more savvy with where we're going. As I said to some of my staff about blended learning: 'The whole sector has gotten over the why. We just need to work on the how.'

(University X)

It was clear from across the set of DVCE interviews that there was general agreement that new designs for integrated physical and virtual learning space were a key component of what was required for universities in Australia to achieve their aspirations for students and staff, and that the integration of these elements is very under-developed. However, when asked to describe exactly what was needed, there was less clarity on the specifics of learning space solutions for new course designs. Nor were there insights into what should be done to build the capability to achieve a better fit between educational needs and learning spaces. To better understand the challenges involved, the next chapter considers what the IT and facilities leaders think is required for the creation of effective learning spaces.

Summary of Chapter 3

The aggregated views of the DVCEs provide a snapshot of current and emerging education issues facing the Australian university sector. It was clear from the interviews that effective teaching and learning systems require strategy, governance, policy and management to work in an integrated manner: focusing on the needs of students and teachers and the aspirations of the education mission. Disturbances to established 'ecologies of learning' are being brought about by new demands, new pedagogies, new learning resources, and new course designs and credential structures. Together, these challenges and opportunities are requiring a renewal of strategy, governance, policy and management approaches in universities.

A common issue for all of the institutions involved was the difficulty of connecting the learning challenges identified in courses (the micro) to the goals expressed in strategy for the whole institution (the macro). This too requires a better understanding of how to align the needs of students, teachers, the learning activities of the curriculum, the physical and virtual learning space in which the learning and teaching takes place and the necessary support services. The next chapter looks more closely at some additional challenges in achieving this alignment.

4

The views of university technology and facilities leaders

With Kenn Fisher and Bruce Meikle

In this chapter, we share insights gained from analysing the interviews with technology and facilities leaders. The format is similar to Chapter 3, with variations that reflect the different priorities and preoccupations of the people involved. While we treat technology and facilities leaders together in this chapter, we should stress that they are quite different professions and constituencies. There are many similarities in observations from the two groups but there are also some distinctions. For this reason, the extracts from the interviews presented below identify whether they come from technology or facility leaders. For ease of reference, we have used the terms 'technology leader' or CIO (chief information officer) and 'facilities leader' in this chapter and we use the term 'professional leaders' to include both groups. A description of their roles and other titles used can be found in Chapter 2.

Many leaders from both groups acknowledged the rapidly growing overlaps between their areas of concern. Indeed, most saw as a pressing challenge the need to demolish unhelpful boundaries between the physical and the digital. Our interviews with the technology and facilities leaders began with the meanings (to them) of 'learning space' (see question schedule in Chapter 2).

Speaking at cross-purposes: developing a shared language for learning space

When teaching and learning systems are disturbed with new ideas and activity, one of the first noticeable aspects is the introduction of new language. In many cases, the more popular and influential an idea appears to be, the more the language surrounding it is co-opted by different advocacy groups in the institution to support a variety of causes. This is just one of the many pressures in an education enterprise which can lead to confusion.

The first section of this chapter provides some examples of the challenges of developing coherence in the language and concepts of learning space. The provision of effective learning space for students, teachers and courses is a shared strategic goal for technology and facility leaders and a desired outcome from faculties. However, one of the main challenges is variation in terminology and the underpinning ideas that are intended when even the same words are used. Three sub-themes emerged when we looked across the full set of transcripts:

1. Defining the elements of learning space
2. Adapting a student perspective on learning space
3. The language of innovations involving learning space

I Defining the elements of learning space

The technology and facilities leaders felt that without developing a shared language and common concepts for learning space within their institutions, time, resources and goodwill can be wasted and the education strategy impeded. A shared vocabulary and concepts for learning space have become increasingly important because of the strategic benefits provided through integrating the physical and virtual in university teaching and learning models.

In contrast to the education leaders, these two groups of professional leaders generally had a more tangible concept of learning space. Amongst the CIOs, there was general agreement about the material elements of learning space.

> Learning space is both on-campus and off-campus, it's timetabled and non-timetabled, it's wired and wireless. It's more than the LMS [learning management system] because the internet can provide as much through other services through YouTube or through Khan Academy or whatever other things you want to point to. It is much more than just the traditional sit in a lecture and then go to a lab or sit in a lecture and go to a tut (tutorial).
>
> (Technology leader, University H)

Some of the facilities leaders had a similar understanding.

> Learning spaces are both physical and virtual. Students of the university engage in both formal and informal learning … from our point of view it's not limited to the sort of physical and formal teaching spaces, learning spaces, but sort of the whole campus and even beyond that to off campus.
>
> (Facilities leader, University LL)

> I'd take it as sort of the combination of the physical and the digital. Probably with an additional dimension around time in terms of where some of these things take place. And so for me this all leads to the notion of the student experience, at the end of the day probably a better sort of notion or indicator of what we're talking about with learning spaces.
>
> (Facilities leader, University N)

Other facilities leaders did not elaborate on their concepts of learning space in ways that fully reflected students learning in combinations of physical and virtual learning space. Some tended to emphasise learning space as being predominantly physical, on-campus space.

> That would include lecture theatres, you know flat-floor spaces, tutorial spaces, but also a much more of an awareness of lab spaces and then informal spaces, the importance of informal spaces. And that's really I would say come about through interaction with students … we're giving students a lot more group work, there is a lot more interaction … So I would take learning space personally as both the formal teaching spaces and also the importance of the informal on-campus experience spaces.
>
> (Facilities leader, University A)

> It's really any space on-campus that the students occupy. So it's a social space, it's the library space, it's the labs, it's the formal classrooms, it's anywhere where they'd engage with their content, their peers or their academics.
>
> (Facilities leader, University C)

While it was clear to many of the leaders that it was strategically and practically useful to conceive of learning space as both the physical and virtual from the point of view of students, such an integrated conception was not always prevalent throughout their institutions.

> I think the reality is they are considered to be completely separate things; the online world and the physical world.
>
> (Technology leader, University B)

> Learning space development is really getting people away from fixating on just the physical spaces and rather thinking about the virtual spaces and the learning management system, all the interactions there, as an equally valid area for learning and teaching … You can do different things and better things in that combined environment sometimes than you can do face to face. So there is still that discussion in the sector about 'Can real teaching occur online?'… things like connecting with work-integrated learning. So thinking of the space of professional placements, thinking of students who are doing their physiotherapy clinic, how do we connect and bring them into the spaces of the university?
>
> (Facilities leader, University X)

As a group, the facilities leaders did not elaborate on the constituent parts of virtual learning space. In comparison, the most common concept of virtual learning space amongst the CIOs was some sort of a university-wide management system for learning, used by all students and at the centre of an ecosystem of other technologies that integrated with, and extended, its educational functions.

The centrepiece would be the learning management system and the surrounding sort of ecosystem of tools ... portals and so on, that present that formal digital learning space ... Everything from our media capture and streaming capabilities to Blackboard collaborate, right through all the web cameras, tools and components that go into that.

(Technology leader, University F)

2 Adopting a student perspective on learning space

Some of the concepts of learning space held by the professional leaders were closer to the ideas expressed by the educational leaders. Some of the technology leaders conceived of learning space as being constituted in relation to *where the student is* at any time. This conception does not separate the participant from the idea of learning space.

To us a learning space is a place where the learner chooses to be. So that might be in a 300-seater lecture theatre or that might be on the train or sitting at their office desk or any of those things and we've got that history.

(Technology leader, University L)

Well I guess very briefly, learning space would be anywhere a student learns ... So if I think of an informal digital space that could be watching YouTube at home on the tablet using Facebook or whatever. But I think there are informal digital learning spaces as opposed to formal digital learning spaces that might be the learning management system or using Blackboard to collaborate and so on.

(Technology leader, University F)

Similarly, a few facility leaders also emphasised a student perspective on how learning spaces are connected and can be used to join up experiences across formal and informal contexts.

Learning space means any sort of spaces or any space that is intended to contribute to that learning opportunity and experience... learning is an experience that goes beyond the formal and so we create learning spaces to promote and support the informal learning as well.

(Facilities leader, University K)

Spaces anywhere where a student is undertaking some learning activity. So it can be under a tree, in a coffee shop, on a park bench in the grounds or anything. It has a very broad meaning ...There are some old big lecture theatres, I think there's one around 500 seats. The other sort of learning spaces are the un-tiered ones, that have tables of five, six or seven, typically with a computer on them and then they link back to the main computer screen in the room. They're becoming more and more common ... And then the specialist areas, like laboratories, have far more flexible spaces, whether it be the super lab in the science area or in the engineering area, where everything is on wheels. So you bring in and out the equipment ... You have that natural sort of grouping and people group and regroup, and by having things on wheels, it makes it very easy to do that on tables, equipment and on chairs.

(Facilities leader, University C)

When conceptions of learning space across a university were not comprehensive and did not put the learner at the centre, the professional leaders reported finding it much harder to communicate and plan effectively with stakeholders.

And certainly one of the key measures that facilities always held up was actually student density, so how many students could you actually cram into a space of a certain size, because that was for them an efficiency measure. But it bore no relation to the pedagogy associated with what you actually wanted to do in that space, right? It was really just a brute-force metric that they were using.

(Technology leader, University J)

I wish to wave a magic wand and improve my ability to communicate ... At a meeting on Friday where I went hammer and tongs at our president of the academic board. At the end of 45 minutes we realised that we shared something in common. We both agreed, but she was using a vocabulary that was unfamiliar to me ... I need to share language, and improve my ability to learn their language. Not just use mine.

(Facilities leader, University K)

We're still not really thinking as the DVC (Education) thinks about teaching. And in terms of approach to courses, I think we're still struggling a bit too, really. It's like we do stuff and staff say they're happy, but I still think we can improve on it. I don't think we've quite got there in terms of understanding really where they're coming from. I think they're still working through some things in the whole small-group experience.

(Facilities leader, University A)

3 The language of innovations involving learning space

A student-centred view of innovations in learning space was emphasised by the professional leaders. In this view, the student experience is being supported by the innovation, while the curriculum requirements spur the innovation.

Well, I guess innovation will be really finding new ways of making students think, feel involved. People who often go a scenario where you've got a co-hort in the classroom on-campus and a cohort off-campus watching now or watching at a delayed time to make that off-campus cohort feel that they are engrossed in that learning opportunity.

(Technology leader, University L)

Innovation is 'how students are learning now?' or 'how do we want them to learn?', 'what has changed?' and then 'how do we configure either spaces or virtual environments to accommodate that?' That really changes the way you've got to think about the learning process. I mean it's immediately going to be more collaborative and ... the emphasis has shifted from the sort of cu-rated, instructor-led learning, to 'give me a whole bunch of tools and a topic and a team and I go out and learn kind of on my own with your support'.

(Technology leader, University A)

We've got a very major curriculum renewal project under way at this uni-versity. It is in recognition that we are probably not well set up to deal with that anywhere, anytime, any-place type learning methodology that is the anticipated mode going forward. And that the starting point of that would be to look at our curriculum and try and model up some more flexible as-pects of what the curriculum should be aiming to provide. And then out of that giving a more cohesive requirement to what are the services that need to go along with that.

(Facilities leader, University H)

When facilities leaders discussed concepts of innovation in learning space, more variation in what drives university-level 'innovation' was apparent. Some facili-ties leaders thought innovation was largely driven by technology.

Some of the innovation I see is driven out of the students bringing their own devices. Which means that campuses have been set up to provide the fixed classroom and provide the computer labs and provide online library catalogues. The innovation for me is where you decouple that, where anyone can have any device and you can access the online learning shell at home or on-campus. They can access their resources in classrooms, they can display their content, they can use all the tools without institutional impediments is probably where I see the innovation.

(Facilities leader, University C)

Others perceived learning to be at the centre of all learning space innovation.

I think the discourse so far has been, not completely, but largely driven by technology. What we're starting to investigate at the moment is the challenge of including the activity-based designs, the spatial, the furniture components of a room to manage a transition towards deeper learning approaches, particularly group-based learning modalities. Moving from traditional infrastructure, which is principally laid out didactically, towards more a group-based learning dynamic.

(Facilities leader, University LL)

So innovation then is driven by our understanding of learning ... That meant, for example, moving much more to campus-wide timetabling was important because no longer could the physics department have the physics lecture theatre and a physical classroom and then control their use. We want people wandering in and out of buildings because we want them to bump into different bodies of knowledge. So now we're beginning to define spaces that support this kind of innovation.

(Technology leader, University K)

Some particularly experienced leaders recognised the importance of using curriculum design as a driver for learning space innovation: allowing students to pursue ideas back and forth amongst physical and virtual space.

As far as discussions around curriculum development and how our spaces both within the formal classroom and the informal area best supports that, we still are in some of the early discussions about really supercharging the relationship between where we want the curriculum to go and how our physical and digital facilities can support that.

(Facilities leader, University FF)

At its heart, it's about spaces that are flexible in which students can go from one mode of learning to another quite seamlessly. So they might go from an academic giving instruction or directing an activity, to students working in a group and being able to manipulate that space and the resources within it to choreograph those shifts... So the virtual environment needs to foster that collaboration and connection. The physical environment ought to extend that and in some way supplement it. So students who want to, and some might be required to, can extend whatever activity they're undertaking in the virtual world with their peers and be academics in the physical environment on-campus. So the campus environment needs to reflect that need more so, and move away from the traditional kind of model of a lecture theatre supplemented by tutorial space. It needs to bridge that gap I think, create something different.

(Technology leader, University U)

Both technology and facilities leaders emphasised the difficulties created by an absence of a common language and ideas amongst stakeholders. If there is not a general understanding of the associations between student learning, the design of activities and how teachers can help students achieve learning outcomes by pursuing disciplinary understanding across virtual and physical space, then strategising and planning for effective learning space, can be significantly impeded. A lack of common concepts and a common frame of reference for learning space, one that was holistic, constituted from a student perspective and understood to be driven by innovation in learning, added to the confusion and fragmented thinking in the conversations that the professional leaders had about learning space across their institutions. As the interviews with the professional leaders in universities progressed, the view emerged that alignment of concepts and ideas amongst stakeholders also needed to be complemented by alignment of other elements of learning and teaching systems, if there was to be effective learning space development and innovation and serious progress in the area.

Throughout the interviews, the technology and facilities leaders described important capabilities their universities had, or capabilities they wished their universities had, that would enable the innovation, development and sustainability of learning space provision to meet the needs of new course designs. The capabilities that were mentioned aligned with the organisational elements identified in the interviews by the researchers: strategy, governance, management and funding. While the professional leaders felt that having significant capabilities in each of these areas was essential, each area by itself was insufficient. Analysis of the interviews indicated that more than individual element capability was required, and led to the conclusion that a close interdependency and alignment amongst all of the elements was necessary for each to be effective in its own right. For example, a learning space strategy alone without effective governance, implementation through management and sustained funding was unlikely to result in the outcomes sought. Similarly, funding without the other three elements working together would also be ineffective.

The next four sections present technology and facility leaders' views on effective strategy, governance, management and funding of learning space. As with other parts of the discussion, the shared background to these issues was a concern to meet the needs of students and teachers and new course designs.

Technology and facilities leaders' views on effective strategy for learning space

Both the technology and facilities leaders stressed the importance of a learning space strategy which addressed both physical and virtual instances of learning space and its integration from the perspective of course design and the student experience. Five sub-themes are associated with this organisational element:

1. a sufficiently detailed strategy;
2. visioning for strategy development;
3. appropriate sponsorship;

4. developing teaching staff capabilities as part of the strategy;
5. uncertainty and strategy development.

1 A sufficiently detailed strategy

The professional leaders reported that effective learning space provision was dependent on a clear university learning and teaching and/or student experience strategy, but in most cases the strategic context had not caught up yet, and the detail was insufficient.

> So we have a teaching and learning plan, which is an overall university strategy, but that plan is probably somewhat light on the detail. It's very heavy in detail in terms of development of digital learning and digital learning strategies, what's to be delivered online, what might be delivered online to support on-campus delivery. And it also has a bit to say about increasing needs in informal learning space and the need to create a sticky campus. But it's not extremely definitive in laying out how on-campus delivery is going to change in a specific way.
>
> (Technology leader, University LL)

> So I mean we have some broad sort of teaching and learning strategies and in mission statements, et cetera, or strategic plans around the improvement of the student experience. For my money those are often not specific enough to engage with this sort of more nuanced notion of what a space might be or what an experience might be, and I think they need to be made a little more practical.
>
> (Facilities leader, University N)

While sufficient details were essential, the strategy also needed to align to other key university-level strategies and policies for it to have sufficient impact.

> So we've got the university strategy more broadly, we've got the learning and teaching strategy, and we've also got the IT strategy, and I think they're pretty aligned in terms of achieving that direction.
>
> (Technology leader, University J)

> So we have a quite well-defined direction in terms of blended learning. We have a blended learning policy and we have standards for blended and online subject designs and so on. We've got quite a level of appropriately prescriptive detail around minimum standards, desirable standards in all of these sorts of things across curriculum, assessments, student interactions and educational technology and so on ... the biggest thing that helps me is the clarity of direction from the learning and teaching strategy piece.
>
> (Technology leader, University F)

A lack of a university learning and teaching or student experience strategy that explicitly guided learning space development could contribute to fragmentation throughout the institution.

> We'd have to say that, until now, we haven't had a joined-up defined student experience strategy at the university. It's been pretty much piecemeal. It's been very much driven by individual faculties and how they've approached pedagogy within their schools. But that's, we hope, certainly starting to come together in a more joined-up approach.
>
> (Technology leader, University B)

> The problem is strategy development for learning space is not coordinated. So the university does have a vision 2020 for learning and teaching but that doesn't specify the physical space. It talks about the activities they want for students and the academics to engage in in the future, but it doesn't (have enough detail) to inform the spaces we build. It says we want more real-world activities, and says we want less lectures and more collaboration-type activities, but it's not sufficiently detailed to inform the development of learning space. The IT strategy also does not specify what physical spaces we have to provide.
>
> (Facilities leader, University C)

Key amongst the observations about detailed strategy development is the importance of having student experience and defined learning outcomes driving, or at the very least informing, the integrated strategic plans. This is necessary to ensure that priorities across the various functions and disciplines across the institution have a common point of reference for priority-setting and decision-making.

2 Visioning for strategy development

The lack of ability to provide a detailed strategy for learning space was linked to a preference to 'do things as they have always been done', rather than imagine things differently.

> A thing I'd highlight is we're trying to drive the conversation around learning transformation to be more open … we're trying to drive that conversation to be a little bit more explicit and out in the open because there's quite a lot of reluctance and push-back from various areas in the university … their dominant mode is large lecture
>
> (Facilities leader, University LL)

> I look at it and think it's a real challenge because the academics probably see less about what they could do and more about what they've always done. And I don't think it's just the academic world. I think it's just human

nature. It's 'the way we've always done it and it works for me', so therefore it has to work for everybody else. And it's trying to change that sort of culture and that will only change through experience and being open to other options. So I think it's not going to happen overnight, but I think it'll ultimately change.

(Facilities leader, University M)

Developing a creative vision was difficult if key areas of the university were construed as mere service providers rather than strategic collaborators. For example, having learning space as part of a learning and teaching strategy could be undermined if the university IT unit was conceived of as a service at the level of schools rather than a strategic resource at the level of the whole institution.

Yeah, so I'd say that's less, you know not as good as it could be. The narrative I'd say is IT at our university was kind of perceived as a utility service and therefore it was resourced as a utility service. And part of my reason to come has been changing that mindset to make sure that IT is actually a strategic enabler. And you know it had reasonable traction but large bureaucratic organisations take a while to change their culture and mindsets.

(Technology leader, University F)

One of the things I'm working on right at the moment is reworking the planning around our digital strategy and this is to try and lift the whole thing up to get disruption at a business level across the organisation ... instead of having the digital themes fragmented across the organisation as we are to some degree. So we are still not good using the digital theme or the digital technology in an integrated way, even though we have mechanisms for governance in place. In fact, late this afternoon we reviewed that again as to whether we need to lift it up a level to ensure that our digital planning is well and truly encompassed within the top-level business directions that they want to take.

(Technology leader, University D)

3 Appropriate sponsorship

The professional leaders generally agreed that the right sponsor for learning space was the university's senior education leader, who needed to provide a clear vision for both learning and teaching and how learning space should help achieve the vision. Only then would strategy engage the right stakeholders and effectively shape governance and management.

Our DVC (Education) has a strategy focused on learning and innovation. So for us it's actually, it's working together with the academics, working together with the DVCE, to get the best possible outcome. It's not us work-ing alone. We also work very closely with our information technology pro-viders, to identify the best technologies with the best innovation that our academics are coming up with. So for us it's about putting those compo-nents together to actually to build great student spaces and just enhance that student experience. So it's about us working as a team and not doing it by ourselves.

(Technology leader, University S)

With the new vice-chancellor coming on-board and really promoting the small-group experience, we've got, to me, a clear direction from the top. And then each of the faculties demonstrate how they are working in this direction with their approach. And then from there we have developed a teaching space master plan which has come up with a number of key princi-ples. We've also developed what we call teaching space precincts.

(Facilities leader, University A)

However, just having the education leader involved was insufficient. The com-plexity and number of stakeholders meant that other senior members of the executive needed to be involved, including heads of faculties.

We've got a very close working relationship with all the members of our senior management group. It's an iterative process where a strategy might be developing under the leadership of a senior management group member, a provost, chancellor or a deputy vice-chancellor. Or it might come from the bottom up where we might be working with our peers across other divisions and units formulating masterplans and bringing those two things together. And we'll invariably be involved in development of all of our master plans, our senior management group leadership as well as our peers, the directors and heads of schools and their staff as well on that on that journey. So it's very much a collaborative effort.

(Technology leader, University U)

The CIOs emphasised that if all the key stakeholders of learning space did not feel connected to the strategy, its implementation and acceptance would run into a variety of problems. It is essential to ensure all senior stakeholders feel a sense of shared ownership of the learning space strategy.

So we engage with the schools. We call it our 'engagement model' rather than a 'governance model', to have some open discussions about their plans, understanding their strategic plans, et cetera. So there's a sort of a loop where we engage with the deans of schools and then the schools generally at the lowest level to bring forth what needs to be done from a technology perspective, and facilities do it too for what needs to be done from a facilities perspective. Then that goes up through the chain and ultimately the deans of school are the ones that say yes we will or we won't. And so therefore there's an ownership, I guess, of that initiative and that investment right from the word go.

(Technology leader, University G)

I think we're an organisation where, right from the vice-chancellor and the majority of his executive group, the PVC (Education) spent some very good time in educating up at that level and getting that understanding and acceptance of the digital strategy. There's still some naivety around understanding it I suppose, but the acceptance is there.

(Technology leader, University D)

4 Developing teaching staff capabilities as part of the strategy

A number of the CIOs acknowledged the importance of accompanying change management and staff development processes in learning space strategy development. The design of new activities which require students to move back and forth between physical and virtual contexts involves new ways of teaching and new course designs. The everyday teaching practices of staff can change in unexpected ways. Without these changes being managed carefully, take-up and ongoing development of new course designs would be likely to stall and university learning and teaching goals put into jeopardy.

I think a decent amount of the money would need to go into the curriculum redesign and the change management associated with getting the academics comfortable and familiar with teaching in these environments, because I don't think we should underestimate the change management impacts associated with that.

(Technology leader, University J)

I think from my perspective it's a much greater investment in training. I think whatever projects we do, we'll get the funding to do the project, but very little more and we probably need an equal amount to actually do the training on that solution, so ... change management. If you get one million dollars for a new education technology system, you probably need another million dollars for the change management and training on that, getting staff to be able to use all of the capability.

(Technology leader, University L)

Without change management and staff development, the benefits of learning space for new course designs and the student experience are unlikely to flow.

Change is dependent on the capabilities of the people involved, not just the technology.

> The take-up of new technologies is dramatically increasing, as a new generation of academics and lecturers come into university. I would suggest that, as always, you've got that 10 per cent to 20 per cent who would be pushing the boundaries of technology. There'd be another 40 per cent to 50 per cent that utilise technology, and then there's the 20 per cent to 25 per cent who push back and like to keep some of the old ways.
>
> (Technology leader, University D)

> So having a really good rigorous, realistic prioritisation approach and a sensible discussion around how long things might really take and most of the effort is going to be about change management. It's not always necessarily the technology that's the critical path. When you've got up to ten thousand staff and fifty thousand students, the bigger issues now, I think, are around change management and how much change the university can bear. Because things change at the 'people rate' of change, not the 'systems rate' of change. So that prioritisation is really important.
>
> (Technology leader, University C)

5 Uncertainty and strategy development

Some facilities leaders reported that practical concerns, and responding to rapid changes in uncertain times, can impede effective strategy development.

> The last few years, our growth in student numbers and size of the cohorts have been of such significance that we've just been literally trying to create spaces to house the students together with a bit of IT and AV [audio-visual] to allow the course to be delivered. So it's been very much the investments, decisions have been driven by timetabling.
>
> (Facilities leader, University FF)

> Our strategy, our learning space plan is not part of a master plan. The strategic context for our university is so subject to change that we can't have a master plan. We don't know what's coming up next. Things could hit us rapidly. So what we have is more of a response plan and a long-term navigational strategy that tells us where we want to go, how we want to get there and also gives us a tool that when a priority hits us. Like recently, the city decided it was going to invest several billion into building a railway line and put a railway station smack in the middle of our campus. It completely wiped out any ideas of a master plan we had.
>
> (Facilities leader, University K)

If capacity needs fluctuate unexpectedly, or external influences change the campus planning process, a strategic focus on developing the right type, quantity and location of learning and teaching spaces can be thwarted.

Another practical impediment to aligning learning space to the needs of the education strategy comes about through engaging in short-term (copy-cat) responses to what competitor universities are doing.

> We often come up against competitive forces in the higher education market. So if a competitor university develops highly innovative great quality learning spaces, the expectation is that we're here to well follow suit or offer something better to attract and retain students. So that's sort of changed the planning horizons for us in that, well, the planning horizon has been shortened considerably. The university wants to respond within a very short period to student demand. Whereas in the past, we were able to sort of plan with the understanding that student load would be at 'this level' across these different courses and we would eventually have additional data and time, et cetera. That's all gone out the window. Now I think it's fair to say for all universities, you're sort of struggling to come to terms with being the first to be adaptive, reactive and proactive.
>
> (Technology leader, University LL)

Uncertainty in the operating environment requires careful proactive strategising. Otherwise, events can thwart otherwise well-laid plans, and/or seriously delay decision-taking.

Technology and facilities leaders' views on effective governance of learning space

The technology and facilities leaders reported that while strategy is essential, without governance at the right level involving the right stakeholders, the university education goals and the contribution of learning space to those goals would be at risk. Establishing the leadership and membership of governance was a critical piece of the puzzle, and was often a difficult proposition. As discussed by these leaders, governance involves five sub-themes:

1. an absence of governance;
2. appropriate representation in governance;
3. developing the right governance committee structures;
4. university-wide leadership from governance;
5. fragmented governance.

1 An absence of governance

A notable observation from facilities leaders as a group was that there was generally not sufficient governance and leadership for the learning space agenda in most universities. When large amounts of money were involved in one specific project, there was usually clear governance for that project. However, while there might be a committee structure that notionally had responsibility to implement a unified strategy across the institution, it often proved difficult to identify *where* decisions were made and responsibility resided.

> I mean this one I think is a little fluid at the moment. I think we've got groups that are creating, have created, spaces in the past. I'm sure there's some governance documents ... there's a little bit of documentation, but the governance does need to be strengthened... I think we do need a better governance structure I suppose in terms of what we're doing, the implementation of the learning space.
>
> (Facilities leader, University U)

> We developed governance ... to have a reference group that was on the ground and included teachers who we'd identified had progressive approaches to learning and teaching and some of our more conservative divisional staff; partly as an educative process for those latter staff but also so that we had a great deal of operational involvement in the decision-making process by faculty ... Governance in the traditional academic sense was very limited in that it was me. I would turn up to the academic board and say 'Look at what we're doing'.
>
> (Facilities leader, University KK)

2 Appropriate representation in governance

Where governance exists, a difficulty commonly occurs if there is no real leader designated to pull the different areas together into a coherent whole.

> Each of our campuses has a campus infrastructure committee which is chaired by a person whose title is associate vice-chancellor ... however, there is a cross-over between areas of responsibility for the DVC (Education), DVC (students) and associate vice-chancellor of the campus. But there's no one particular leader.
>
> (Technology leader, University P)

> We've been trying to get leadership for learning space from the central education portfolio area for a long time and I think it's happening for the first time in my career. In parallel with that, the learning spaces governance group actually drove benchmarking and setting the standards around learning spaces... They involved two groups: one was an external consultant company, and one was an internal learning space specialist. So for the facilities area, when we're developing projects, we use the education portfolio as the subject matter experts for learning spaces. We don't try and tell them

anymore. We don't try and push them anymore in terms of the horizons. They're now telling us.

(Facilities leader, University O)

For most of the professional leaders, there was a desire for clarity and leadership of learning space to come from the university education leaders, with university facilities and IT units as partners, and teachers and students as clients: all of whom should be represented on governance.

Probably the good thing, though, was that the deputy vice-chancellor (education) at the time had set up a learning spaces committee. So that was her attempt, four and a half to five years ago, to try and actually bring together all of the disparate voices about what a learning space is. And so capital works were in that and so was IT as well as the faculties and other student representatives.

(Technology leader, University J)

I think we are very aligned. It hasn't always been the case in the past and we've done a lot of work around that in the last few years. ... we have governance in place that ensures that we're driven by the needs of the school and if a school needs a particular type of space, then we will work with facilities around the building and the technology requirements for that space.

(Technology leader, University G)

3 Developing the right governance committee structures

Where there is clear leadership, having the right relationships amongst the key university-wide committees was essential for the professional leaders.

The teaching space committee meets fortnightly to work through the teaching space master plan and links in with the DVC (Education) and the technology group. That gives us the sort of governance on how we say what we're planning for next year. The teaching and learning plan comes under facilities but there is a close coordination with DVC (Education) area who helped prepared it. So it actually is the two groups working together on it with technology sitting on the teaching space committee. And so we've got a couple of technology people who have been involved with teaching spaces for quite a while now.

(Facilities leader, University A)

The professional leaders reported that effective governance was more than just appropriate representation and functioning of the governing committee overseeing learning space. The committee also needed to be sufficiently senior and have sufficient influence on the other senior committees of the university. Without this, effective governance of the learning space strategy would be impeded. The experience of CIOs in this area was uneven across their universities.

> We have a central IT governance committee that has all of our executive on it, our DVC plus representation from the schools ... The deans of schools are represented on the technology governance committee but the deans of school also sit on the university executive. So we will endorse stuff in the technology governance committee but the final approval of that goes up through to university executive. So there's a sort of a loop where we engage with the deans of schools and then the schools generally at the lowest level, to bring forth what needs to be done from a technology perspective... Therefore there's an ownership of the initiative and that investment right from the word go.
>
> (Technology leader, University G)

> As most universities, we have a huge amount of committees and there are governance committees and all of those sorts of things. How they tie together to actually take that strategy and interweave it between every area of the organisation, I would say isn't achieved. And for a lot of us, I think we participate in some committees and don't get visibility of what's happening in others and there's some quite big gaps there. We try to use the IT governance committee as a lever to push things the right way where we can. But, yeah, I think that's a major gap that we have.
>
> (Technology leader, University L)

4 University-wide leadership from governance

An important dimension of effective governance is its ability to lead the disciplines in the faculties, many of whom would prefer to develop their own local solutions for learning space. This approach typically does not achieve economies of scale or suit the needs of other disciplines who would also like to use the spaces concerned. The balance between replication of services and the need for real discipline-specific variations needs to be carefully managed.

> I think the interesting challenge in universities is often working out where local diversity is required to fit particular inherently value-adding practices, and where local diversity is essentially just duplication and waste and should be gotten rid of. So around something like curriculum management, for example, we worked quite hard with the school of medicine because they have some quite distinctive needs that other disciplines don't have.
>
> (Technology leader, University F)

So that's been the major impediment, because from my perspective, it's been more driven by local requirements than it has by a university approach to these things. That's probably the main issue we've faced.

(Technology leader, University B)

Effective governance was assessed as being able to resolve tensions between the needs of individual faculties and university-wide requirements.

I think the campus learning spaces committee, moving directly under the leadership of the DVCE, is a way in which the university is trying to grapple with the tension between individual faculty and university-wide requirements. So that any teaching space that's put up, regardless of whether it's a general teaching space or specialist. Because otherwise our observation is that a faculty will try and maximise the amount of amenity that it has, that best suits their convenience and their needs in delivery. Whereas obviously if you have to develop infrastructure separately for each faculty, it'll never be as efficient as it would be with a whole-of-institution approach.

(Facilities leader, University LL)

The key message about institution-wide and local requirements for learning space seemed to be one of balance; that most spaces should be designed to be shared in ways that met the common requirements of all faculties, and that this needed to be complemented by discipline-specific spaces, which were sufficiently valued and used by particular disciplines to warrant a place in the overall space inventory.

5 Fragmented governance

A common problem reported with governance of learning space arose when it was seen as failing to join the physical and digital together. When fragmented concepts of learning space were common, separate governance structures for learning space, which did not seem to meet at an appropriate level in the university committee structure, were also common.

We've come up against that challenge here. So for instance we've got two separate committees at the moment for online versus the physical environment. We've got the infrastructure committee, which has got all the money, and you know physical infrastructure costs a lot of money by comparison.

(Technology leader, University B)

If the governance does not have sufficient specialised knowledge represented, relationships essential to the governing of learning space break down.

> Firstly, the only thing that was passing between the facilities and IT was a lot of mud-slinging. The relationship was difficult … we couldn't see eye-to-eye, as far as I could tell, on pretty much anything.
>
> (Technology leader, University J)

When we looked back at the concepts of learning space reported by the professional leaders, it was often the universities operating with fragmented conceptions of learning space that also had separate governance committees involved in guiding new course designs and the physical and virtual learning space they required.

Technology and facilities leaders' views on effective management of learning space

Looking at the interview transcripts as a whole, management of the development and support of learning space to meet the needs of new course designs is an area of rapid change in Australian universities, with intense demands coming from stakeholders. However, the internal systems in universities are not seen as fit for the task of managing the changes occurring, partly because of their pace and partly because demands are coming from many directions. Seven sub-themes emerged from this part of our analysis:

1. Uncertainty caused by disruption
2. Managing sector-level change
3. Managing a changing professional staff profile
4. Managing relationships with faculties
5. Managing the integration of facility and IT project processes
6. Disseminating effective learning space designs
7. Freeing up time for teaching staff to engage with new learning space designs

I Uncertainty caused by disruption

One of the main drivers of change mentioned by all the professional leaders is digital technology. The rate of digital disruption and the effects on student experience were commented on, as was the impact on effective management. Understandably, this was a very significant matter for the CIOs.

> Now as far as digital disruption goes, 100 per cent of the student experience will be tied up with it. Because whether they're physically on-campus or not, they're still very heavily involved in the whole digital or virtual learning space capability. All of their services are delivered online, you know 'drop the course', 'add a course', all the administrative side. All of their learning materials are digitised.
>
> (Technology leader, University D)

The demand for these kinds of innovative spaces is outstripping supply and one of the concerns that I've got is that we've got the funkiest possible teaching spaces in the new campus, but it almost creates a digital divide within the university. Because if you go to the nearby campus, there isn't anything. I think we've got to share the love around. So part of the money would be used to actually convert some of the existing traditional spaces into these next generation teaching spaces, because we genuinely believe it gives the students absolutely the best experience and that's what we want.

(Technology leader, University J)

The disruption associated with technology is occurring in all areas of learning space, in formal and informal space as well as in virtual learning space. Dealing holistically with the disruption to the student experience can be problematic when line-management accountability for it is separated.

Then when it comes to learning space infrastructure ... buildings or technology, there are central funding funds set up which are administered by governance bodies. Line-management accountability is, of course, assigned. For example my CIO has line-management accountability for the asset management plan for IT. There's no way that we'd have a DVC (technology) with line-management accountability for buildings. The line-management accountability of buildings goes to the director of facilities management.

(Technology leader, University C)

2 Managing sector-level change

An important area of change to manage, raised by the professional leaders, are external disturbances that drive sector-level activity. A current example emphasised by the CIOs is the growth of cloud services across the Australian higher education sector. This change is having unforeseen internal impacts on the funding sources that CIOs require to provide and support learning space sustainably. The growth of cloud services, such as the provision of software-as-a-service and outsourcing other IT responsibilities, are turning out to be key sources of influence on the way management and operations for learning space are occurring.

So we've actually outsourced our data centres, we've outsourced the management of our network and we're about to buy a cloud service for our collaboration capabilities. So we're on a bit of a mission to do that and a lot of that is about the agility and flexibility it gives us but it's also about sustainability. So we have contracts in place now, so this is what the management of your network costs you. It's irrefutable.

(Technology leader, University E)

We now have somewhere around 130 services that are either platform-as-a-service or software-as-a service... the capital costs and project costs that would normally be incurred within the capital programme are noted for that tranche at least within the capital management projects. For example, in my next year's capital project, I will have a project called 'Recurrent Cloud', and where we've said that we would be making a saving of a hundred thousand dollars next year by moving this item out to the Cloud, the capital projects that benefit will have a hundred thousand dollars there. When we come to next year's finance, we will move that capital money across to the recurrent budget. When we come to the end of the [three-year] tranche, then they'll rebalance a new baseline.

(Technology leader, University D)

The trend towards purchasing professional services from external suppliers is well established in the IT sector. In recent years, most Australian universities have followed suit, sometimes with unfortunate consequences for education strategy. In many cases outsourcing makes economic sense. The diversity and level of expertise in many areas means that it is nearly impossible for an in-house function to provide expertise across everything that is required for delivering an effectively functioning service. Because of limited resource pools, regional universities also struggle to attract all the skills necessary for a modern-day IT service.

The main issue that is emerging is the capacity to support the needs of the education goals of a university if too many skills are commoditised or outsourced. Creative IT people who understand the needs and intricacies of the education ecology of a particular university are required for appropriate innovation, support and industry connections. If universities do not retain a sufficient breadth and depth of local and industry knowledge to deal with disruptions and exploit new technologies in contextually appropriate ways, then the success of the education strategy will be at risk.

Ensuring that appropriate skills and capabilities are retained and developed is a balancing act. Institutions need to find the right sourcing models for commodity services or highly specialised services for which skills are not generally available, while retaining and developing appropriate innovative, integration and support skills. We return to this in Chapter 8.

3 Managing a changing professional staff profile

With changes in new technologies and in how services are provided, the profile of professional staff required for effective learning space provision is changing rapidly. A growing use of cloud services is one of the drivers creating a tension between whether to use internal or external staff for the development of learning space. Cloud services remove the need for salary costs but also reduce the in-house skills of people in the area being served by the cloud solution.

I think that the problem is that as we go 'cloud' and we start doing stuff, we're starting to lose our smart agile knowledge-workers that have expertise. We can't lose those people because we're 'clouding-out' so much that there's nothing for them to do. There was sort of a wave of outsourcing and then a subsequent one with 'cloud' that I think confused us about where our bread is buttered ... It's ultimately down to knowledge and creativity. And I think if we're going to be agile organisations, we need smart people ... It is important to have smart people in technology as it is to have smart people as your principal investigator researchers. The organisation will get held back if you don't have either one of those things.

(Technology leader, University A)

In some universities, the difficulties of providing effective project management for work on learning spaces has prompted them to close down internal capacity in favour of bringing it in from external suppliers. When this has occurred, universities often find they need to reinstate internal project management capability later on.

For the university to get behind an IT unit's ability to deliver and engage with them properly, they have to have confidence that the IT unit can deliver projects soundly ... About two years ago I believe this university made a decision that they couldn't deliver projects and disintegrated their project capability. So the whole project office, project managers and all that sort of thing were culled. And they tried to run projects just organically from within the group. Now to me, I've come from a project background, it's an incredibly efficient and scalable way to get objectives delivered within your organisation. And so what I'm seeing is the most important issue to me here is to demonstrate a sound project framework and delivery capability. It's not just about sticking a project manager there and delivery some boxes and cables to the right place at work. It's about all of that engagement and doing so right throughout the life of that project. So that capability is essential.

(Technology leader, University H)

Instead of closing down internal project management capability in favour of external contractors, many universities are seeking to find a balance between the two. As one of the CIOs noted, a university's capacity to provide innovative, integrated learning space suitable for new course designs is not a passing fad, but rather a fundamental shift in how education is provided. It is directly related to the success and cost of the university's learning and teaching model. As a consequence, it is important that universities retain some internal capability and talent for the design and provision of innovative learning spaces and draw on external vendors were appropriate.

I believe in bringing IT into the organisation. I think we are going to be in a technology-rich teaching and learning context for the next 20 years and

I don't like to look at these efforts as projects done by contractors. I really think we want a group of very highly skilled technology people who are in the space of teaching and learning and we want the intellectual horsepower for building learning environments both digital physical in our own shops. It's not something we contract or get architects to design once and then we go out to the market again and do it again. I just feel like we need our own. To be agile and to do this right we need our own long-term thinking teams that have this expertise.

(Technology leader, University A)

Internal project management is a better methodology of meeting the stakeholders' expectations from a teacher and learning perspective, and meeting their requirements. So if you have a good project methodology for addressing business-value items and you have adequate resources, small, medium, large, to meet those, you've got a much higher chance of meeting your organisation's expected outcomes.

(Technology leader, University H)

4 Managing relationships with faculties

For management of learning space to be effective, the facilities leaders emphasised the importance, and the difficulty, of getting clear requirements from faculties, teachers and students. Amongst other things, post-occupancy evaluation of new spaces is very problematic if the initial requirements are not well specified.

It's one thing which we put a lot of effort into and it's something which we invest quite heavily in, the relationships with our faculties. So that strategic planning involves the pro-vice-chancellors, the members of the senior management group, to firstly develop the capital works programme of which all the individual projects and the portfolios are comprised. And often the proposals will be developed together with those faculty heads and with the staff, the end-users who are directly affected by the work. So a lot of time is spent talking with people and often the brief is developed in a partnership style. So if we're finding challenges in getting the information, my team will remain engaged with those people that need to be providing information. And if we can't get what's required working with them, well then we'll find other ways, whether it be through heads of schools, deans or the senior management group members.

(Technology leader, University U)

While engagement with teachers and students in projects was seen as essential, they said that this was not always easy to achieve.

I think there are different cultures in the different areas of thinking across the university. There's different understanding of engagement and listening. When you come to engaging the academics ... it's always the same two or three, no matter who you approach, who would have the interest in actually becoming a part of a learning space project.

(Technology leader, University D)

When we're re-profiling our learning spaces, changing from the traditional didactic to informal peer learning, often that depends upon funding and priorities set by our facilities committee. That can occasionally feel quite disconnected from what a particular academic discipline wants to achieve at a particular time.

(Technology leader, University F)

As a group, the CIOs mentioned the importance of a close working relationship with facility and property units in universities. If there was not good communication, with integrated project management and a shared sense of purpose, then the actual mechanics of getting project management to work well for learning space innovation and development could prove to be very difficult, and faculties and their students would be left dissatisfied.

That is something that is working less well at our university. There is good intent but when we get down to project management level, operating within constraints is proving to be more of a challenge than perhaps it should be ... And I think IT, property and learning strategy need to spend longer working together before we get to projects. Because once a project starts up, when you talk to the physical guys, you can do planning and conceptualising for so long, but you just know they're itching to start the bulldozer. And so projects acquire a momentum of their own, they acquire constraints and it's very challenging sometimes to work within those constraints. So one of my reflections ... is we need to spend more time conceptualising physical or virtual learning models before we necessarily have a project standing up with a whole set of momentum around it.

(Technology leader, University F)

In some cases, processes are seen as insufficiently mature in the organisation to manage student-centred and timely input into project development.

When we are identifying space that needs to be refurbished and refreshed we tend to not really clarify how the curriculum can be developed in a manner that's as engaging as possible. So it does tend to be either a solution that's something that the consultants are happy with or something that we've done 'over there', without necessarily really working hard with our colleagues in academia about: 'Well is this the best we can do? Have we really thought hard about how we can get the highest degree of engagement with our students?' and 'How does the space and the facilities (and I'd say it's as much the technology as the physical space) contribute to that?'

(Technology leader, University P)

5 Managing the integration of facility and IT project processes

A key dimension of success in providing the type of learning space required by students and teachers emphasised by the CIOs is the agility, responsiveness and collaboration between university facilities and IT units. Facilities and property units in universities have long had the responsibility for providing physical learning and teaching space. In the past, when the intensity of technology supporting learning and teaching activity was lower, IT used to be treated as a service to the provision of physical learning and teaching space, much in the same way that lighting or security were treated.

With the evolution of new ways of learning and teaching that are more heavily dependent on IT systems, the old ways of providing IT in learning and teaching space no longer work. Rather, the design of new buildings and the design of projects to improve the university's online learning environments start with an education or learning concept, so that the whole project is geared towards the space enabling the education and learning outcomes sought by the key stakeholders.

If a learning concept is guiding the management of a learning space development project, then this has significant implications for the project management process of such projects. It often requires a rethink by the university executive about how IT and facility areas should integrate their project management processes. This is proving to be a difficult proposition and is likely to be a key area of development over the next decade in successful universities.

In terms of managing the practical difficulties of learning space redevelopment, universities have had to integrate the project management processes of specialists in facilities and IT units, one way or another.

> So I influence the capital works decisions and timetabling decisions by saying, we need to increase the number of collaborative learning spaces and collaborative classrooms and meeting rooms and we need less traditional flat floor classrooms. They will then upgrade the fabric of the room which is basically carpet and paint and whiteboards and tables and chairs and I can come along then and say well we can add mobile technology in 'Collaboration on Wheel' or COW units.
>
> (Facilities leader, University C)

We wanted to avoid the situation where facilities would refurbish rooms first, and then technology coming along and chasing the walls and putting their cabling and stuff in. I would say that services and resources as a whole division from the top has realised there's still a lot of, there was a lot of 'silo' stuff happening and so both the head of infrastructure and the head of technology have agreed that things needed to be much more integrated.

(Technology leader, University A)

6 Disseminating effective learning space designs

University professional leaders who report a satisfactory approach to the management of learning space planning and development mention using typologies for the educational functions of different learning space designs. Faculties can then choose from these and adjust to meet their requirements. The benefit of this approach appears to be in the simple presentation of ideas and consistency of language used: a major issue that we mentioned at the start of this chapter.

We meet with the architects and designers before they come back with a plan, and we also strip out the technology components of design briefs and we manage them in-house. Right! So that's allowed our university to drive a catalogue approach to all our learning spaces, a building-blocks approach, which allows us to develop new spaces through prototyping with the academics. They prototype design, furniture and technology. And once we get that model right we'll make that a category item. And then with our vendors we can scale-up and build as many of those as the university needs rapidly.

(Facilities leader, University C)

The typologies of learning space designs gaining most acceptance are those that have been derived from prototyping activity with students and teachers, involving both facilities and IT specialists.

At the moment we're working on a model for what they're calling 'web-blended rooms'. So that's a room where you can have some of the students doing activities in it, students off-campus whether they're at home or other sites and being virtually in the room. So the approach we're taking is we find a stakeholder who has come to us and said that's a need … I try and identify a stakeholder group or a group of people who've got that need and get a ground-swell of interest because I've got to convince capital works facilities management that this is a real need. So that's where we actually then say to facilities management, 'We'll prototype it!' …We'll show enough demand, we'll develop it into a new category. We actually develop the room so that it's scalable and sustainable at the lowest cost that delivers the academic what they need, not necessarily for what they want, and in a way that it will run with very light-touch support.

(Facilities leader, University C)

7 Freeing up time for teaching staff to engage with new learning space designs

Many universities can provide examples of new learning and teaching spaces that have not (yet) succeeded because neither the established approaches to teaching nor the existing learning activity designs take advantage of, or work well in, those new spaces. In many cases, time for staff to redevelop their approaches to teaching is seen as the key problem.

> From my side, a key issue is time with the academics. Their workloads are phenomenal and it takes time to change. It takes time to give people the reflective period that they need to think about making change and then to action it. That time just doesn't exist anywhere in anyone's diary, so we have to find ways of accelerating what we want to happen, which we do now. We run a lot of boot camps followed a lot with these accelerator sessions and we try to keep pushing forward. But for me the thing that stops the academic, that holds back the academic adoption of the new spaces is just their time to think about what they need to change and that's my biggest problem.
>
> (Facilities leader, University F)

> The academic staff have to really redesign their academic degree programmes. You can't just turn up for a chalk and talk using the new technology. It just doesn't work. You can't just do it. Our university has been good in giving people time. They're taking them off-line from teaching for six months to allow them to rework all their programmes so they could be rolled out in a new way. But that comes at a cost and it requires the academics to be interested in doing it that way. So that was something that was a strain.
>
> (Technology leader, University C)

Technology and facilities leaders' views on strategic and sustainable funding approaches for learning space

Designing flows of funding to best meet the education mission of the university was a theme raised by both the technology and facilities leaders. While there are similarities in the concerns of the two areas, there are noticeable differences in how funding impacts on IT operations and facilities operations. For IT, disturbances in the sector caused by continuing technological advances created ongoing difficulties for effective budget planning. For facilities leaders, the scale of backlog maintenance has a systemic impact on many areas of operations. We identified six sub-themes:

1. Designing effective budget structures
2. Institutional acceptance of learning space budgets

3. The true cost of learning space provision
4. Sector-wide backlog maintenance of learning space
5. Maintaining separate budgets for physical and virtual learning space
6. Measuring outcomes

1 Designing effective budget structures

Summarising broadly, professional leaders revealed that strategic and sustained funding models for learning space are changing in particular ways in two main areas: operations expenditure (a significant proportion devoted to staff costs, licences, equipment leases) and capital funding. For example, changes to capital funding include determining what technology items should be bought outright, what should be leased and what should be licensed. Some of the CIOs argued that there is a strategic benefit in dividing operating costs into two further areas: the costs of running central IT, such as salary costs, and university-wide costs which are directly connected to faculty operations but which are managed by central IT so as to benefit from economies of scale. An example of this in the IT area is the funding strategy associated with software-as-a-service costs.

> I get an operational budget which is ... probably about 90 per cent staff costs ... there'd be somewhere around about 400 to 450 staff ... to run everyday operations. I get another fund called a recurrent fund, an electronic infra-structure recurrent fund which covers all of our support agreements, licence agreements, et cetera. I get a capital plan, an electronic infrastructure capital plan fund which can range anywhere from twenty million dollars to thirty million dollars a year depending on the work that's being done and that fund is managed through what we call the chairs of those four portfolios. So the four of us come together as the chairs of portfolio and we look at the split across the key theme areas, across student research at our university and infrastructure of where that money should go and then the appropriate, if you like, champions or sponsors and the DVC look at what their money has to be spent on and where they want to take it.
>
> (Technology leader, University D)

When technology is a particularly important part of learning space design, the absence of CIO input into the design of the capital funding model can create problems downstream for the IT component of projects.

> When we come to actually doing, I'm just talking about physical spaces at this point in time, when we come to either building new or renovating current physical spaces, the budget is held separately for all of that. What we find on many occasions is that the technology component of that, because it normally comes towards the fit-out in the last stages, that it gets squeezed

because of the budget. There may be a budget overrun in the physical aspects, so therefore there's less money for the technology in the virtual fit-out
as we go through all of that.

(Technology leader, University D)

Specialist knowledge during budget design processes is required in order to
manage budgets strategically. For example, the transition from capital to operational budgets for learning space needs attention, so that building and technology budgets can deal with conflicting external and internal pressures more
effectively.

So there is a single funding model for large projects. If we're doing a new
building, the new building has a budget for physical construction and technology, which are out of the same capital budget. Of course we then transition to different operating budgets, but there is a single design, there is
engagement and so on. It is, in my view, something that we need to continue
to work really hard at because it's not as smooth as it should be right now.

(Technology leader, University F)

Budget planning for learning space is also being influenced by new drivers and
competition in the area. Some of the facility leaders explained that they were
expected to use capital budgets on short notice to provide new learning spaces,
as a drawcard to maintain or increase student numbers. This is an approach to
campus development for which they are not always prepared.

In terms of offering something that appeals to a student market, if a competing university develops highly innovative great quality learning practices,
the expectation is that we're here to well basically follow suit or offer something better to attract and retain. So that's sort of changed the planning
horizons for us in that, well, the planning horizon has been caught short
considerably in that the university wants to respond within a very short
period as to demand. Whereas in the past, we were able to sort of plan with
the understanding that load would be at 'this' level across these different
courses and we would eventually have additional evidence, et cetera. That's
all gone out the window.

(Facilities leader, University LL)

I was talking to a facilities leader yesterday from the one of the Go8 universities and he said they had evidence for one room, that when they changed
it from a lecture theatre to a group work area, it showed less drop-out rate
and better student satisfaction. They're using that evidence to then convince
[stakeholders] about what they are going to do in the next stage. So I think
it's going to be challenging.

(Facilities leader, University X)

2 Institutional acceptance of learning space budgets

Professional leaders who report a university-wide governance structure overseeing their budgets have less friction and resistance in maintaining the distinctions and levels amongst their capital and operational budgets. The existence of a strategic framework providing the context for governance and budget, in a way that is related to the needs of new course designs, is essential. If things are working well in terms strategy and governance, then the real issue to be discussed amongst stakeholders is which projects are prioritised and funded in which order.

> So we've got the university strategy more broadly, we've got the learning and teaching strategy and we've also got the IT strategy and I think they're pretty aligned in terms of achieving integrated learning space. The key issue though is cost. I mean we don't have the funding immediately available or the capacity to convert 550 rooms into this style … prioritisation tends to come out of the capital planning process. So we've got a capital plan that spends a hundred million dollars a year on new and refurbishments of spaces so it really ties into that.
>
> (Technology leader, University J)

When IT elements that are part of operational or capital funding envelopes are not well understood, the CIO can be placed in a difficult position trying to maintain a quality of service and support to students and teaching staff. Having a university strategy on learning space is essential to deal with the difficulties.

> I've had to go forward to win funding and win the resources to do things … really structured around the university's strategy. Recognising that I'm not going to be able to satisfy all faculties and all schools in that, but at least if we provide a foundation that then they can, in an agile way, apply their own pedagogical approach to teaching and learning. Then that satisfies a certain requirement. But yeah I guess … we haven't had a defined strategy and therefore we haven't had to define an investment plan in these kind of things and it's been very piecemeal up until this point.
>
> (Technology leader, University B)

Without defined strategies for learning space, derived from the teaching and learning strategy, it is difficult for the CIOs to sustain minimum levels of support and standards of technology. In part, this is because the total cost of providing, supporting and replacing technologies is not made explicit.

3 The true cost of learning space provision

The technology leaders argued that criteria for prioritising learning space projects should be based mostly on strategy. Many used student and/or staff numbers as a way of allocating funding and priority for projects, which was felt to be problematic.

There was, however, a call for identifying the true cost of learning space provision to faculties by some of the CIOs, so that elements of equity and rationality could contribute to decision-making about which projects were prioritised.

> Our central services costs at this university are apportioned based on FTE (full-time equivalent) across the university. To me that's actually a very unfair allocation … because some schools are very low users of technology who don't require much technology to do what they do and there are other schools who really push the boundaries in their use of technology … we've implemented some IT service costs in software to start capturing that sort of information … it's not about a user-pay system, but it is about the university having a better understanding of the true cost of delivering a course in any particular area because at the moment what's happening is cost subsidisation.
>
> (Technology leader, University G)

Without understanding the true costs of servicing technology in learning spaces for faculties and schools, the university executive and faculties are likely to have divergent expectations about what variety of learning space designs and levels of service the different disciplines could reasonably expect.

> I think that (cost allocation) is a decision, it's a business decision. What I want to know is what is the true cost of servicing the different parts of the university … So at the moment there's a disconnect between the constraints we have in supplying the services and the demand for the services. There's an unrealistic expectation that we can deliver those services for that dollar amount. So we need as much information as we can to show that. What will happen is you never meet expectations, or conversely your service levels will start to slip away because you're neglecting some work to do the stuff that the noisy, you know the noisy ones, are wanting you to do. So it's really just for the university to understand the true cost of what we do, for the university to be able to make choices about whether we will do, or we won't do, that.
>
> (Technology leader, University G)

The true cost of learning space, one that is often an impediment to its effective provision and support, is related to the total life costs of assets purchased with capital funding. In the facilities budget, this would involve calculating how frequently rooms can be renovated, such as every eight, ten or twelve years. For the IT budget, it is often the case that a capital project can fund significant growth in technology and service provision to students and teachers, but the operational costs of continuing to support those technologies as part of normal operations are not factored into annual operational budgets.

> From a funding perspective we have challenges in that new capital for buildings may often include some provision for the initial purchase of new technology

under the capital programme, under the building programme. But there is a very big disconnect when you go and buy millions of dollars' worth of new technology, but the operational budgets aren't modified to factor in the ongoing maintenance ... Unless you're also looking at the total cost of ownership and you're looking at the future requirements, year-on-year requirements that are supportive of those environments, then I think we have some major disconnects that can occur. If it's not attended to properly, it can cause operational issues and also increasing support and maintenance cost issues which place pressure on other programmes if it's not dealt with holistically.

(Technology leader, University C)

The problems emanating from total life-cycle costs of technology provision in learning spaces can be exacerbated with 'software-as-a-service' models. Software-as-a-service and cloud computing models replace the procurement of software, hardware and ongoing support costs of new technologies with contracts in which the external vendor manages all of these aspects and makes the software available to students and teachers as a supported service. Problems can occur when funding of previously capital-based activities are no longer funded from capital budgets, but need to be funded from operational budgets. This means that after the capital project concludes, the subsequent annual costs are considered operational costs. Funding models that do not recognise this shift diminish the funds for available for operations.

We have difficulty in moving costs from capital to operational ... we don't capitalise intangibles. So there is already recognition that if you have a physical piece of property you can capitalise that and take all of the advantage of defraying your costs over the useful life of the asset. But if it's not a physical asset so a piece of software or a bit of infrastructure reliant on software and implementation, that's an operational expense and so you have to acquit that out of your operational, your annual operational budget ... it potentially opens up what you can implement under a capital model versus what you have to acquit within your operational annual budget.

(Technology leader, University H)

Identifying the true cost of learning space provision, including its support, was deemed to be a key contributor to helping a university shape its behaviour and expectations about what was sustainable and strategically acceptable.

4 Sector-wide backlog maintenance of learning space

Most of the facility leaders, and many of the IT leaders, had significant concerns about the size of backlog maintenance of learning space, which were thought to be creating a serious impediment to raising general standards across the sector. When designing flows of funding to improve the overall quality of the learning space inventory, the size of the budget required to bring up aging stock to new minimum standards is often prohibitive.

> Probably the biggest one, and I've no doubt the biggest one for a lot of universities, is the budget. Obviously the cost is significant and competes with a lot of other priorities, which means you have to move in waves across an institution when you're starting from a fairly low base. You've got the minimum standards which have to be dealt with fairly urgently across huge numbers of teaching spaces, and then on top of that, you want to do things that are actually going to advance practise. And that's far more expensive, particularly the integration of technology and when you start moving walls and ripping out lecture theatres. So budget is a major issues in terms of how fast and how well we could progress.
> (Facilities leader, University KK)

The sustainability implications of renewing aging stock and dealing with backlog maintenance is magnified when old is swapped for new and the new is technologically richer.

> They're expensive spaces. All that educational equipment they have on the student benches cost a lot of money and these days it gets dated very quickly particularly because it's driven by computers and things are changing. So the idea is to have equipment and spaces that could be shared. For example, the idea of a super teaching laboratory in the sciences is that you can have several different classes in there using the technology with a capacity of 150–200 seats … So if you make sure that your expensive teaching laboratory space is used more heavily than it was in the past, then you can afford to replace the equipment more quickly and so it stays contemporary rather than out of date because you can't afford to change your equipment.
> (Facilities leader, University C)

Cost increases in new physical learning space designs are not only related to technology. There is a growing awareness of the potential benefits of removing or reducing lecture theatres, but the additional teaching costs that arise when teaching smaller classes can prove to be a barrier.

> The business model I think for, say, the large lecture theatres could be one aspect. I think what we're talking about for our learning and teaching strategy in the future, we're talking about shaping what we're doing in these spaces with the blended environment. I think there are some challenges … I think one of the things that we're going to have to do is be convincing to people on the financial side, that although it's financially viable to teach 1:500 students, is it the best thing that we want to be known for? And I think in some ways, I'd rather have classes of 50.
> (Facilities leader, University X)

5 Maintaining separate budgets for physical and virtual learning space

In contrast to conceptualising and designing physical and virtual learning space as an integrated whole, there was a preference amongst the professional leaders for differences in how to fund the development of physical and virtual learning space. For large projects like buildings, there was some appetite to integrate capital sources of funding. For smaller projects, including systematic renewal of technologies, there was a preference for separate budgets.

> When we do planning, like if the university demolishes a building like the science and engineering building or the new education precinct, it will bundle the capital and the IT funding for the whole building together ... So for the new buildings and new precincts, it's capitalised altogether, if that makes sense. For the bread and butter refurbishment [of existing space] that happens on big campuses, it's separate.
>
> (Facilities leader, University C)

One of the reasons for maintaining separate budgets in some cases is the different timelines for new builds versus refurbishment, and the knock-on effects for the student experience.

> So the major precincts builds are only like every five years and that's capitalised together, so the build and IT costs are a big bucket. But a lot of what the students experience on a day-to-day basis comes from refurbishment and is separate.
>
> (Facilities leader, University C)

Another reason for not combining the operational budgets of learning space include the different project management risks and approaches to professional practice between facilities and IT.

> Facilities and IT operational budgets were combined until I got here and part of my remit as the new CIO was to separate IT. And to be honest, that was good for IT and for the organisation because IT was sort of the poor step-child ... It was that sort of fate-sharing that wasn't working. I used to run property at my previous university in addition to IT ... Property's three, four or five times as big with huge lumpy capital flows and while IT is big and getting bigger, it's really not the same scale of beast.
>
> (Technology leader, University A)

> There's a really deep cultural division. Whereas IT is largely self-managed with some help from the outside world, the property world is almost all [external] contractors. And it's really a series of vendor negotiations, contracts

and control of those contracts. What I was finding was the executive were tending to think the same way about IT and so you wanted to make a simple change to a webpage and we would hire a contractor to do it, with all the unintended cost and control elements.

(Technology leader, University A)

Adopting a separate approach to funding responsibility and management between the areas of facilities and IT in universities means projects for the innovation and development of new learning space have to be managed in carefully integrated ways, otherwise the outcomes are likely to be less than satisfactory. In addition to managing quality assurance of contractors' work in facility projects, one of the strategies that the professional leaders suggested to address this was to have student- and teaching-focused outcome measures attached to projects that deliver integrated learning space. The facilities and IT staff would have to address the same set of outcome measures, rather than each answering to more technology- or facility-centric targets. None of the leaders saw this as a simple matter.

6 Measuring outcomes

One of the most contentious areas of funding management was how to define and measure outcomes from learning space projects. Finding direct measures of investment in learning space that relate to the benefits for new course designs is problematic. When measuring the benefit of learning space projects, a number of the CIOs argued that the accounting treatment of IT costs should be assessed in relation to the income generated from student enrolments and other educational benefits. Some technology leaders reported that IT costs for innovative learning space design were continuing to be treated solely as a cost, and not a strategic ingredient which made the income from new course designs possible.

Different universities have different models with the way they manage their budget. The way ours is managed here is the greater proportion obviously goes to the school, then what's left over gets divvied up. We've got a very centralised service delivery model for our common services across the university and there's some resentment from the schools about how much money the service centres get, but ... we don't create the demand for that technology and I think that's a bit of an issue. I think from a cost effectiveness way, our model's not bad, but I think the understanding that technology's actually integral to teaching and learning and research. It's not something that 'we do' that creates this added cost that everybody resents.

(Technology leader, University G)

To assist the argument for improving the design of university learning space, some universities have brought a number of different metrics to bear: to convince the different stakeholders involved, particularly finance.

I know the vice chancellor is on the same page, I think she's very keen. The first discussion I had here probably 12 months ago was 'How do we get rid of large lecture theatres?' I think it's getting the pieces together to allow that. I think facilities will be fine, I think it's going to be the finance side, the timetabling, the modelling in terms of return on investment. I think things like retention, employability, student satisfaction, the failure rate, et cetera, all the KPIs [key performance indicators] that are evaluated are going to be so important.

(Facilities leader, University X)

We also collect a lot of data, universities are exceptionally good at data collection, and using some of that data to help us understand the movements of students and what they do and don't like ... like the thermal counters that we have in a lot of our classrooms which provides data on how many students attend courses. And we know factually that for the first three, maybe four weeks of a semester they attend religiously, numbers dropping off, and then by week four to five they've dropped off significantly, and it's trying to work out what that means. So that data there provides us some support in developing strategies around teaching.

(Facilities leader, University M)

Summary of Chapter 4

Chapter 4 has reported on the views of technology leaders and facilities leaders from across the Australian university sector. The concept of 'learning space' was used as the initial focus for discussions because it provides a student-centred, common point of concern for IT and facilities leaders. It enabled a way of thinking about their combined efforts to achieve the outcomes sought by education leaders, who are themselves looking to improve the student and teaching experience, in part through new course designs and new combinations of integrated learning spaces.

The professional leaders shared with us their views on concepts and language for learning space, strategy development and the governance, management and funding required to implement strategy. Taken together, the views reported by the professional leaders contribute to our growing sense of the challenges involved in integrating education, IT and facilities thinking. We take this forward in the next chapter, where we try to summarise a number of the high-level concerns that have emerged in this chapter and Chapter 3, and look more closely at variations in capability, alignment and maturity.

5

Emerging issues

Balance, integration, capability and alignment

With Bruce Meikle

Chapters 3 and 4 shared the perspectives of Australian university leaders responsible for education, technology and the built environment. What they said in their interviews was prompted and framed by consideration of the needs of new course designs and more integrated learning spaces. In this chapter, we summarise the cross-cutting issues identified in the interviews and we examine the maturity of the universities with respect to each of the five organisational elements: strategy, governance, policy, management and funding. We define maturity as a two-dimensional construct, consisting of capability and alignment. For example, highly capable management needs to be aligned with the other four elements – strategy, governance, policy and funding – if it is to function properly. It turns out that very few universities are good on all fronts and that aligning organisational elements is hard, not least because of the lack of robust underpinning models of how learning and teaching systems function.

Key issues for education, technology and facilities leaders

In this section, we provide a summary of the areas identified by our interviewees as being most significant and, in one way or another, problematic. We start with some overarching issues that appeared frequently in the transcripts and that were clearly of considerable importance to the interviewees. After that, we summarise the main issues for each of our three sets of interviewees, under the headings of strategy, governance, policy, management and funding.

Five overarching issues

The single most substantial area of concern, for most of the deputy vice-chancellors (education) DVCEs in particular, relates to the balance between innovation and quality assurance – in other words, resolving tensions between the need to change and the need to be confident about the quality of educational experiences on offer to students. DVCEs spoke about how quality frameworks were better evolved than frameworks for educational innovation. They identified the bureaucracy of course approvals processes as a systemic disincentive to educational innovation. They also expressed concerns about the ways in which student evaluations of teachers can make teaching staff risk-averse: over-reliance on quantitative student evaluation data in academic promotions processes, for example, can deter innovation, especially where a change takes time to bed down. (Since these interviews were conducted, a number of universities, particularly in North America, have begun to decouple student evaluations of teaching from promotions processes, driven in part by doubts about whether the evaluation data are fit for purpose.)

The professional development (PD) of teaching staff also emerged as an overarching issue for all three groups of leaders. DVCEs spoke about the need to balance PD aimed at longer-term cultural change with PD aimed at enabling incremental developments in teaching and learning. They also referred to shifts in teacher identity and practices – from 'teaching the content' to 'teaching the student'; from didactic to design-oriented methods and from teaching alone to working in collaborative, inter-professional teams. The technology and facilities leaders also spoke about the need to allow ample time and funding to support teaching staff in adopting and adapting to new ways of working – including involvement in the design and use of new kinds of learning space as well as new technologies. They revealed a concern that new spaces and new technologies would be attributed (by others in senior management) with causal powers that they do not possess – as if student outcomes would magically improve without any change in the mediating processes of teaching and learning. Technology leaders, in particular, spoke about the importance of having an in-house cadre of expert and experienced IT staff, knowledgeable about the institution, its people and needs, without whom the IT service could not provide leadership or respond in an agile way to new opportunities and challenges.

The third overarching issue concerns the need for student learning – and teaching – to be able to move seamlessly between different kinds of space, both material and virtual, on-campus and off-campus. Interviewees framed this desire for more thoroughly integrated learning space as a crucial but really difficult area.

The fourth issue concerns aligning strategy, governance, policy, management and funding. Technology and facilities leaders emphasised the difficulties that flow from poor integration between these areas. They also spoke emphatically about the need for strategies, including teaching and learning strategies, that addressed space and technology issues at a sufficient level of detail. The importance of, and difficulties involved in, connecting macro and micro level issues – as well as thinking holistically – were also reflected in these comments.

The fifth and final overarching issue we will mention here could be regarded as a special instance or corollary of weak alignment. We single it out because it mattered deeply to technology and facilities leaders but scarcely came up at all in the DVCE interviews: funding. More specifically, technology and facilities leaders drew our attention to structural and procedural issues with budgeting, such as failure to integrate technology and facilities budget planning in major new building projects and overlooking recurrent costs when approving large capital projects.

These overarching issues were accompanied by some issues specific to the organisational elements of strategy, governance, policy, management and funding. In the next part of the chapter, we identify salient issues for education, technology and facilities leaders under each of these headings. Recall that the overall framing for the interviews was established by talking about (a) new course designs and (b) better integration of learning space.

Strategy: salient issues for the education leaders

- The need to simplify programme structures and pathways; removing 'obscure' options; redesigning programmes around a disciplinary core, interdisciplinary options, and a capstone course for generic and employability skills.
- The difficulty of translating educational strategy into the means for achieving learning outcomes (LOs). Quality assurance is better on intended outcomes than on the processes for achieving them.
- Difficulties in integrating and stimulating innovation in learning and teaching frameworks orientated towards quality assurance.
- Lack of principled approaches to university-wide innovations like work-integrated learning (WIL) and especially for ensuring high-quality outcomes from them.

Strategy: salient issues for the technology and facilities leaders

- The existence of a sufficiently detailed strategy, or strategic plan is necessary to guide the design, integration and development of facilities, both physical and digital (virtual) to enable effective learning and teaching processes and outcomes.
- The importance of executive leadership and buy in from the disciplines: necessary to avoid fragmentation and waste of time and resources
- Alignment between disciplinary, faculty and executive visions for learning space. It is essential to be able to develop a vision for learning space, through imagining alternatives and drawing on all possible expertise, to improve the student and teaching experience.
- Change-management strategies as part of an overall approach: critical in ensuring learning and teaching requirements continue to inform, and are informed by, opportunities created by new types and new configurations of learning space.
- Necessity of finding a way to deal with uncertainty caused by rapid change and external influences – these will otherwise undermine a coherent strategy and weaken the coherence of the end results.

Governance and policy: salient issues for the education leaders

- Lack of attention to, and understanding of, associations between processes and outcomes, especially in relation to governance. (In our words, no shared causal model of how learning and teaching function.)
- Managing risks around involvement of third parties
- Need for more holistic understandings
- Need to see policy development as a tool for implementing strategy and for institutional change.

Governance and policy: salient issues for the technology and facilities leaders

- Education leadership of governance structures is important to capture the attention and provide a legitimate focus.
- Effective governance requires representation from all appropriate areas of the university that have a stake in learning space provision and use; for example, students, teachers, faculties, IT, facilities, finance.
- Effective governance involves developing the right relationships amongst the senior committees at the university.
- Incomplete representations and undeveloped concepts of learning space can lead to fragmented outcomes.
- Finding the right balance between shared facilities and discipline-specific facilities is an important role for the governance of learning space.

Management: salient issues for the education leaders

- Quality management – especially the shift of focus with learning outcomes assessment from course to programme levels.
- Managing the future: broadening digital ecosystems; integration of research-teaching, etc.

Management: salient issues for the technology and facilities leaders

- Digital disruption and new teaching approaches for course delivery need to be planned for and accommodated.
- Sector-level changes, such as use of cloud services, need to be tailored to suit individual institutions and contexts.
- Internal and external drivers of change create further change in the professional staffing profile required for innovative, sustainable learning space.
- Managing relationships with faculties during learning space development is essential for design and support requirements.
- Collaboration and integration of IT and facilities project processes are essential.

- Simple concepts and consistent language are required for effective dissemination of learning space designs.
- Success is contingent on ensuring teaching staff have sufficient time to engage with new course and learning space designs.

Funding: salient issues for the technology and facilities leaders

- To design budgets effectively, funding needs to be managed at a strategic level in appropriate capital and operational areas and integrated across the institution.
- Strategic budget management includes understanding and gaining leverage from sector-wide developments, such as new methods of service provision (e.g. cloud, software-as-a-service).
- The budgets of university service providers (e.g. facilities and IT) will be more readily accepted if they are seen to be driven by strategy and overseen by representative governance.
- The true costs of spaces need to be understood for sound academic business decisions, at institutional, faculty and discipline levels.
- In the Australian sector, backlog maintenance of learning space is a common concern which requires systematic attention.
- There are operational benefits in maintaining separate budgets for physical and virtual space in most cases, and some advantages in combining capital budgets at the outset.
- Universities are engaging in a number of different ways of measuring the outcomes from investment in learning space. Exploring different alternatives is important, but lack of agreed methods is also problematic.

It is clear from the interviews that the five elements (strategy, governance, policy, management and funding) are inextricably related to each other. Addressing any element without understanding the impact on all the others is futile because of their interdependency. So for each element, we looked at both the capability and the relationship to the other elements in developing the overall maturity model in Figure 5.6. In our view, the fact that technology and facilities leaders run parts of the university that have to translate abstract requirements into real infrastructure means that they are more exposed when this process goes awry, or is perceived as having failed to deliver. Encouraging the university to adopt stronger and more capable governance, management and funding approaches is both a rational risk-management strategy and a plea for better articulation of how technology, facilities and education come together to shape valued outcomes. We return to this fundamental issue of articulating 'how things actually work' in the second part of the book.

Before that, we offer an analysis of the maturity of the universities involved in our study, with respect to each of the five organisational elements and their alignment.

Mapping maturity

In this section, we share outcomes of the analytic process described towards the end of Chapter 2 to map the maturity of the universities. In brief, members of the extended research team rated each of the 39 universities on a number of measures. To do so, they drew on the interview transcripts but also on an array of documents produced by each university. Researchers' ratings were compared: inter-rater reliabilities are presented in Chapter 2. That said, the ratings have to be understood as *subjective expert judgements* made by people with unusually deep experience in the areas concerned. We are not holding them up as objective measures. Neither are they directly linked to objective data on institutional processes, contexts or outcomes. They are mediated by what our informants told us about how major issues are handled within their institutions, warts and all.

In each of the next five subsections, we present a graph that plots each university's position in a two-dimensional space: *capability* x *alignment*. We use the term 'maturity' to combine both (a) the level of capability of each university with respect to the organisational element concerned, and (b) the degree of alignment between that organisational element and the other four organisational elements. Once more, we remind the reader that consideration of new course designs and integrated learning spaces, quality and innovation issues provided a common background for the interviews. The graphs are based on good coverage of the Australian university system. We cannot claim that the questions we used to focus the analysis of each of the five organisational elements would be exactly right for universities in other countries, but we have included them to both illuminate the current analysis and provide a basis for researchers in other systems to try out the approach we have used. We have anonymised the universities. The identifiers used in these graphs are different to those used in earlier chapters to ensure the anonymity of the participating institutions.

Strategy readiness

The following criteria guided the researchers' *capability* maturity ratings with respect to strategy:

1. The university teaching and learning strategy is sufficiently comprehensive; encompasses new course designs as well as the integrated learning spaces in which they occur.
2. The university teaching and learning strategy is sufficiently student-centred. The underlying concepts of course and learning space design focus on the needs of students seeking to achieve their learning outcomes.
3. The university teaching and learning strategy is sufficiently teaching-informed. The strategy supports changes in the teaching roles created by new course designs and integrated learning spaces.

4.   The university teaching and learning strategy is sufficiently clear. The university teaching and learning strategy provides sufficient detail to shape activity by all relevant stakeholders.
5.   The university teaching and learning strategy is perceived as being owned by the relevant stakeholders. The implementation of the strategy ensures that relevant stakeholders feel they are represented and have a stake in the university teaching and learning strategy.

The researchers' ratings for *alignment* maturity reflected their judgements about the extent to which strategy appeared to be aligned with the other organisational elements of governance, policy, management and funding. Together the capability and alignment ratings capture maturity in terms of 'strategy readiness'.

The distribution of strategy readiness ratings in Figure 5.1 suggests significant variation across the sector. To help summarise the pattern, we can refer to the four quadrants of the figure: top left, top right, bottom left and bottom right. (For presentation purposes, when the dots representing a university sit on the same location as each other, we have moved their positions slightly to reveal that there is more than one institution at that point. The raw data can be found in Appendix 2.)

There are rather few universities in the top-right quadrant in Figure 5.1. This quadrant is occupied by universities in which strategy is both well developed and well aligned. Only three universities stand out as being rated as excellent in both strategy capability and the alignment of strategy to the other organisational elements. Universities in the bottom-right quadrant have reasonably well developed strategies but their strategies are not as aligned as those in the top-right quadrant. Overall, four of the universities stand out as high on alignment amongst the key organisational elements necessary for effective strategy deployment.

As we will see, strategy rated somewhat higher than the categories of governance, management and funding, and lower than policy. While most institutions have a strategy that encompasses learning and teaching, there were varying levels of completeness, clarity and detail in both the discussion with the leaders and the documents reviewed. While clarity and detail are important in guiding an institution's direction and investment, the alignment with the other categories appears to be a serious inhibitor to success.

Governance readiness

Figure 5.2 plots the researcher ratings of governance readiness. The following criteria guided the researchers' ratings about governance *capability*:

1.   All relevant stakeholders were appropriately represented on university teaching and learning governance.
2.   The university teaching and learning committee is sufficiently integrated in the committee structure to influence the other senior committees of the university through iterative discussion, evidence and decision-making.

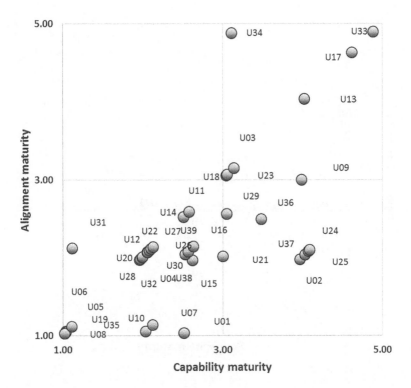

Figure 5.1

3. The make-up and decision-making of the committee ensures effective pro-gress of the university teaching and learning agenda by removing roadblocks for management and prioritising activity appropriately in relation to strategy and stakeholder interest.
4. Governance ensured all areas of the university works collaboratively in ways that promote the strategy and education mission of the university.

As before, the researchers also assessed alignment: this time, of governance with the other organisational elements of strategy, policy, management and funding. Together the capability and alignment dimensions locate 'governance readiness'.

Using the four quadrants of Figure 5.2 as a frame of reference, there are three universities in the top-right quadrant. These have relatively well-developed and well-aligned governance arrangements, with five having good governance capability but relatively poor alignment. But 24 universities in the bottom-left quadrant have relatively poor alignment of governance across their institutions.

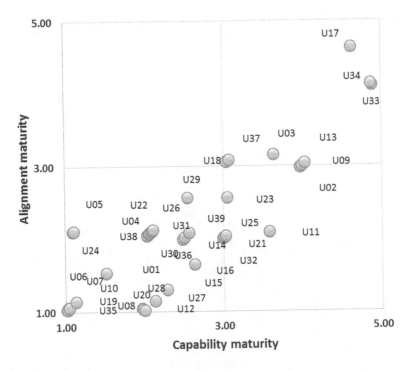

Figure 5.2

Overall, the ratings on governance capability are lower than for strategy capability, reflecting the views of the university leaders about the difficulty of arranging for all areas of the university to move in the same direction. Within the bottom-left quadrant, there are five universities that stood out as having very low governance capability and very poor alignment. In general terms, capability of the governance function is better than its alignment with the other organisational elements.

Effective governance is critical in linking strategy and policy and in tracking and guiding priorities and implementation through management and funding practice.

Strong and aligned governance models connect strategy and policy to effective delivery of environments and practices by guiding management practices and funding priorities.

Policy readiness

Figure 5.3 plots the ratings on 'policy readiness'. Note that the facilities leaders did not discuss policy issues systematically, and policy did not merge as a thematic category in the professional leader interviews. This results in fewer plots on Figure 5.3 (n = 19).

The criteria guiding the researchers' ratings about policy capability were as follows:

1. Policy informs processes and products which are practically achievable in situ.
2. Policy is informed by best-practice knowledge internationally.
3. The policy framework adopts a student perspective in how it orientates its purpose, implementation and evaluation.
4. The policy framework is designed to guide tangible outcomes that benefit some aspect of the learning and teaching experience.
5. Policy is designed so that it is consistent with external national and international educational requirements that the university needs to address.

Three of the universities stand out as strong on both capability and alignment. Another seven sit on the borders of the top-right quadrant, being relatively strong on one or other of these dimensions. Looking to the weaker bottom-left quadrant, a similar (inverse) pattern appears – with two universities scoring very poor on both dimensions and seven others being somewhat stronger.

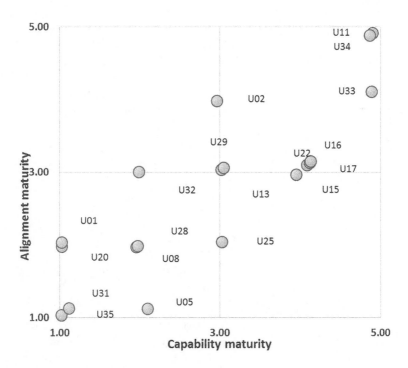

Figure 5.3

Education policy maturity guides practice and influences decisions. It provides a barometer for the educational culture of a university. Strong policy frameworks improve the ability of managers to manage.

Management readiness

Figure 5.4 plots the researcher ratings of management readiness. The criteria used by the researchers in determining their ratings of management capability were as follows:

1. Management processes are sufficiently agile, responsive and flexible to respond quickly to changes in faculty and student demand, new technologies and course design requirements for integrated learning space.
2. Management processes successfully engage all student, teacher and other relevant stakeholders in project processes.
3. Management processes operate within a quality-assured and policy-led framework.

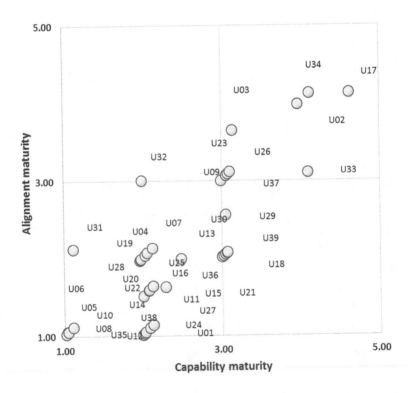

Figure 5.4

4. End-to-end processes for learning, teaching, course and learning space development successfully integrate education strategy, policy and direction from governance.
5. Project management, delivery and operational services result on time and within budget.

Just three universities are firmly in the top-right quadrant; most of the remainder sit at or below a score of three on both capability and alignment of management processes. Arguably this reflects the growing complexity of university teaching, learning, IT and space arrangements, with knock-on effects for both management capabilities and alignment between management and the other key organisational elements.

Project pressures and differing project priorities and approaches were often cited in the interviews as areas of concern for successfully managing the implementation of strategy. The interrelationship between management and funding was also one of the significant dependencies raised in the interviews.

The relatively low score for the management element is not surprising as this, above all the other elements, depends upon their alignment to achieve results. It is where the action (delivery) takes place, and if any of the other elements are not aligned, then education management processes are put at risk.

Funding readiness

Figure 5.5 provides a snapshot of university teaching and learning funding capability and how well Australian universities align their funding approach to their teaching and learning strategy, governance, policy and management. The criteria used by the researchers in rating funding capability were as follows:

1. Funding envelopes were well-structured, enabling business-as-usual operational expenditure, strategic growth in operational expenditure (e.g. software as a service) and capital expenditure on strategic developments for teaching and learning.
2. At the level of the institution, there is a balanced allocation of funding to new course design, the accompanying staff development processes as well as the physical and virtual learning space that is required to enable the realisation of the courses.
3. Normal limitations in funding and time in the academic year motivate a shared prioritisation of projects by all stakeholders.
4. The educational and professional leaders have sufficient control over the different purposes of funding to manage strategic and operational risk.

The appraisal question used by the researchers about funding alignment was the extent to which it appeared to be aligned with the other organisational elements of strategy, governance, policy and management. Together the capability and alignment issues defined the idea of 'funding readiness'.

Only one university was rated in the top-right quadrant (both capability and alignment above 3). A second institution rated 4 on capability but was weaker – only 2 – on alignment. Eight more universities sat at the mid-point on capability and the rest fell into the bottom-left quadrant: rather weak on both capability and alignment.

Rapid change in ownership, expectations and applications of IT, shifts away from traditional lecture spaces, and the knock-on effects for both capital and recurrent funding decisions probably explain how it is that so many universities are struggling to get funding models and the balance of funding allocations right. This has implications for both capital development and the refreshing of physical and digital infrastructure. Proper funding of appropriate support functions is a critical factor in the effective delivery of capability and services. Also, if the balance of capital between physical and digital does not reflect actual use and needs of students and teachers, the desired outcomes will not be achieved.

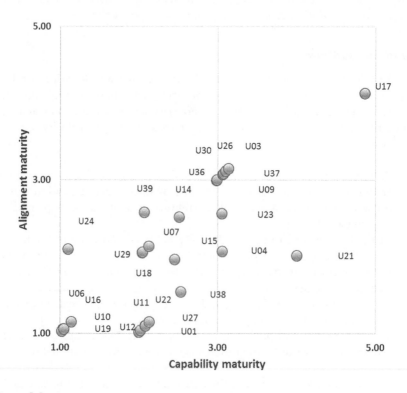

Figure 5.5

The interviewees emphasised that to achieve an effective funding model is extremely difficult as demand almost always exceeds supply. Balancing and assigning priorities is full of compromise. Given the extent of change-management requirements alluded to in the interviews, this highlights the challenges associated in achieving balance between change and sustainability, quality assurance and innovation within funding envelopes.

Understanding the maturity of teaching and learning systems in Australian universities

While recognising that the ratings given for capability and alignment across these five organisational elements depend upon expert judgement rather than objective indicators, we think it is worth pushing the analysis one step further. Figure 5.6 combines the scores across the five organisational elements to give an aggregate picture of institutional maturity.

While a linear relation between capability and alignment can be glimpsed in the earlier figures, it comes through very strongly in Figure 5.6. In other words, when we combine and average across the five organisational elements of strategy, governance, management, policy and funding, there is a solid relationship between capability and alignment. Only three universities stand out as doing very well on this aggregate measure. The majority sit in the bottom-left quadrant, with only two more scoring above the 3 line on both capability and alignment.

Figure 5.6 provides a generalised sense of the maturity of Australian universities' teaching and learning systems – including their digital and physical components. It is a snapshot of a system coping with dramatic changes in both external environments and internal practices. The higher-education system is witnessing and having to respond to changing aspirations, changing pedagogies and educational support systems, changing accreditation requirements, disruptive technologies, changing expectations of services and uncertainties about funding. It is not surprising that many universities have some way to go in adapting their internal systems to cope with such changes. The performance of the three universities in the top-right quadrant show that there is much that can be done.

Figures 5.7 and 5.8 provide a view of some of the differences between the organisational elements. They show that:

1. Overall (Figure 5.7), the average score for maturity across all the organisational elements for the entire sector was 2.32 out of 5: 2.49 for capability and 2.15 for alignment.
2. For each of the five organisational elements, maturity scores higher than alignment. Logically, developing the capability of one element is easier than ensuring its alignment to all the other elements.
3. Policy is rated higher than any of the other elements. This may reflect external pressures associated with quality assurance; universities being required to develop policies to meet national standards, for example.

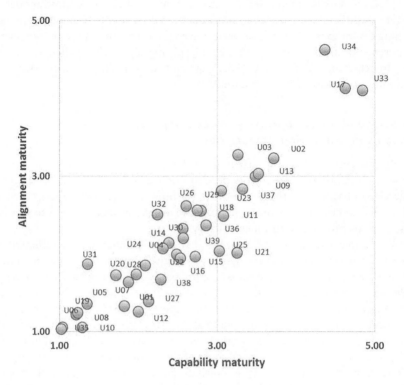

Figure 5.6

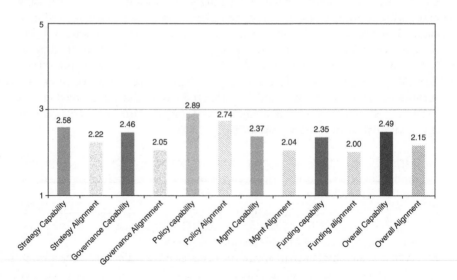

Figure 5.7

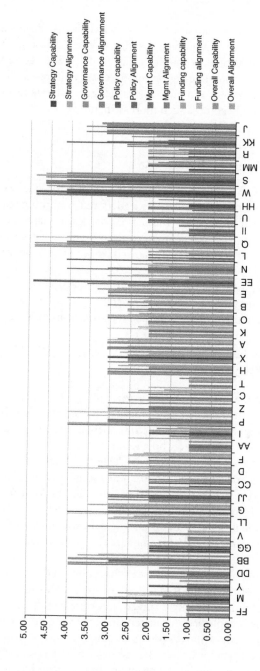

Figure 5.8

4. Management is rated low, relative to the other elements. This may reflect the challenges in implementing strategy when several areas of the university are involved.
5. Funding is rated lower than any of the other elements. Problems with the structure and levels of funding may be due to the increasing diversity and complexity of educational, technology and facilities arrangements. In particular, where better integrated learning spaces are required in order to meet the needs of new course and curriculum designs, uncertainties grow and estimating funding becomes much more difficult.

Summary of Chapter 5

Chapter 5 provides two complementary overviews of what our research team discovered through interviewing university leaders and examining relevant documents produced by their universities. In the first part of the chapter, we identified four overarching themes that were areas of concern for many if not all of the leaders interviewed, and a fifth that was emphasised by the IT and facilities leaders:

- balancing quality assurance and the need for innovation;
- the professional development of teaching staff;
- the need for student learning to be able to move seamlessly between learning spaces;
- problems in aligning strategy, governance, policy, management and funding;
- funding and budgeting.

In the second part of the chapter we used expert ratings of each of the five organisational elements – strategy, governance, policy, management and funding – to map capability and alignment. In combination, these measures give a sense of the maturity of universities in the sector: how well they can perform in each of these areas and how well the areas are connected. Using these reported experiences as whole, Appendix 1 at the end of this book offers some questions as a guide for universities interested in investigating similar issues in their context.

The issues arising from the alignment (or, more accurately, the misalignment) of the five organisational elements highlight the danger of focusing on outcomes alone. While effective educational outcomes are the goal, achieving them occurs through processes of education.

The interview material, and the analyses it has supported, provide a rich and complicated picture of the challenges of leadership in education, IT and facilities. It is not easy to pull out a single thread, but we will risk doing so. Underpinning much of the complexity and uncertainty, we suggest, is the absence of a shared sense of how educational systems function. In other words, there is a sense of mystery about the processes that actually produce valued educational outcomes. This diagnosis provides the rationale for the second part of our book.

Part II

This second part of the book – Chapters 6 to 9 – contains our response to the main challenges identified in Chapter 5. In each of these four chapters we offer a new perspective on the complex task of integrating educational, IT and facilities leadership and planning. We frame this as a task that must be driven by educational purposes, though some of the main conceptual difficulties arise from the need to expand consideration of educational thinking, to take proper account of how learning depends upon interactions within a rich ecosystem of tasks, tools, places, ideas, methods and people. This is now a strategic priority. University leaders can no longer delegate to others an understanding of how students actually learn, and how the circumstances in which they learn affect their outcomes. Without the insights from the learning sciences that have been accumulating over the last three decades, leaders are ill-placed to shape systems that can support current needs and deal with uncertainty and change.

We are very focused on what we take to be the main underlying difficulty: finding ways of understanding, representing and improving the processes, entities and relationships that constitute educational ecosystems. We offer sets of ideas, and links to further reading, that collectively build a sense of ecologies of learning: how to interpret them and how they can be strengthened; how they evolve and are interconnected; and how to generate actionable knowledge about them. These challenges are keys to unlocking the processes that lead to valued educational outcomes. As we explained in the first part of the book, a capacity to enhance these processes in informed, sustainable ways depends upon rejecting the 'black-box' approach to learning systems: tweaking the statistical correlates of a small set of (sometimes dubious) outcome measures is no longer a tenable position.

The ideas in each of these chapters are offered as *resources for discussion* among those responsible for leadership and for advising leaders in universities. They need fleshing out and adapting to local realities. The processes involved in discussing and modifying these ideas, and testing their potential for local application, may in themselves prove helpful.

The central themes in each chapter are interconnected. Chapter 6 introduces the idea of service design, and then focuses it on the design of services for a specific kind of service 'user' – with a reconceived and rather more complex user in mind. We move away from an image of the (student) user as an individual *customer to be managed*, in order to open up perspectives on *designing services for activity systems*. That becomes the core theme for Chapter 7, where we share some insights from activity theory and introduce activity-centred analysis and design. Chapter 8 provides a summary of foundational ideas for a new specialism: introducing educational ecology as an applied science. We develop this further in Chapter 9, offering four approaches to analysing and strengthening educational ecosystems, and sketching a way of connecting research and its application through forms of research–practice partnerships.

Each of the five organisational elements that surfaced in our interviews – strategy, governance, policy, management and funding – has to be *grounded* in the realities of contemporary student learning. Decisions have *material* consequences, as the IT and facilities leaders kept reminding us. Educational work in today's universities is inherently complicated and responsibilities are more distributed than ever. It is impossible for any one person to understand the whole complex ecology; rather, the enterprise depends on the meshing of partial and provisional views. When we also take into account the value of having students partner with teaching staff in co-designing and co-creating educational opportunities and environments, it becomes clear that enquiring into how the learning ecologies actually function is of direct concern to everybody.

Service design

This chapter falls into six sections. We start by arguing that it may prove easier to integrate educational, IT and facilities leadership and planning around service design rather than product design. We go on to explain service design in more detail and how it can be understood in educational settings. Designing services begs the question of who the services are for, so we dig more deeply into the question of services and service users in higher education. This leads naturally to a discussion of how services are co-produced and even co-designed. We push the argument a little further at the end of the chapter, showing how the goal of helping students become better at co-designing knowledge-rich services can act as a novel and productive focus for higher education; an image we develop further towards the end of the book.

Conceptualising university leadership in relation to service design

Some of the most debilitating issues identified by the university leaders (Chapters 3 to 5) concern the difficulty of integrating educational, IT and facilities planning and evaluating the quality and effectiveness of planning processes and outcomes. Part of the problem is that these areas of university practice have different ways of forming and implementing plans and evaluating their consequences. Indeed, they focus on very different kinds of things, even though benefits to clients (students, academic staff and others) are front of mind – or at least back of mind – for the personnel involved. Planning, monitoring and evaluation depend upon assumptions, and sometimes on informal theories, about the main entities that exist in each of the domains concerned, and about interactions and other dependencies between those entities. These assumptions and informal theories are often implicit, but can be quite powerful in shaping how work gets done. The term 'ontology' can be used to refer to this question of what entities, relationships and processes exist within a domain. Ontological claims are claims about what exists. We think that one of the difficulties in integrating educational, IT and facilities planning is that these areas of professional practice have different ontologies; or, at best, they have ontologies that only partially overlap. In consequence, the concepts and language available to those working

Table 6.1 Diverse ontologies in the fields of educational, IT and facilities planning

	Examples of characteristic entities in each field of practice
Education	Graduate attributes, learning outcomes, curriculum, assessment, pedagogy, teaching and learning, learning resources, teachers and students
IT	Hardware, software, networks, systems, tools, infrastructure, databases, interoperability, access, scalability, reliability, (cyber)security, technical staff, users, user support, emerging technologies and trends, obsolescence, budgets
Facilities	Classrooms (and other teaching spaces), libraries, learning commons, informal learning spaces, AV facilities, grounds, (new) building projects, refurbishment, maintenance, occupancy rates, budgets

across these three areas are not fit for purpose, as Chapter 4 so clearly revealed. Table 6.1 illustrates the point.

Another way to express this would be to say that the vast majority of attention in each of the three fields goes to the kinds of entities listed on the right-hand side of Table 6.1, and to note that there is little or no overlap between the three sets of entities and only a shaky or uncertain sense of how to make rational connections between entities that sit in different rows.

While there are some similarities between how these three fields of practice design, plan, monitor, evaluate, and so on, there are enough differences that it is very challenging to see how better integration might be achieved. It is not just that different technical languages are in use, but different worldviews are in play. From time to time, serious efforts have been made to develop integrative architectures to do this (e.g. Ford et al., 1996; Ellis & Goodyear, 2010; Bain & Zundans-Fraser, 2017). But integration remains a difficult and unsolved problem, as our interviews show. A further complication arises from the fact that designing and managing for other people's learning involves *dual ontologies*. We explain this more thoroughly in Chapter 7. For now, it is enough to say that the world as imagined during planning and design work is not the same as the world eventually experienced by students and teachers. This under-acknowledged source of complexity makes it even harder for education, IT and facilities leaders to establish common ground and integrate their tasks.

From organising around product design to organising around service design

One shared characteristic of designing and planning across the three fields of practice is that core problems and solutions are often *product* focused. For example, in the area of educational design – also known as instructional design, or design for learning – there is a long tradition of focusing on the design of instructional resources, such as textbooks, audio-visual materials and computer simulations. 'Message design' still plays a significant role in the curriculum for instructional designers. Even when design is oriented towards learning activities, it tends to approach this through designing *things*, like task specifications or collaboration scripts. Similarly, design in the IT area is sharply focused on the design of tools and systems, networks and architectures. And practices in the facilities field are strongly influenced by the master of all design disciplines: architecture. So while the final purpose of educational, IT and facilities planning can be expressed in terms of desirable educational outcomes, most of the attention in day-to-day work is on shaping products: syllabus documents, descriptions of graduate attributes, IT tools and infrastructure, the furnishings in learning spaces, and so on.

We do not want to push this argument to extremes. For example, all three fields have an interest in understanding *users*, though we would not be the first to note that architects have no agreed term-of-art for the people who use their buildings. Both IT and educational design show a growing interest in user experience (UX) and learner experience (LX). Moreover, user-interface design and the broader discipline of human–computer interaction (HCI) have made substantial contributions to our collective understanding of relationships between people, technology and work. Nevertheless, one can still argue that much of the discussion – particularly at a strategic level in higher education – is discussion of *things* (and their associated costs).

Service design: a brief introduction

Much of the literature on design is also dominated by the consideration of *products*, to the extent that many people assume all designers are product designers, even if some of them design very big products, such as buildings, ships and airplanes. Over the last 40 years or so, a different line of thinking has opened up in design studies and in writings about innovation. Work in this area goes by several names, but much of it can sit under the umbrella of 'service design' (see, e.g., Shostack, 1982; Gallouj & Weinstein, 1997; Secomandi & Snelders, 2011).

Service design emerged in recognition of a transition in Western economies from markets dominated by the exchange of tangible products (*goods*) to markets, and other social arrangements, in which intangible or less tangible *services* play an increasingly important role. Shostack's pioneering work was partly a response to the difficulty that marketing departments faced in figuring out how to promote services. Similarly, economists like Gallouj were motivated by the difficulty of specifying exactly what a service consists of – a problem for anyone wanting to quantify costs and benefits or frame service innovation policies.

> Products are tangible objects that exist in both time and space; services consist solely of acts or process(es), and exist in time only ... Services are rendered; products are possessed. Services cannot be possessed; they can only be experienced, created or participated in ... Though they are different, services and products are intimately and symbiotically linked.
>
> (Shostack, 1982, 49)

For Shostack, the distinction between product and service depended heavily on the balance between the tangible and intangible elements. In her view, goods and services are generally hybrids. A preponderance of intangible elements suggests the essence of what is being offered and purchased is a service.

But how does a consumer know that they are getting a good service, or a service of any kind, if the essence of what is being provided is intangible? Shostack's response to this is to focus on tangible 'service evidence' – not the service itself, but the ways in which a consumer can sense that a service is being provided, and whether it is of good quality.

Three core characteristics of services and service design

Secomandi & Snelders (2011) summarise the essential elements of service design and service innovation under three broad headings: exchange relations, interface and infrastructure, and materiality.

While the exchange of goods may involve little or no contact between producer and consumer, service production typically involves an 'intertwining of stakeholders' (Secomandi & Snelders, 2011, 29). In other words, services are very often *co-produced*.

> Exchange relations establish the context for attributing particular roles to the stakeholders involved in service co-production. Typically, providers devise and market services; clients purchase and use them. Furthermore, an investigation of the circumstances of exchange relations reveals a host of sociotechnical resources that are required for service production.
>
> (Secomandi & Snelders, 2011, 29).

This idea of co-production turns out to be rather more complicated and, more important, in education, where students have to be active co-producers of 'learning services'. We return to this theme later in the chapter.

Many service-design researchers distinguish between two aspects of service production: interface and infrastructure. The interface can be thought of as the *locus* of exchange or of service co-production. It is the site where Shostack's tangible evidence can be sensed. In contrast, service infrastructure can be thought of as the 'back office' of service production – necessary, but out of sight to the service consumer or client. Both infrastructure and interface are necessary, but the service interface 'actualises' the co-production of the service.

> In sum, exchange relations between providers and clients require the mobilization of infrastructure resources but, ultimately, are realized through the interface. For this reason, the interface becomes subtly prominent as the end-point of all service design deliberations.
>
> (Secomandi & Snelders, 2011, 30)

Crucially, the service interface has *material properties*. Intangible services are experienced through tangible manifestations at the service interface. This includes services that are co-produced by interpersonal encounters – as when a teacher and their students are working together in a classroom.

> for the production of services, intangible resources must be actualized through an interface that is material and available to bodily perception ... service exchange relations between providers and clients are grounded on the materiality of their interfaces, even in the case of interpersonal encounters.
>
> (Secomandi & Snelders, 2011, 31–32)

So services may conventionally be deemed intangible, and on that basis distinguished from goods or products, but actually service (co)production requires a material interface. A better distinction between exchange of goods and exchange of services is to say that the service interface does not simply offer a well-bounded material object (as tends to be the case with products). Rather, the service interface is characterised by material heterogeneity: it is usually complex, unevenly distributed in space, multi-channel/multi-media.

An important point to add here is that the term 'experience design', as in 'user experience design (UX)' or 'learner experience design (LX)', cannot be taken literally. It is impossible to design someone's experience, just as it is impossible to design their learning, their wisdom or their happiness. Experience is a *relation* between a person (having the experience) and a thing or event (that which is experienced). This caveat applies to service design in general, and has special implications in relation to design for learning. As Sangiorgi puts it, when talking about a clarifying focus in service-design thinking: 'Service design therefore iteratively moves from designing intangible experiences to designing the tangible elements that enable the desired experiences to occur in a coherent way' (Sangiorgi, 2009, 416). In other words, learning and learning experiences cannot be designed, but they can be designed *for*.

Service design in (higher) education

We said near the start of this chapter that design and planning in the education, IT and facilities fields of practice have historically tended to focus on tangible products, even if the eventual goals (desired educational outcomes, student satisfaction, etc.) are much less tangible. However, there has been some work in higher-education settings inspired by service-design theories and methods. A little of this work is closely connected to core educational activities, but much of it is restricted to ancillary services like student enrolment (Baranova et al., 2010; Radnor et al., 2014), catering and cleaning. Though these are important to the effective functioning of the university, they are not at the heart of our current concerns.

A few researchers have come closer to analysing learning services. We mention these briefly here. For example, Kuzmina (2014) uses a service-design approach to understand education as a service, and to make recommendations for change in aspects of primary (elementary) school education. Although much of Kuzmina's treatment of education and change is specific to primary education, her thesis provides a powerful illustration of how design thinking can reframe problems and open up fresh opportunities for reconsidering what have been taken-for-granted as intractable difficulties or immovable obstacles.

Turning to the higher-education sector, Felix (2011) contrasts the sophistication of design practices and design outcomes associated with the *physical* aspects of new learning spaces with the more rudimentary nature of design work that addresses the *educational* use of those spaces. In particular, he comments on the lack of integration between space design and service design.

> The design of learning spaces is focused mostly on … the proportion and configuration of the space, the materials and furniture, and the technology. When services are considered – such as in learning commons spaces within libraries – they are often developed after the space, designed from the provider rather than user perspective, and considered individually rather than as a system
>
> (Felix, 2011, n.p.)

Felix sketches a number of service-design processes and tools that can play a stronger role in integrating space design and student activities, such as the use of personas ('representative users based on research into motivations and behaviors'), journey maps (which map service use over time, identifying key 'service touchpoints') and blueprints (which provide guidance on delivery of a service across different staff and systems channels). Felix is influenced heavily by Shostack's early work on service design (e.g. Shostack, 1982). Where Felix and Shostack talk of 'touchpoints' we prefer to follow Secomandi & Snelders (2011), using the richer construct of complex, material service interfaces.

Ng & Forbes (2009) come rather closer to our own perspective on understanding aspects of educational planning from a service-design perspective. Their focus is very firmly on educational service *marketing*, and their goal is to find a better way of framing what it is that universities offer, in order to market those services more effectively. While that leads them in a different direction from us – they are explaining what services exist, rather than thinking about how better services get designed – they nevertheless pick up on some distinctive aspects of higher education as a service and the role of students in co-producing those services.

(Re)configuring the user: from managed customer to activity system

Researchers who analyse the evolution of technologies, and of technology-rich workplaces and social practices, have spoken about how design involves processes of 'configuring the user' (e.g. Woolgar, 1990). This phrase has several sets of implications. For one thing, members of design teams have to imagine who will use the outcomes of their work (products and/or services) and will conjure up scenarios in which what they design gets used. This allows members of a design team to discuss, and come to resolutions about, the capabilities, needs and preferences of their intended users. Another implication is that these imagined users and uses flow through into the reality of use. For example, users of a new tool or service may adapt their preferred ways of doing things to better align with the way the tool or service functions. The imagined user reconfigures the actual user.

When implementing education strategy, the experiences reported by the university leaders in Chapters 3 and 4 revealed that much of their activity was influenced by a goal of meeting student needs: the student was often front of mind. Design and planning practices in higher education configure their users in many ways, of course. The interviews showed there is no simple orthodoxy about this.

However, we need to prepare the ground for the argument developed in Chapter 7: that service design should take as its focus not the individual student but whole-activity systems. There are two main steps to this argument: (1) a conceptual shift away from the individual student as the default focus of attention – the user as 'managed customer' (Macfarlane, 2017); and (2) an opening up of the world of 'situated learning' – where learning involves complex activity systems in which people, tasks, technologies and spaces entangle (Goodyear & Carvalho, 2014; Greeno & Engeström, 2014).

Universities have clung tenaciously to the idea of the individual student as the focus, beneficiary and outcome of their educational work. When a student graduates, they take with them their university's warrant (certification) – attesting to their achievements as captured by the assessment system. The rationale for much of a university's educational work is that it will prepare the student to act, with an acceptable level of capability, in other contexts. A key assumption is that the student, on their own, will be able to take knowledge and skills learned in academia and display them in workplace, community and other significant settings. In other words, it is expected that their academic learning will *transfer*. Implied in the university's warrant for the student is that what they can transfer to the workplace (etc.) is a *personal* accomplishment, not dependent on the help of other people or tools. The idea of knowledge and skills as personal possessions aligns with some conventional disciplines of assessment, best illustrated in the time-limited, formal, unseen exam. Many universities these days have reduced their use of, and dependency on, formal terminal exams (Tomas & Jessop, 2018). But there are still deep and widespread anxieties about what is being tested and warranted through assessment. Worries about plagiarism, contract cheating and impersonation abound (Dawson & Sutherland-Smith, 2018). Academic integrity focuses on the capabilities and character of the solo student. In a system where universities test and warrant capabilities, these anxieties are understandable and it is quite rational to manage risks – whether to reduce the risk of reputational damage, or out of concern for safe practice.

The preoccupation with the individual student, their learning and capabilities, is also a reflection of how psychologists have tended to frame their object of inquiry. There are mutually reinforcing tendencies between psychological research on how people learn and assessment and certification practices in education.

> In traditional psychology, learning is studied at the level of the individual. This is true of behaviorism, which studies behaviors of individual organisms, and also of cognitivism, which studies mental processes and structures within individuals' minds.
>
> (Greeno & Engeström, 2014, 128)

This predilection for focusing on what the solo student can do, unaided by other people and things, is not without its critics. On the one hand, as lists of contemporary graduate attributes attest, the ability to work capably with other people, using increasingly complex 'tools of the trade', is highly valued (see Chapter 1). On the other, some of the strongest scientific accounts of human action and capability are cast in terms of the 'extended mind' or the 'person plus'. If the human cognitive system is not bounded by the skull or the skin (Clark, 2011), but extends out into the person's environment, then some forms of assessment – like the time-limited, unseen, pen and paper exam – disable that system. Put another way, some core assessment tasks tell us little or nothing about how good a person is at assembling the epistemic environment – including tools, materials and people – needed to solve complex problems efficiently.

A default focus on the individual student is not simply an issue for assessment regimes. As Macfarlane (2017) argues, it permeates thinking, policies and procedures relevant to the whole sweep of educational provision and quality assurance. His preference is for reconfiguring the user from customer to novice scholar.

> university students should be regarded as novice scholars, not as 'customers'. They are autonomous adults who have chosen to further their education at university for a variety of reasons. Yet their primary identity as novice scholars is being submerged beneath a new identity as a *managed customer*, one of several so-called stakeholders that higher education institutions seek to satisfy and placate. Ironically, behind the rhetoric and marketing hype, this identity weakens rather than strengthens the rights of students as learners. They are domesticated, or made docile, in their roles as managed 'customers' and subject to constraints as learners rather than as adult members of an academic community. While it is popular to contend that students enjoy heightened rights as customers, the reality is that their rights as student members of an academic community are in retreat.
>
> (Macfarlane, 2017, 2; emphasis added)

We agree with Macfarlane that the 'student as managed customer' has taken a dominant position in university management, quality-assurance and quality-enhancement practices. It was also a 'lament' of many of our interviewees. This is a clear consequence of the market-centred ideologies that have been foisted upon universities, and other kinds of public institutions, over the last 40 years or so. Managing customer expectations and responding to customer experiences (as communicated through evaluation questionnaires and quantitative measures of engagement) form much of the organisational logic for the work of educational, IT and facilities leaders. But we now want to take the argument in a different direction.

In short, we believe that thinking about service design in higher education needs to shift its default focus away from the individual student (the managed customer) as user. It needs framing or reframing in terms of co-design for *activity systems*. We mentioned activity systems in the Introduction and we have more to explain about them in Chapter 7. At its simplest, we can consider just a tripartite system: a subject (a person) working towards an object (a goal) with the use of a mediating instrument (a tool) (Kaptelinin & Nardi, 2006) or an agent (a person), working on a task with the help of an artefact that makes the process more efficient (Bonsiepe, 1999). In an educational setting, we can say that an activity system typically consists of one or more students working on a task, together with the material, digital and social resources they are using in tackling that task. Having such an image of an activity system in mind will be helpful in considering what we say next about co-produced and co-designed services, and the relevance of these ideas to framing the challenges of strategic educational leadership.

Service co-production and co-design

We mentioned service 'co-production' earlier in the chapter, suggesting that many services are co-produced insofar as the client has to actively participate if the service is to succeed. For example, doctors offer medical services, but patients have to take their medicines, and/or follow a recommended diet or exercise regime. Investors may seek financial advice, but they then have to interpret and act upon it.

> Co-production is a core element of the service delivery process – an essential and intrinsic process of interaction between any service organization and its service users at the point of delivery of a service ... co-production [is] 'the moment of truth' of services delivery
>
> (Radnor et al., 2014, 408)

Some services demand very little productive activity from the client. For example, having a massage requires the client only to lie still and relax. Admittedly, the client still has to be there; their body plays a vital role in materialising the service interface. But in educational contexts, active participation in service co-production is vital.

> Education fails completely if the student is not actively constructing their own understanding during educational transactions. Most models of effective learning give the learner a central role in co-configuring

> their actual learning activities, learning relationships and learning environment
>
> (Carvalho & Goodyear, 2018, 42)

In other words, students have to be actively engaged or there is no learning. Learning cannot be delivered. A teacher can lecture to an empty room, but that does not constitute an educational service. A teacher can record their lecture and post it on a learning management system, but the educational service does not materialise until a student engages with the recording. If they watch the lecture on the train home, while taking notes on a laptop and shutting out the ambient noise with headphones, they are playing a serious and skilful role in co-configuring a congenial service interface and co-producing an educational service.

A special case, or perhaps an extension, of service co-production is co-design. To the extent that students play a significant role in the early stages of shaping an educational service, they can be said to be participating in co-design. In recent years, there has been a steadily growing interest in participatory design in education: partly as a way of making educational services more relevant to students and partly as a way of helping students learn to do more of the design work themselves – becoming more autonomous as learners, and better able to create their own environments for learning and problem-solving in the future. Markauskaite & Goodyear (2017) describe how this activity of participating in co-design can help students learn to create their own epistemic environments: drawing together the people, tools and other resources needed for specific kinds of knowledge work. Co-design is also proving particularly important in situations where students are coming to school or university from a culture that has been badly under-represented. Among other advantages, it allows better tuning of curriculum, assessment and pedagogy and provides students with a mandate for speaking up about their own needs, expertise, perspectives and experiences (Bang & Vossoughi, 2016; Zavala, 2016; diSalvo et al., 2017).

We have more to say about the practicalities of co-design and co-production, and about the co-creation of knowledge, in Chapter 7. We also sketch some more radical forms of participatory design in Chapter 9.

Social innovation and relational services

One of the reasons that we attach special importance to service co-design and co-production is that it aligns with a fundamental educational goal of helping students become more capable of working with others to tackle major social challenges: to strengthen their 'moral know-how'. Insofar as this can be done with university staff, and as part of the university's broader social mission, it also strengthens the university community and acts as a corrective to the fragmenting forces that separate research, teaching and service. University life often seems to be structured around some resilient, taken-for-granted ideas or models, such as that teaching is for the passing on of established knowledge whereas research is where new knowledge is created, and that the two are necessarily in competition for time and other resources. Another powerful almost taken-for-granted idea is that teaching is most *efficient* when students are organised into large, homogeneous, undifferentiated cohorts. A related assumption is that most students hate group work (Clinton & Kelly, 2017) and are risk-averse, preferring educational activities and assessment tasks that are familiar, and over which they have a high level of personal control; not ceding control to unreliable peers and putting their grades at risk (Chapter 1). These anxieties are understandable, especially when the university culture has become one of exchanging work for grades, and high grades have a special value in the job market. So part of what we are arguing here is for the introduction of other approaches that can reshape assumptions and meet anxieties head on.

There is a growing body of literature on social innovation, understood as 'people creating solutions outside the mainstream patterns of production and consumption' (Cipolla & Manzini, 2009, 45). Manzini (2015) provides a compelling analysis of why social innovation is becoming essential in finding paths towards more sustainable ways of living. One of Manzini's goals is to rethink the role of (expert) design in times when everybody needs to be proactively involved in social innovation or, in his words, what should expert design be when everybody designs? 'Design for social innovation is everything that expert design can do to activate, sustain, and orient processes of social change toward sustainability' (Manzini, 2015, 62). While we agree with Manzini that the democratisation of design thinking should not be allowed to delegitimise design expertise, or the hard-won tools and methods of design practice, we also think that higher education should be offering opportunities for all students to learn how to participate in collaborative social innovation. One of the ways they can be helped to do this is by playing a more conscious and increasingly more expert role in co-designing their own learning situations, while simultaneously expanding their learning situations to include local and networked communities.

There are plenty of examples of educational practices that get students to work together to solve complex problems. This is quite common in business studies and engineering, for example, and in other professional and/or science, technology, engineering and mathematics (STEM) education areas that lend themselves to complex project work. There is also a growing interest in setting up student group projects, especially in later years and in capstone courses, that are focused on solving real problems experienced by companies, non-profit organisations or community groups (Dutson et al., 1997; Fung, 2017). Much can be learned from these experiences – by the students themselves and the external clients, but also by academic staff who are supervising the work and university leaders who can synthesise and disseminate lessons learned across the whole institution.

In a way, we are merely pushing this line of development a few steps further. Following Manzini (2015), we can argue that if university graduates are to play productive roles in helping resolve the wicked problems created over recent decades – climate change, displacement of peoples, pollution of the oceans, misuse of antibiotics, food insecurity, obesity, precarious and exploitative employment, spiralling inequality, and so on – then they need to master the methods and toolsets of social innovation and socially responsible design (Cipolla & Bartholo, 2014). In addition to gaining a deeper understanding in their specialist area(s), they need to experience working with others on complex problems that involve both enquiry and practical action: building a consensus for action among groups of people whose lives are tightly meshed with the problems concerned (Goodyear & Markauskaite, in press). Cipolla & Manzini (2009) analyse social innovation projects in terms of the *design of relational services by creative communities*. Relational services are services which depend for their success on intensive social relations.

> An analysis of the social innovations ... organized by these communities revealed that they are prevalently organizing services – which range from childcare to care of the elderly, from looking after green spaces to alternative forms of mobility, from the building of new solidarity networks to the realization of unprecedented housing typologies – that indicate an emerging new service model deeply and profoundly based on the quality of interpersonal relations between participants.
>
> (Cipolla & Manzini, 2009, 46)

Relational services cannot be designed directly. They can only be 'enabled'. In other words, 'they need to be designed in such a way as to start up, support, and continuously sustain interpersonal encounters between the participants' (Cipolla & Manzini, 2009, 50). Moreover, as we have seen, the services created by and for communities do not only depend upon social relationships. They usually also involve quite complex service infrastructures and interfaces – sociotechnical resources – which originate in, and are sustained by, processes of co-design and co-production (Secomandi & Snelders, 2011; Baek et al., 2018).

Learning to participate in social innovation – to collaborate with others in designing relational services – is clearly non-trivial. It is likely to benefit from well-judged combinations of direct instruction, modelling by experts and opportunities to practise on authentic problems. Rather than bolt this on to an already overcrowded university curriculum, we are arguing for a closer alignment between learning to design for others and learning to design for oneself. Learning to act '"where you are" to transform your own situation by establishing dialogical relations with those who live in the same context' (Cipolla & Bartholo, 2014, 1). On this view, service design should take a central place in integrating educational, IT and facilities planning, and students should be expected to co-design and co-produce these services and be guided, encouraged and supported in doing so. If that happens routinely, then a number of forces that currently compete for time and money can be resolved and there can be better alignment between what the university provides and what graduates will want to be able to do in the future.

Summary of Chapter 6

This chapter marks a shift in the orientation of the book – from eliciting issues that bedevil the work of education, IT and facilities leaders to creating a better framework for thinking about and acting upon those issues. The heart of our argument in this chapter is that smarter integration of leadership and planning, across these specialist fields, can be achieved by taking a *service-design* perspective. Naturally, the educational outcomes and experiences of the university's students maintain their position as ultimate sources of value and purpose. That is not in dispute. Chapter 6 helps with the challenging task of 'opening up' the black box of *process*. There are many ways in which students' activities enable them to learn. Many of these activities benefit from interactions with peers and with more capable guides – academic teachers and others – and depend upon timely use of good tools and resources, all fitting together to make a supportive learning environment. The service-design perspective that we are promoting helps provide a core organising concept around which leaders and their teams can work in a more cohesive fashion. Rather than having two parts of the enterprise focus heavily on the performance characteristics of tools and infrastructure, all parts can cohere around the co-design and co-creation of services for activity systems. As we will try to show in the chapters that follow, the larger grain size involved in planning for the needs of a manageable number of activity systems (rather than the averaged needs of diverse individual students) can help university leaders find a balance point: realistic and grounded.

References

Baek, J. S., Kim, S., Pahk, Y., & Manzini, E. (2018). A sociotechnical framework for the design of collaborative services. *Design Studies, 55,* 54–78.

Bain, A., & Zundans-Fraser, L. (2017). *The self-organizing university: designing the higher education organization for quality learning and teaching.* Singapore: Springer Nature.

Bang, M., & Vossoughi, S. (2016). Participatory design research and educational justice: studying learning and relations within social change making. *Cognition and Instruction, 34*(3), 173–193.

Baranova, P., Morrison, S., & Mutton, J. (2010). *Service design in higher and further education: a briefing paper.* Derby: University of Derby.

Bonsiepe, G. (1999). *Interface: an approach to design.* Maastricht: Jan van Eyck Akademie.

Carvalho, L., & Goodyear, P. (2018). Design, learning and service innovation. *Design Studies, 55,* 27–53.

Cipolla, C., & Bartholo, R. (2014). Empathy or inclusion: a dialogical approach to socially responsible design. *International Journal of Design, 8*(2), 87–100.

Cipolla, C., & Manzini, E. (2009). Relational services. *Knowledge, Technology & Policy, 22*(1), 45–50.

Clark, A. (2011). Supersizing the mind: embodiment, action, and cognitive extension. Oxford: Oxford University Press.

Clinton, V., & Kelly, A. E. (2017). Student attitudes toward group discussions. *Active Learning in Higher Education.* doi:10.1177/1469787417740277

Dawson, P., & Sutherland-Smith, W. (2018). Can markers detect contract cheating? Results from a pilot study. *Assessment & Evaluation in Higher Education, 43*(2), 286–293.

DiSalvo, B., Yip, J., Bonsignore, E., & DiSalvo, C. (eds). (2017). *Participatory design for learning: perspectives from practice and research.* New York: Routledge.

Dutson, A. J., Todd, R. H., Magleby, S. P., & Sorensen, C. D. (1997). A review of literature on teaching engineering design through project-oriented capstone courses. *Journal of Engineering Education, 86*(1), 17–28.

Ellis, R., & Goodyear, P. (2010). Students' experiences of e-learning in higher education: the ecology of sustainable innovation. New York: RoutledgeFalmer.

Felix, E. (2011). Learning space service design. *Journal of Learning Spaces, 1*(1). Retrieved from: http://libjournal.uncg.edu/jls/article/view/284/174

Ford, P., Goodyear, P., Heseltine, R., Lewis, R., Darby, J., Graves, J., . . . King, T. (1996). *Managing change in higher education: a learning environment architecture.* Buckingham: SRHE/Open University Press.

Fung, D. (2017). *A connected curriculum for higher education.* London: University College Press. Retrieved from: www.ucl.ac.uk/ucl-press/browse-books/a-connected-curriculum-for-higher-education

Gallouj, F., & Weinstein, O. (1997). Innovation in services. *Research Policy, 26*, 537–556.

Goodyear, P., & Carvalho, L. (2014). Framing the analysis of learning network architectures. In L. Carvalho & P. Goodyear (eds), *The architecture of productive learning networks.* New York: Routledge.

Greeno, J., & Engeström, Y. (2014). Learning in activity. In K. Sawyer (ed.), *The Cambridge handbook of the learning sciences* (2nd edn). Cambridge: Cambridge University Press.

Kaptelinin, V., & Nardi, B. (2006). *Acting with technology: activity theory and interaction design.* Cambridge, MA: MIT Press.

Kuzmina, K. (2014). Investigating opportunities for service design in education for sustainable development. PhD thesis, Loughborough University.

Macfarlane, B. (2017). Freedom to learn: the threat to student academic freedom and why it needs to be reclaimed. London: Routledge.

Manzini, E. (2015). *Design, when everybody designs: an introduction to design for social innovation.* Cambridge, MA: MIT Press.

Markauskaite, L., & Goodyear, P. (2017). *Epistemic fluency and professional education: innovation, knowledgeable action and actionable knowledge.* Dordrecht: Springer.

Ng, I. C., & Forbes, J. (2009). Education as service: the understanding of university experience through the service logic. *Journal of Marketing for Higher Education, 19*(1), 38–64.

Radnor, Z., Osborne, S. P., Kinder, T. & Mutton, J. (2014). Operationalizing co-production in public services delivery: the contribution of service blueprinting. *Public Management Review, 16*(3), 402–423.

Sangiorgi, D. (2009). Building up a framework for service design research. Paper presented at the 8th European Academy of Design Conference, Aberdeen.

Secomandi, F., & Snelders, D. (2011). The object of service design. *Design Issues, 27*(3), 20–34.

Shostack, G. L. (1982). How to design a service. *European Journal of Marketing, 16*(1), 49–63.

Tomas, C., & Jessop, T. (2019). Struggling and juggling: a comparison of student assessment loads across research and teaching-intensive universities. *Assessment & Evaluation in Higher Education, 44*(1), 1–10. doi:10.1080/02602938.2018.1463355.

Woolgar, S. (1990). Configuring the user: the case of usability trials. *The Sociological Review, 38*(1 suppl.), 58–99.

Zavala, M. (2016). Design, participation, and social change: what design in grassroots spaces can teach learning scientists. *Cognition and Instruction, 34*(3), 236–249

Learning in activity systems

This chapter helps make the second part of the argument about furthering educational strategy by refocusing the integration of educational, IT and facilities planning. Whereas Chapter 6 moved the focus from products to services, this chapter shifts attention from managing (for) the solo student to designing for activity systems. We introduce some ideas about situated learning, activity systems, activity-centred analysis and design, and the connections between what can be designed for learning and what must be left to emerge in learners' activities. We aim to dislodge some elements of the 'folk psychology' that pervades university discussions of teaching and learning and help readers construct more robust ways of thinking about the core concerns of educational, IT and learning space strategy.

The conditionals of learning

In Chapter 1 we summarised a number of perspectives on desirable graduate attributes: how employers, university leaders and others describe what they want graduates to be able to do when they enter the workforce. One of the attributes that comes up quite frequently is the ability to work as a productive member of a team. For this and other reasons, it has become increasingly common for university courses to set group-work tasks.

This begs a question: do group-work tasks improve the team-working skills needed in the workplace? What evidence is there, in the very substantial literature created by decades of research into group work, that it reliably leads to the formation of team-working skills? One can ask a number of parallel questions about other valued graduate attributes – communications skills, IT skills, the ability to work with a wide range of other people, the ability to manage one's own workload, take initiatives, yet be responsive to business priorities, and so on. Does working with a small group of classmates on a joint presentation reliably improve oral presentation skills and/or the ability to link words and images in forming a persuasive argument? Does a week-long internship in a community organisation improve empathy?

One can push the questioning further. What evidence do we have for the success of problem-based learning (PBL), or case-based learning, or flipped classrooms, or work-integrated learning, or reflective practice, or learning in communities of enquiry? Do any of these popular educational approaches reliably produce the outcomes desired?

The educational research literature contains a very large number of studies on many of these approaches. There are also a large number of meta-analyses, quantifying the average effects of each approach, as well as systematic reviews that aim to provide best-practice guidelines based on evidence of efficacy. (See, for example, Donia et al., 2018, on peer feedback and teamwork; Betihavas et al., 2016 on 'flipped classrooms'; Koh et al., 2008 on problem-based learning.)

However, other research summaries can be found that question and/or contradict these findings. Kirschner et al. (2006) and Mayer (2004) have mounted a strong argument that most if not all varieties of 'minimally-guided instruction' or 'discovery learning' have such a poor record of demonstrating educational benefits that they should be dropped entirely. They include discovery learning, experiential learning, problem-based learning and enquiry-based learning. Indeed, Mayer (2004) argues that these are essentially rebrandings of what is fundamentally the same (failed) approach.

We mention this not to boost the argument against 'minimally guided instruction' but to point out that it is understandable if teachers in higher education begin to doubt whether educational research is actually capable of informing educational practice. To the question 'does PBL work?' the best answer is 'it all depends …'.

This may seem like a very unsatisfactory attempt to dodge responsibility. After all, medical research seems able to produce robust guidelines about treatments, using randomised controlled trials (RCTs). Why cannot education do the same (Connolly et al., 2017)? The best response to this is to note that: (a) RCTs are not very good at handling complex (multi-part) interventions: (b) the findings from experimental research in psychology labs, while sometimes reliable and replicable, rarely have much power outside the lab: (c) lab findings can improve our understanding of some fundamental cognitive and learning processes, but environmental or contextual variations tend to overpower their effects on real-world performance (Bronfenbrenner, 1979; Sandoval & Bell, 2004). For example, cognitive load theory (CLT) has been very successful in pointing out the educational problems that arise when working memory is overloaded – as when a student works with too demanding a mix of information sources (e.g. Paas et al., 2004). But CLT does not tell us how to stop students trying to multi-task; and they do, even though their work suffers.

In the rest of this chapter, we propose a way out of this dilemma. On the one hand, we want to help university leaders and teachers give up their addiction to sprinkling pedagogical fairy dust – which is one way to describe the belief that group work magically generates team-working skills. On the other hand, we want avoid a situation in which only pedagogical guidelines that have been validated by RCTs are treated as useful knowledge.

The middle path is found by looking more closely at that seemingly timid phrase 'it all depends'. Informed professional action needs to be sensitive to the *conditions* that apply to statements about what works. Understanding the effects of nested contexts on the connections between learning activities and learning outcomes is key. In other words, one needs an *ecological* understanding of how to promote good learning.

In this chapter we examine student learning as a *situated* activity, to open up discussion of how the activity systems in which student learning takes place can be understood and improved. We introduce a specific approach known as activity-centred analysis and design (ACAD). After presenting the ACAD architecture, we turn to constructs that are needed to explain the relationships between structures that can be designed and activity that emerges in and around those structures. These kinds of constructs are necessary tools for rational design and for analysing and evaluating learning activities and activity systems.

The importance of the unit of analysis: activity systems and activity theory

Fleetwood (2005) stresses the role of ontology in framing research. How one conceives of the nature of reality – and the kinds of entities that exist and constitute it – is crucial because ontology affects

> what we think can be known about it (epistemology); how we think it can be investigated (methodology and research techniques); the kinds of theories we think can be constructed about it; and the political and policy stances we are prepared to take.
>
> (Fleetwood, 2005, 197)

A central ontological question in research concerns the nature of the *unit of analysis*: it plays a crucial role in defining what we can and cannot see, what we can and cannot enquire into, in any investigation. Thus it makes a difference if our thinking about student learning focuses on (i) the learning outcomes for each individual student, or (ii) what students say about their educational experiences, or (iii) whether the average grades for a class are falling or rising, or (iv) the relative costs of teaching courses in different disciplines – to give just four examples.

Also, the unit of analysis for such enquiries tends to define and place constraints on what are seen as candidate areas for change: there is a flow-through from the ontology of enquiry to decisions about what design, management, leadership, policy, funding and governance should focus on. If action is to be evidence-informed, then there has to be a degree of consistency between the unit(s) of analysis used to organise evidence gathering and those framing subsequent action.

In principle, it is important for university leaders to be able to range across a wide array of problems and opportunities, to conceptualise these in ways that make sense within the institution, and to focus information gathering and recommendations for action on units that vary in scale and diversity, from the individual student, course, technology, space or assessment task up to whole-of-institution issues. However, energy cannot be dissipated across all kinds of foci and levels.

We suggest and explain why we see *activity systems* as being useful entities for design and other processes to focus upon.

> instead of focusing on individual learners, the main focus of analysis is on activity systems: complex social organizations containing learners, teachers, curriculum materials, software tools and the physical environment.
>
> (Greeno, 2006, 79)

An activity system can be understood as a complex mix of people, tools and tasks in the here and now. But there is also an important historical dimension.

> rather than the socially mediated individual being taken as the basic unit of analysis, the *historically located* activity system should be the fundamental unit ... this approach features the essentially social nature of activity and the centrality to it of durable cultural artifacts
>
> (Blackler, 2009, 29; emphasis added)

Sannino et al. use this missing historical dimension to distinguish cultural-historical activity theory (CHAT) from other forms of sociocultural theory.

> Sociocultural theories ... focus on action rather than activity ... a focus on action does not account for the historical continuity and longevity of human life. Activity theory conceptualizes actions in the broader perspective of their systemic and motivational context and, thus, aims at going beyond a given situation ... activity theory is a practice-based theory ... [and] a historical and future-oriented theory.
>
> (2009, 3)

In our previous work on analysis and design of complex learning systems (e.g. Carvalho & Goodyear, 2014), we have not paid sufficient attention to either the historical development of the systems, and their sub-systems and super-systems, or to the constraints, contradictions and opportunities for change embedded in such systems. We take some initial steps to remedy this when we describe activity-centred analysis and design later in the chapter. Before that, we need to go a little more deeply into the roots of CHAT.

The situative view

The situative view represents a deliberate opening up or broadening of perspective, so that a better account can be given of the influence of a person's social and physical setting on what they do, think and learn. Its origins can be found in the work of Lev Vygotsky, who aimed to put psychology on firmer foundations by incorporating history, society and culture, including material culture, more thoroughly into explanations of the development of mind.

The person and mind understood from the viewpoint of cultural-historical psychology

> Vygotsky's ideas defined a new perspective in psychology. This perspective attempted to find the origins of mind in culture and society. Instead of considering the social world an external context in which mind originates and develops according to its own immanent laws, cultural-historical psychology considered culture and society to be a generative force shaping the very nature of the human mind. Many other approaches took (and are still taking) for granted that the subjective processes of the individual constitute a separate world related to objective reality mostly through perception. It is up to the individual to decipher sensory inputs and transform them into a meaningful picture of reality ... Cultural-historical psychology takes a radically different stance. It postulates that reality itself is filled with meanings and values. Human beings develop their own meanings and values not by processing sensory inputs but by appropriating the meaning and values objectively existing in the world ... The border between the mind and the physical world, between the individual and other people, is not closed. It is being dynamically redefined on a moment-to-moment basis ... Meaning and values can cross these borders – and of course, are creatively transformed along the way.
>
> (Kaptelinin & Nardi, 2006, 50)

Although Vygotsky and his followers acknowledged that the material world plays a significant role in human development, their treatments of human culture tend to foreground social relations and language. The importance of specific properties of material objects in shaping brain and mind has been relatively neglected, but it is of growing interest among archaeologists, anthropologists and others involved in studying the evolution of material culture. For example, in creating a niche for Material Engagement Theory, Malafouris argues that 'the human brain is as much a cultural artefact as a biological entity ... the brain, far from a hard-wired modular organ, emerges as a dynamic co-evolutionary process of deep enculturation and material engagement' (Malafouris, 2013, 45). Taking materials seriously is particularly important when thinking rigorously about pedagogy, educational activity, learning spaces and digital tools.

Scholars developing what have come to be known as situated or situative perspectives have not all focused on the same aspects of human activity, though one might argue that their main areas of attention overlap substantially. For convenience, we can summarise published work as primarily concerned with situated cognition, situated action and situated learning. It is important to note that referring to something as – for example – 'situated learning' does not imply that some forms of learning are not situated. Rather, the term is a reminder to attend to the situated nature of the activity concerned, if one wants to understand human activity and development without recourse to a damaging separation of person from context.

Cognition as situated

In its heyday – roughly, the 1980s and early 1990s – cognitive science proposed and defended models of the (human) mind as an information-processing system, not unlike a digital computer. On this view, people solved problems, and carried out other forms of intelligent action, by manipulating representations in the mind.

> Individual problem solvers are hypothesized to have constructed cognitive structures called 'problem spaces' that represent the task, including objects of the problem, arrangements of the objects in different states, operators, goals and strategies. Problem solving is understood as a process of searching in the problem space for a path from the initial state to the goal.
>
> (Sawyer & Greeno, 2009, 349)

In contrast, a growing band of researchers, studying how real people solve every-day problems in the real world, began to see, and insist on, the importance of *things* in that real world for the processes of everyday cognition. Rather than positing a problem space as a stable mental construct – a kind of map in the mind of the problem-solver – these researchers reframed the problem space as 'dynamically co-constructed by the problem solver in collaboration with material resources, sources of information, and (very often) other people in the situation' (Sawyer & Greeno, 2009, 349).

There are several aspects to 'situatedness' in studies of cognition. These include preoccupations with one or more of: embodiment (cognition depends on the body not just the brain); embedding (cognition habitually takes advantage of structures in the physical and social environment); the extended mind (that cognition has ways of extending 'beyond the skin'); distributed cognition (that cognition can be distributed across multiple people and/or across tools, devices, instruments, etc. in the environment) and enactivism (a focus on the dynamic coupling between an agent and its environment). Separately or in combination, these perspectives challenge rather seriously the adequacy of the (folk) psychological concept of the 'solo' learner.

Action as situated

It would not be an exaggeration to say that Lucy Suchman's anthropological research at Xerox Palo Alto labs in the 1980s brought about a paradigm shift in conceptions of how people plan, act, talk, think and learn. Her work had profound effects in the R&D communities working on artificial intelligence, cognitive science, intelligent tutoring systems and human–computer interaction. Suchman's 1987 book *Plans and Situated Actions* demolished the foundations for work in these fields that assumed intelligent action in the world depends upon prior planning – that action is essentially the execution of pre-existing plans. Through careful observation of the details of human–human interaction and human use of machines, Suchman showed how action is emergent, and is not predetermined by plans or scripts. If anything, plans are resources for action, and for post-hoc explanations of action: 'The organization of situated action is an emergent property of moment-by-moment interactions between actors, and between actors and the environments of their action' (Suchman, 1987, 179) and 'every course of action depends in essential ways on its material and social circumstances' (Suchman, 2007, 70). Suchman's account of situated action is neither a behaviouristic not a mentalistic perspective. It is not behaviouristic because it does not assume that the significance of action is reducible to 'uninterpreted bodily movements' (ibid.) and it is not mentalistic because it takes the significance of action to be based firmly in the physical-social world.

Learning as situated

These insights about situated action and cognition soon found applications in educational research, particularly where researchers were interested in how people solved problems in everyday settings.

> solutions of problems ... were better understood as emerging from interactions between people and resources in the setting than as products of mental operations with and on symbolic representations ... Situative research provides an alternative to the mentalist idea that considers cognition as an internal mental process – one that may be influenced by the surrounding context but that is, at its root, internal. The situative approach shifts the focus: situated action within activity systems is central, with individuals and their actions considered constituents of the activity system.
>
> (Sawyer & Greeno, 2009, 348–350)

Lave & Wenger (1991) popularised, and argued persuasively for moving beyond, the term 'situated learning'. For one thing, all learning is situated. Some early adopters of the idea of 'situated learning' took it to mean the opposite of classroom learning. Some advocates of getting students to work on 'authentic tasks' are misled by a similar notion. Learning can be situated in a classroom or a psychology lab, or anywhere. For this reason, Sawyer and Greeno use the term 'situative' – to mean a perspective that recognises cognition, action and learning are always somehow situated – rather than 'situated' (which would imply that cognition, action and/or learning are sometimes *not* situated). The other part of the argument that made 'situated learning' a transitional term for Lave and Wenger reflects their commitment to seeing learning as an aspect of all or many social practices, rather than singling it out as an odd and autonomous process. Learning 'is not merely situated in practice – as if it were some independently reifiable process that just happened to be located somewhere; learning is an integral part of generative social practice in the lived-in world' (Lave & Wenger, 1991, 35).

Or as Greeno puts it: 'From the situative perspective, all socially organized activities provide opportunities for learning to occur, including learning that is different from what a teacher or designer might wish' (Greeno, 2006, 80).

Lave & Wenger also introduced the idea of legitimate peripheral participation in communities of practice as 'a descriptor of engagement in social practice that entails learning as an integral constituent' (1991, 35). This is a powerful idea that has spread widely in higher education thinking, influencing the organisation of professional education programmes, both pre-service and in-service. It has also given theoretical strength and clarity to educational approaches based on forms of apprenticeship in communities of enquiry. We believe it can be applied more generally in higher education, to bring together apprenticeship in an academic discipline (cf. Macfarlane's idea of the 'novice academic'), apprenticeship for future knowledge work and apprenticeship as an active citizen (Fung, 2017; Macfarlane, 2017; Goodyear & Markauskaite, in press).

Taking a situative view has scientific as well as practical implications, of course. It sharpens vision and clarifies what needs to be analysed: 'the core commitment … is to analyse performance and transformations of activity systems that usually comprise multiple people and a variety of technological artifacts' (Sawyer & Greeno, 2009, 348). But this is far from simple. It requires tools and methods. So in the next section we present an approach to analysis and design that we have been developing for some years: ACAD.

Activity-centred analysis and design (ACAD)

In Chapter 6, we introduced the idea of service design and, more specifically, the design of the *service interface*. We defined this as the locus of exchange for services, or as the site where services are co-produced. Since services can only be experienced through tangible elements – available to be perceived by those co-producing the service – we can get a firmer grip on service design by examining the characteristic elements constituting the service interface. We now want to connect this with the idea of analysing and designing for learning in activity systems.

There are various ways this can be done, just as there are numerous approaches to design for learning (e.g. Goodyear & Retalis, 2010; Laurillard, 2012; Dalziel, 2016; Bower, 2017). The approach we offer here is an extension of the design approach described in Ellis & Goodyear (2010). In the intervening period, it has come to be known as activity-centred analysis and design, or ACAD (Goodyear, 2005; Carvalho & Goodyear, 2014, 2018).

Figure 7.1 provides a high-level schema for ACAD. The service interface consists of three kinds of elements, which can be designed ahead of time, though at 'learn-time' they typically become entangled with one another and are also modified by students through and for their activity. The three kinds of designable components of the service interface are tasks, physical resources (material, digital and hybrid) and organisational forms (such as roles and divisions of labour).

Tasks

Tasks can be thought of as suggestions for things that are worth doing. They are the primary structuring resources – the most salient design component – in most

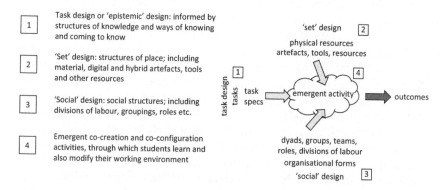

1	Task design or 'epistemic' design: informed by structures of knowledge and ways of knowing and coming to know
2	'Set' design: structures of place; including material, digital and hybrid artefacts, tools and other resources
3	'Social' design: social structures; including divisions of labour, groupings, roles etc.
4	Emergent co-creation and co-configuration activities, through which students learn and also modify their working environment

Figure 7.1 The ACAD framework: design perspective

cases of design for learning. Generic kinds of tasks include such things as writing an essay (on such-and-such a topic), carrying out a lab experiment, preparing a presentation, solving a set of problems, discussing a controversial issue, or creating a resource to be used in future work. Strictly speaking, a task is somewhat abstract: it gets realised in concrete, perceptible, form as a *task specification*. The task specification is part of the service interface. In many learning situations, students adapt tasks. They may customise them, to make a better fit with their needs and interests. For example, a student nurse may have more specific knowledge than her teachers about the hospital in which she is going to do her next work placement (internship). She can use this knowledge to fine-tune the requirements of a task she has been set, to better match the working practices in the hospital to which she will be attached. Or a student of philosophy may choose one of a number of available theoretical concepts to use in scoping an essay. This kind of customisation of a task is generally regarded, in higher-education settings, as educationally valuable. It is one aspect of co-designing and co-producing a service that generally brings additional educational benefits. However, there are other forces at work that can have less beneficial effects. We summarised our research on the nature and effects of a number of these influences in Ellis & Goodyear (2010). For example, some students may take a surface or strategic approach to a particular task, and end up working on an impoverished version of the task.

For good or ill, this slippage between a task as designed and what the student then does, means that one cannot safely assume that the *task* is identical to the student's subsequent *activity*.

Physical resources

The second kind of designable component includes all the different sorts of physical resources that the designer(s) believe may be useful in carrying out the task. 'The structure of a tool itself, as well as learning how to use a tool, changes the structure of human interaction with the world' (Kaptelinin & Nardi, 2006, 56). For example, writing an essay may benefit from access to a word processor, a bibliographic database, easy access to online journal articles and electronic books, a desk and a quiet place to work. Carrying out an experiment in biochemistry may benefit from access to a safe, properly equipped and well-supervised lab space, but also from protective glasses, an electronic notebook and a video demonstrating the correct procedures.

Physical resources may be material (like a pipette or lab bench) or digital (like a word-processing program or an e-print) or some kind of digital–material hybrid (as with a laptop or an iPad). Physical resources also tend to be 'nested' or arranged in some other spatial pattern. For example, the biochemistry lab bench and student workstation will be located in a lab that also contains many other workstations, as well as shared resources like fume cupboards. The lab may be in a building that contains a mix of research and teaching facilities. And the building will be on a campus, to which the student may have to travel. The spatial arrangement of physical resources can have significant consequences, over and above the mere availability of those resources (Luckin, 2010).

(Social) organisational forms

The third kind of designable component concerns people, who are not, of course, designable. (Though as Snelders et al. (2014, 9) put it: 'different gradations of designerly control over human relations can be exercised in practice'.) What can be designed in the social domain are such things as roles and divisions of labour. For example, to tackle a certain designed task, in a learning place that has been equipped in a certain way, it may be suggested to students that they should work in pairs, or in groups of four, or strictly on their own. In the case of group work, it may be suggested that each person in the group should take turns in being the person who creates a record of the group's discussion and decisions; or someone may be selected to be chairperson. On a larger scale, students are often arranged into year groups – all the first year students following the same curriculum – and into groups based on their major subject(s). These are based on design decisions, though sometimes the arrangements can seem so engrained in practice that they are assumed to be part of the natural order of things. Other designs in this social/organisational space may result in such things as the formation of a community of practice, or a community of enquiry.

Activity

These three *kinds* of components that feature in design for learning – and which become realised in what we can think of as the service interface – can be labelled 'set design' (for the physical), 'social design' (for the social/organisational) and 'epistemic design' (for the design of tasks).

At 'learn-time' the designed, provided and/or recommended elements of set, task and social become resources that students (re)configure to better suit their needs and/or wants. For example, students can be asked to work as a team of four, but their first act may be to break the task up into four components and then work independently. Or students may get a list of 'essential readings' with 20 journal articles on it, and only skim read four of them. They may take their laptop to a lecture, so that it is available for taking notes, but end up using it to check their social media feeds. In relation to tasks, it is not unusual for students to interpret a task as specified, work out what they think the marker(s) will really value, and focus on that.

In short, they modify the tangible elements that feature in the service interface. Their learning activity emerges in and from this work of reconfiguring; they co-produce a specific instance of an educational service (Carvalho & Goodyear, 2018). Their activity is triply situated – by the physical architecture (set design), social architecture (social design) and epistemic architecture (epistemic/task design) – and, as the activity emerges, so these elements become entangled. An activity system comes into being, or more accurately a local activity system comes into being for the duration of a specific educational activity, forming as a subset or a moment in the life of a larger, more sustained activity system. (It is important to note that the activity in an 'activity system' is not restricted to what students do in response to so-called 'active learning' tasks (Freeman et al., 2014). Students in lectures are usually active: listening critically, taking notes, posting on Facebook (French & Kennedy, 2017). The activity may not be perfectly aligned with the lecturer's sense of the task, but it is still an activity.)

The distinction between tasks (as specified) and activity (emergent; as realised) derives from the writings of the French ergonomist Alain Wisner. Goodyear (1999) introduced it into the educational technology and higher education literature, to help analyse divergences between university staff expectations and students' actual use of educational innovations. In studies of workplaces, Wisner (1995) found it useful to distinguish between the task – meaning the work as prescribed by managers and/or formal procedures – and the activity – meaning the work as actually performed. Wisner himself derived the ideas from his reading of Lucy Suchman's research into plans and situated actions. 'plans are resources for situated action, but do not in any strong sense determine its course' (Suchman, 1987, 52). In the same way, tasks or task specifications are resources for (situated) learning activity. They do not determine those activities. They are used by agentic students in improvising their work.

Outcomes

What students learn through participating in learning activities can be varied, complex and uncertain. For any one activity, there may be several outcomes. For example, group-work tasks may simultaneously strengthen understanding of a problem from the discipline, and improve communication and team-working skills. In design for learning, it is common to work backwards from some ideas about desirable learning outcomes to activities that are congruent with the attainment of those outcomes. Since the activities themselves are not designable in advance, design thinking then has to shift to considering the three design components mentioned above – task, set and social design.

Outcomes and activities

In the ACAD lexicon, 'activity' is used to denote *what students actually do* at learn time. It can be *imagined* at design time, to allow some reasoning about plausible links connecting desirable outcomes to situated activities to task, set and social design. But activity is not realised until learn time, and can only be known during and after the event. This usage of the term 'activity' is not entirely consistent with the tenets of (Cultural Historical) Activity Theory, within which one can find an insistence that what people do should only be classed as 'activity' when there is an object – a goal or motive – in mind. Our preferred usage is more inclusive than this.

> In this broad meaning, any process of a subject's interaction with the world can be qualified as an activity. However, in activity theory, the term also has a narrower meaning ... a specific level of subject-object interaction, the level at which the object has the status of a *motive*.
>
> (Kaptelinin & Nardi, 2006, 59)

From an ACAD perspective, what people *actually do* is important in explaining what they learn. What they actually do may have no clear object or motive, or it may have many. What they set out to do may be different from what they actually do, but it is the latter that matters for learning: it leaves a trace.

Figure 7.2 is an expansion of the representation of the ACAD framework. It shows how the service interface comes together through combinations of epistemic design (shaping tasks), 'set' design (shaping the material and digital environment) and 'social' design (shaping the social environment), melded with the co-configuration work of the students. Through their co-configuration work, students help co-produce the service interface and bring into being a live activity system.

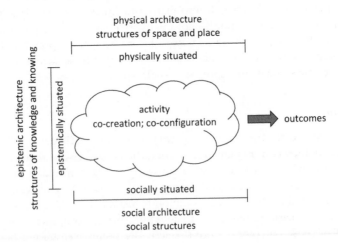

Figure 7.2 ACAD: co-configuration of service interface and activity system at 'learntime'

Indirection in design: how is activity influenced by what has been designed?

The connections (arrows) in Figures 7.1 and 7.2 imply that there are causal processes at work. Only rarely are these deterministic processes. But they are not random. For design to be possible, designers have to be able to think about the likely effects on learning activity of their epistemic, set and social design decisions. Design for learning is an *indirect* practice. As we have said, the really important things – the outcomes and the activity – are not directly designable. This need to be able to work indirectly in relation to complex activity systems means that designers have to make decisions based on a mixture of experiential knowledge, research-based evidence and hunches. There is no shame in this. All designers are in a similar position, able to affect some things directly, but rarely able to touch some of the things that really matter. Architects cannot determine in advance how people will use or feel about their buildings. Aircraft designers cannot guarantee that passengers will enjoy their flights.

For designers to reason about relationships between things that they can design and activities and outcomes, they need 'connecting constructs' – well-theorised concepts tuned to linking these different kinds of elements (Goodyear et al., 2016). Some of these constructs are applicable to relationships between physical entities, and these *tend* to be more stable and predictable. Some are applicable to relationships between people, or between designed elements and emergent activity, and these tend to be less predictable. What sometimes makes them more dependable, however, is that students who are participating in a learning activity – if they are told about the rationale underpinning its design – may act in ways that *realise* the design logic. In simpler terms, if students know why they are being asked to do something, provided that they believe it is in their best interests, they may put effort into making the design work – when it might otherwise have failed. Students are, or can be, reflexive and agentic: they co-design and co-produce the service.

A very important caveat here is that students' attention is not infinite. If they are overwhelmed by the challenge of working out what they need to do to co-produce the service – to make a success of the intended activity – then the activity will fail. A crucial function of good design for learning is to avoid overloading students, so that they can focus on what is to be learned. (There are circumstances where overload and failure can stimulate better learning down the line, but if students are forever mystified and/or distracted by working out task management requirements, then many opportunities for learning will be lost.)

Structure and agency

Relationships between what has been designed and what students then do are a particular manifestation of a much larger set of issues concerned with action in the world: issues which researchers in fields such as sociology, political science, human–computer interaction as well as education refer to as problems of 'structure and agency' (e.g. Giddens, 1984; Archer, 2003; Jones & Karsten, 2008; Ashwin, 2012; Overdijk et al., 2012).

Accounts of how structures influence what people do, how structures are constituted and change, what agency consists of, and what its limits are, tend to operate at a high level of abstraction. While this can help explorations of the scope of their applicability, it makes it unnecessarily difficult for newcomers to be sure they understand what is being said, and can contribute to discussion without looking foolish. Because we are interested in ideas that can play a productive role in real-world organisations, we will take a moment now to introduce 'structure and agency' in more vivid and shareable terms: to help readers help colleagues *use* these ideas locally. (If you already understand the relations between structure and agency, you can skip this section, though you may still find the analogies useful in explaining the ideas to other people.)

Structure, agency and wayfinding in complex landscapes

Imagine yourself walking in the hills. There are no walls or fences and just a few rough paths, made by the boots of other hikers. You are free to walk wherever you want. Imagine also that you plan to walk to the top of one of the highest hills in the area. You have a goal in mind, but the walk itself is the point. If one of the paths leads to your chosen hilltop, you might decide to go that way. But you might also see a more direct, or less steep, or more attractive but less trodden route. You set off in the general direction of your chosen hilltop. The terrain undulates. In general you try to stick to higher ground, following the little ridges so that you do not lose height unnecessarily and have to expend energy regaining it. (A trace of your footsteps, looked at from above by someone who cannot see the undulations, might look erratic and inefficient.) As an experienced hillwalker, you find that you pick your route without much conscious attention. It's almost as if your feet find the best way forward, leaving you free to admire the view and think deep thoughts. Every now and then you realise that you have strayed a bit. You look again at your chosen hilltop and correct your line of approach. This has a tendency to happen where the landscape dips – your feet lead you downwards, when (if you had been paying more attention) you would have skirted the dip and maintained your height. Rough or boggy ground can also cause these deviations. During any walk, you happen upon obstacles that need to be skirted. You also deal with them without much thought, not really noticing that they are there, unless once more you find you have to correct your line of approach to the hilltop.

If this image does not work for you, think instead about wandering through the dense, twisting streets of an old city, with an eventual goal in mind – such as visiting a restaurant recommended by a friend – but where the wandering is (also part of) the point. Or consider sailing a boat upwind to round a headland. In exploring the city, you have an eventual destination in mind, but the process of getting there is not reducible to finding the quickest route. The twists and turns of the streets, the knots of people, the density of traffic, glimpsed views – all of these can affect the route you take. With the sailing boat, the fixed point of the headland to be reached and rounded gives a firm goal; variations in the strength and direction of the wind have moment-by-moment effects on the course you can steer; the direction and size of waves may also favour one course rather than another.

In each of these three examples there are pre-existing structures, some natural and some artificial, some stable and some dynamic, that influence but do not determine the route taken to reach the goal. The route actually taken, and the enjoyability of the activity of getting to the goal, involve interleaved processes of more and less conscious wayfinding. It can be exhausting to have to concentrate, at every step or shift in the wind, on finding the best route forward: on optimising the route. Moreover, this 'economic' optimisation reduces the enjoyability of the activity. Getting to the destination is only part of the point.

Natural and artificial structures, in these examples, have effects in ways that are sometimes subtle and sometimes dramatic. The hiker *has* to walk around a lake, but they may choose to pick their way carefully through a boggy area. The sailor *can* choose to thrash into the wind, close-hauled as possible, but this will not be kind to the boat or the crew. Finding an enjoyable route without overloading one's attention or energy is a key to success.

Translating these ideas to the context of students' learning activities we can note:

1. The walker/sailor's *capabilities* are important – not just in terms of reaching the chosen goal but also of enjoying the activity, including wayfinding without excessive attention to topography or maps. Moreover, for the structures of the hillside, city, sea and wind to have effects on the paths taken, the walker/sailor must have some capabilities. Their agency is needed for the structures to have effects on much of what they do. In educational technology discourses, structure and agency are sometimes framed as being in competition with one another. But structure and agency are relational not oppositional or mutually exclusive (Archer, 2003). Students' capabilities and agency affect how structures in the learning landscape affect them.
2. With learning activity in university settings, the landscape students are navigating is partly composed of material things – buildings, rooms, books, a learning management system – but it is also partly composed of (immaterial) learning tasks and their requirements. Activity, at any time, may be a response to multiple tasks and goals. Using one's time and energy carefully is a matter of wayfinding in complex terrain: taskscapes as well as material and digital landscapes.
3. Some of the landscapes or taskscapes that people navigate are not directly perceptible, or can only be sensed from time to time or in special ways. Think graphically, for a moment, like an economist and see the surfaces formed by supplies of, and demands for, a multiplicity of goods and services. Consumers move across such surfaces, deciding what they can and will buy, substituting one good for another and acting, on the average, in ways that economists consider rational.

4. Students also navigate multidimensional scapes of tasks, materials, digital resources, texts, and so on. The routes they take through the learning landscape depend upon more and less subtle interplays between their own goals and conscious choices (agency) and the contours and qualities of the scapes (structures). On the average, their routes may be predictable – with some acceptable margin of error – but predictability is reduced at the level of the individual student and/or in novel circumstances.

5. Exercise of agency reshapes some structures. The routes students take through the learning landscape can become well-worn paths that others may see and follow. Areas they neglect may become priorities for redevelopment by university staff. Over time, people make, adapt and remake structures, though they usually do so in circumstances that are not of their own making.

6. Not all landscapes are continuous surfaces. Or rather, it can be a mistake to only see them as such. In the example of the city, streets form a *network*. One can move along streets and paths (connections) in the network, but one cannot usually cut through other people's buildings. (If an observer sees a continuous surface, and the agent sees a network, the observer will struggle to see any logic in the agent's path.) Network structures are becoming more important in digital times, in education and elsewhere. However, teachers rarely see more than glimpses of what students are doing in their extended networks. The 'smooth spaces' of the classroom are easier to survey.

In sum, the *products* that IT and facilities staff design and set in place form parts of a landscape that provides structure – constraints but also enabling resources, like scaffolding – for students' activities. This applies to the form of buildings, the functioning of rooms, the digital tools and resources provided, and so on. Working out *what* to set in place, and where, has to be informed by ideas of how students are likely to find their way around within the learning landscape. They *should* be exercising agency rather than merely following directions; after all, their higher education is partly aimed at strengthening their agency. At first glance, it may seem that students' exercise of agency makes designing, planning and managing digital and material facilities problematic. However, focusing on a manageable subset of types of activity and activity system can help with this. Understanding how the products of educational design and teaching add a further dimension to the landscape is important for all staff concerned. But again this is likely to encourage some kinds of activities rather than others: a manageable set rather than an infinity of possibilities. Joined-up thinking about education, IT and facilities provision can benefit from an extra conceptual layer: integrating objects and practices around servicing the needs of a discrete number of kinds of activity system.

Through such integrative work, university leaders may be better placed to help students navigate the very complex, multidimensional, partly invisible landscapes enjoyably, in ways that help them reach their goals. To do so, however, the fundamental unit of analysis of education strategy needs to shift – to activity systems.

We now need to turn to more specific ideas about connections between things that have been designed for students and what they then do. Such connecting constructs are needed at design time – to discipline the design imagination – and they are also needed for later analytic or evaluative work, since they capture important causal processes.

Connecting constructs

Returning to Figure 7.2 in the light of what we have said about structure and agency, we can examine some of the 'connecting constructs' that support reasoning about relationships between what has been designed and what students then do. We do not have space here to review these comprehensively, so we will focus on just two: the role of pedagogy and the affordances of tools and places.

Putting pedagogy in its place

When I hear the word 'pedagogy', I reach for my gun.
(IT director, UK university)

In discussions within universities about educational technology or new learning spaces, it is common for people to say that developments should be 'pedagogy driven'. This article of faith is meant to stand as a corrective to views that technological or architectural innovation will be in the driving seat. The notion that educational needs rather than technological possibilities or fashions in interior design should have priority in the development of new educational tools and facilities seems very sensible. It also helps avoid the worst excesses of technological or architectural determinism; for example, the thought that new learning spaces have agency and will revolutionise how people teach, or that MOOCs will undercut the business model of the majority of universities. But what exactly does it mean when people say 'pedagogy driven'?

If we look closely at Figure 7.2, the *only* connection that involves pedagogical reasoning is the one linking intended outcomes to learning activities. In classic approaches to instructional design, or more recent approaches to design for learning, the heart of the design process is working from intended learning outcomes back to the activities that are likely to promote them. This involves the application of pedagogical knowledge, rooted in research on learning and especially in research that connects specific types of knowledge to specific types of learning experiences. (For example, becoming quicker at the execution of a skill benefits from opportunities to practise and automate that skill.)

Once pedagogically informed decisions have been made about what activities are to be fostered, the rest of the design work has to draw upon other kinds of knowledge. Crucially, the knowledge needed to connect activity to technologies and physical facilities – the design components that physically situate learning activity – is not *pedagogical* knowledge, it is *ergonomic* knowledge. In other words, once the target activities are known, decisions about appropriate tools and places can draw upon generic knowledge of workplace design without any risk of pedagogical obfuscation. If people staffing university IT and campus infrastructure understand the ergonomics of workplaces, then they can understand the ergonomics of learning environments.

Affordances

One of the most useful and most misused constructs that can connect activities to tools and places is the idea of 'affordance'. A tool's affordances are what it offers the user: what it invites them to do. Similarly, many of the attributes of material learning spaces invite certain kinds of activity. Chairs invite sitting. Chairs arranged in a circle invite inclusive discussion. Chairs fixed in long rows, all facing in one direction, invite sitting and waiting for a lecturer to speak. If a room is furnished with small tables, each surrounded by four to six chairs, the room invites small group work. Students entering such a room for the first time will most probably divide themselves up into groups and expect to be given a group task. The qualities of a tool or place do not determine the activity, but they make certain activities more likely and more likely to be productive. Affordances are relational: they exist in the relationship between a tool, or place, and a person. They depend upon the capabilities of the person.

A great deal has been written about affordances, their nature and functioning in the literatures of educational technology, environmental psychology, human–computer interaction and design (e.g. Gibson, 1977; Greeno, 1994; Maier et al., 2009). Some theorists doubt the coherence or utility of the idea (e.g. Oliver, 2005; Dohn, 2009; Collins, 2010), particularly when it is evident that people are capable of making their own interpretations of what a tool (or place) is good for. However, it does seem that design informed by an understanding of affordances can, at a minimum, reduce the interpretive work that students, or people more generally, have to do in tackling tasks. If affordances are intelligently deployed, they allow users to focus on the heart of a task and not on peripheral and distracting aspects of task-management. Goodyear & Carvalho (2013) discuss this in terms of fast and slow cognition – that well-designed tools and spaces support a smooth flow of activity, leaving people free to do slower and more demanding interpretive work where it matters most: on getting the most from the learning tasks that have been set. Writing about the causal powers of the structures within which activity unfolds, Elder-Vass puts it even more sharply.

> when individuals act, that action is the direct and immediate product of non-conscious brain processes ... conscious intentionality is itself a naturally caused phenomenon that acts as an input into this process, but only as one of many such inputs.
>
> (2010, 198)

Understanding the affordances of a tool or space, for the activity of a group of students working on a certain kind of task, ought to be a key part of the intellectual toolkit of IT and facilities staff. Without the concepts and terminology needed to think about and discuss such relations, IT and facilities staff will struggle to connect what they do to what students and teachers need.

Synthesis: integrating educational, IT and facilities leadership through organising service design for learning in activity systems

Core constructs and terminology

In Chapters 4 and 5, we noted how IT and facilities leaders remarked on the lack of a shared conceptual framework and shared terminology for some of the phenomena at the centre of their efforts. In organisational discourse, such gaps tend to get filled from other sources and this can be unhelpful. Language choices matter and the use of one metaphor rather than another can lead people to think and act in certain ways. The language used in committee discussions, strategic plans, policy documents, course outlines and study guides cannot determine what people do. But the recurring use of one set of terms, rather than another, or one set of metaphors and images, rather than another, can reinforce some lines of thinking and action, and make other things harder to express, think and do.

For example, Nardi & O'Day (1999) examine four metaphors used in discussions of technology. They cover technology as: tool, text, system and ecology. Each of these has been theorised in the literature of science and technology studies; each has different implications. For instance, the tool metaphor suggests the idea of a 'device-used-by-an-individual-to-get-something-done' (Nardi & O'Day, 1999, 28). The tool metaphor suggests appropriate tactics to technology users: that it is important to choose the right tool for the job; that one should learn how to use a tool well, and so on. The tool metaphor evokes considerations of utility, usability, affordances, learning and skill.

In contrast, 'technology as text' reframes considerations to those of communication: technology as a carrier of meaning. Writing about the semantic turn in design, Krippendorff talks of how

> a successful design affords the meanings of all those stakeholders who can move an artifact through its lifecycle, making it part of a social process ... In the end, what an artifact becomes is what its network of stakeholders makes it to be.

(2006, 186)

In this way, the technology as text metaphor suggests different tactics to users: that they are responsible for reading the technology to understand what it means, what it prescribes, and so on.

Metaphors matter and it can be dangerous to subscribe to just one metaphor. This point was also made very eloquently by Sfard (1998) in reviewing two powerful metaphors in the literature on human learning: an acquisition metaphor, which foregrounds the personal acquisition of knowledge as an individual cognitive accomplishment and a participation metaphor, which foregrounds learning as participation in valued social practices. Recent trends in higher education towards giving students greater opportunities for 'active learning' (Macfarlane, 2017) and 'authentic assessment' can be characterised as a shift away from instructional approaches informed (tacitly) by the acquisition metaphor and towards approaches informed by the participation metaphor. But in configuring the student as agentic user of technologies, striding capably through a complex learning landscape, we risk abdicating our responsibilities as leaders. Student learning is richer than this. It is not reducible to acquisition or participation. Technology use is trickier than this, particularly if and when we move beyond promoting twentieth-century 'office' tools and take more seriously the array of innovative epistemic tools that are transforming knowledge work outside education.

Paths to integration

Turning to the deeper challenges of integrating leadership in education, IT and facilities, our suggestions include, but go beyond, recommending better metaphors – and more conscious use of them. More specifically, in this chapter and in Chapter 6, we have proposed that conceptual integration may best be achieved through reconceptualising the underpinning work in terms of the *design and co-production of services for students learning in activity systems*. This relocates the central concerns of IT and facilities staff – shifting them to a focus on infrastructures and service interfaces for a manageably small set of particularly valued activity systems. The logic of service design can then draw on more mainstream and well-defined areas of expertise – including the ergonomics of learning environments – rather than being captured by the mysteries of poorly articulated pedagogy. Focusing on what students are actually doing, and what tools, and so on, they need in order to succeed in doing it, clarifies the sightlines and makes the task of integrating education, IT and facilities more manageable.

Moving that up to a leadership level, we suggest that working towards a shared sense of the educational mission can be helped by distinguishing and mapping out the main kinds of activity system that can be supported. For example, if problem-based learning plays a significant role within the university's offerings, then its typical forms and requirements can be specified quite readily. If PBL is not much used and a course team then proposes to introduce it, it will be clear to everyone that part of the preparatory work will be mapping what PBL involves and what the activity systems spawned by it will actually need. Education-driven leadership can ensure that policy, resourcing, quality assurance and governance mechanisms will pay proper attention to such matters, increasing the likelihood that those people who are brought together from different specialisms will be able to see how their decisions feed forward into creating the environment that will be needed.

To drive the point home: education strategies that depend upon unarticulated conceptions of how students actually learn, and what they need in order to engage in productive learning activity, make life unnecessarily hard for everyone involved in implementation, including the students. Such strategies obscure the processes through which educational outcomes are achieved and make the diagnosis of problems more difficult. They can also result in too loose a coupling between educational, IT and facilities strategies, with the danger that the latter become susceptible to being driven by external fads and fashions rather than properly analysed local needs.

The remedy is for education, IT and facilities leaders to take on the shared task of co-designing for their own activity system to make sure they and their staff have the intellectual tools and frameworks needed to succeed in understanding and shaping complex educational ecologies. That way, the higher-level work enacted through policy formation, funding decisions, design of governance mechanisms, and so on can be tackled with greater confidence, knowing it is grounded on firm foundations.

Summary of Chapter 7

This chapter began by questioning one of the taken-for-granted foundations for educational decision-making: the idea that there are widely applicable principles that can be used to justify investments in Technology X or Pedagogy Y. We introduced the idea that design decisions are on safer ground when they are made in relation to the needs of a real activity system: people using resources in their environment to achieve certain object(ive)s that they value. We talked about situated action, cognition and learning, to strengthen the idea that what people do, think and learn is often influenced, in powerful and/or subtle ways, by their physical and social (and epistemic) environment. To render this more concrete, we described an approach to educational design and analysis (ACAD) that centres on situated activity. And to introduce some ways of thinking about relations between what can be designed and what students will then do, we offered some useful ideas about structure and agency, affordances and the ergonomics of learning environments.

These may seem to some people like low-level ideas, concerned with the 'nuts and bolts' of learning, rather than matters for consideration at strategic levels. That may be the case. However, we are arguing that the absence of such ideas becomes a strategic weakness. High-level vision is difficult to implement if no one agrees on how its implications can be realised in practice. Without careful attention to the nuts and bolts, the wheels come off.

Therefore, successful high-level educational leadership needs to encourage better shared thinking about education ecologies and how they actually function. We explore this further in the next chapter.

References

Archer, M. (2003). *Structure, agency and the internal conversation.* Cambridge: Cambridge University Press.

Ashwin, P. (2012). *Analysing teaching–learning interactions in higher education: accounting for structure and agency.* London: Continuum.

Betihavas, V., Bridgman, H., Kornhaber, R., & Cross, M. (2016). The evidence for 'flipping out': a systematic review of the flipped classroom in nursing education. *Nurse Education Today, 38*, 15–21.

Blackler, F. (2009). Cultural-historical activity theory and organization studies. In A. Sannino, H. Daniels, & K. Gutiérrez (eds), *Learning and expanding with activity theory* (pp. 19–39). Cambridge: Cambridge University Press.

Bower, M. (2017). *Design of technology-enhanced learning: integrating research and practice.* Bingley: Emerald.

Bronfenbrenner, U. (1979). *The ecology of human development: experiments by nature and design.* Cambridge, MA: Harvard University Press.

Carvalho, L., & Goodyear, P. (eds). (2014). *The architecture of productive learning networks.* New York: Routledge.

Carvalho, L., & Goodyear, P. (2018). Design, learning and service innovation. *Design Studies, 55*, 27–53.

Collins, H. (2010). *Tacit and explicit knowledge.* Chicago: University of Chicago Press.

Connolly, P., Biggart, A., Miller, S., O'Hare, L., & Thurston, A. (2017). *Using randomised controlled trials in education.* London: Sage.

Dalziel, J. (Ed.) (2016). *Learning design: conceptualizing a framework for teaching and learning online.* New York: Routledge.

Dohn, N. (2009). Affordances revisited: articulating a Merleau-Pontian view. *International Journal of Computer-Supported Collaborative Learning, 4*(2), 151–170. doi:10.1007/s11412-009-9062-z

Donia, M. B. L., O'Neill, T. A., & Brutus, S. (2018). The longitudinal effects of peer feedback in the development and transfer of student teamwork skills. *Learning and Individual Differences, 61*, 87–98.

Elder-Vass, D. (2010). *The causal power of social structures: emergence, structure and agency.* Cambridge: Cambridge University Press.

Ellis, R., & Goodyear, P. (2010). *Students' experiences of e-learning in higher education: the ecology of sustainable innovation.* New York: RoutledgeFalmer.

Fleetwood, S. (2005). Ontology in organization and management studies: a critical realist perspective. *Organization, 12*, 197–222.

Freeman, S., Eddy, S. L., McDonough, M., Smith, M. K., Okoroafor, N., Jordt, H., & Wenderoth, M. P. (2014). Active learning increases student performance in science, engineering, and mathematics. *Proceedings of the National Academy of Sciences, 111*(23), 8410–8415.

French, S., & Kennedy, G. (2017). Reassessing the value of university lectures. *Teaching in Higher Education, 22*(6), 639–654.

Fung, D. (2017). *A connected curriculum for higher education.* Retrieved from London: www.ucl.ac.uk/ucl-press/browse-books/a-connected-curriculum-for-higher-education

Gibson, J. (1977). The theory of affordances. In R. Shaw & J. Bransford (eds), *Perceiving, acting, and knowing: toward an ecological psychology* (pp. 67–82). Hillsdale, NJ: Lawrence Erlbaum Associates.

Giddens, A. (1984). *The constitution of society: outline of the theory of structuration.* Berkeley, CA: University of California Press.

Goodyear, P. (1999). New technology in higher education: understanding the innovation process. In A. Eurelings, F. Gastkemper, P. Komers, R. Lewis, R. van Meel, & B. Melief (eds), *Integrating information and communication technology in higher education* (pp. 107–136). Deventer: Kluwer.

Goodyear, P. (2005). Educational design and networked learning: patterns, pattern languages and design practice. *Australasian Journal of Educational Technology, 21*(1), 82–101.

Goodyear, P., & Carvalho, L. (2013). The analysis of complex learning environments. In H. Beetham & R. Sharpe (eds), *Rethinking pedagogy for a digital age: designing and delivering e-learning* (pp. 49–63): RoutledgeFalmer.

Goodyear, P., & Markauskaite, L. (forthcoming). The impact on work and practice of wicked problems and unpredictable futures In J. Higgs, D. Horsfall, S. Cork, & A. Jones (eds), *Practice Futures for the Common Good.* Leiden: Koninklijke Brill NV.

Goodyear, P., & Retalis, S. (eds). (2010). *Technology-enhanced learning: design patterns and pattern languages.* Rotterdam: Sense Publishers.

Goodyear, P., Carvalho, L. & Dohn, N. (2016). Artefacts and activities in the analysis of learning networks. In T. Ryberg, C. Sinclair, S. Bayne, & M. de Laat (eds), *Research, boundaries and policy in networked learning* (pp. 93–110). New York: Springer.

Greeno, J. (1994). Gibson's affordances. *Psychological Review, 101*(2), 336–342.

Greeno, J. (2006). Learning in activity. In K. Sawyer (ed.), *The Cambridge handbook of the learning sciences* (pp. 79–96). Cambridge: Cambridge University Press.

Jones, M. R., & Karsten, H. (2008). Giddens's structuration theory and information systems research. *MIS Quarterly, 32*(1), 127–157.

Kaptelinin, V., & Nardi, B. (2006). *Acting with technology: activity theory and interaction design.* Cambridge, MA: MIT Press.

Kirschner, P., Sweller, J., & Clark, R. (2006). Why minimal guidance during instruction does not work: an analysis of the failure of constructivist, discovery, problem-based, experiential and inquiry-based teaching. *Educational Psychologist, 41*(2), 75–86.

Koh, G. C.-H., Khoo, H. E., Wong, M. L., & Koh, D. (2008). The effects of problem-based learning during medical school on physician competency: a systematic review. *Canadian Medical Association Journal, 178*(1), 34–41.

Krippendorff, K. (2006). *The semantic turn: a new foundation for design.* Boca Raton, FL: CRC Press.

Laurillard, D. (2012). *Teaching as a design science: building pedagogical patterns for learning and technology.* Abingdon: Routledge.

Lave, J., & Wenger, E. (1991). *Situated learning: legitimate peripheral participation.* Cambridge: Cambridge University Press.

Luckin, R. (2010). *Re-designing learning contexts: technology-rich, learner-centred ecologies.* New York: Routledge.

Macfarlane, B. (2017). *Freedom to Learn: the threat to student academic freedom and why it needs to be reclaimed.* London: Routledge.

Maier, J., Fadel, G., & Battisto, D. (2009). An affordance-based approach to architectural theory, design and practice. *Design Studies, 30*(4), 393–414.

Malafouris, L. (2013). *How things shape the mind: a theory of material engagement.* Cambridge, MA: MIT Press.

Mayer, R. (2004). Should there be a three-strikes rule against pure discovery learning? The case for guided methods of instruction. *American Psychologist, 59*, 14–19.

Nardi, B., & O'Day, V. (1999). *Information ecologies: using technology with heart.* Cambridge, MA: MIT Press.

Oliver, M. (2005). The problem with affordance. *E-learning,* 2(4). doi:10.2304/elea.2005.2.4.402

Overdijk, M., van Diggelen, W., Kirschner, P., & Baker, M. (2012). Connecting agents and artifacts in CSCL: towards a rationale of mutual shaping. *International Journal of Computer-Supported Collaborative Learning,* 7(2), 193–210.

Paas, F., Renkl, A., & Sweller, J. (2004). Cognitive load theory: instructional implications of the interaction between information structures and cognitive architecture. *Instructional Science, 32,* 1–8.

Sandoval, W. A., & Bell, P. (2004). Design-based research methods for studying learning in context: introduction. *Educational Psychologist,* 39(4), 199–201.

Sannino, A., Daniels, H., & Gutiérrez, K. (eds). (2009). *Learning and expanding with activity theory.* Cambridge: Cambridge University Press.

Sawyer, K., & Greeno, J. (2009). Situativity and learning. In P. Robbins & M. Aydede (eds), *The Cambridge handbook of situated cognition* (pp. 347–367). Cambridge: Cambridge University Press.

Sfard, A. (1998). On two metaphors for learning and the dangers of just choosing one. *Educational Researcher,* 27(2), 4–12.

Snelders, D., van de Garde-Perik, E., & Secomandi, F. (2014). Design strategies for human relations in services. Paper presented at ServDes 2014: Fourth Service Design and Innovation Conference, Lancaster.

Suchman, L. (1987). Plans and situated actions: the problem of human-machine communication. Cambridge: Cambridge University Press.

Suchman, L. (2007). *Human–machine reconfigurations: plans and situated actions* (2nd edn). Cambridge: Cambridge University Press.

Wisner, A. (1995). Understanding problem building: ergonomic work analysis. *Ergonomics, 38*(3), 595–605.

8

Educational ecology as an applied science

A dynamic world needs fluid, intelligent structures – ecology shows the way.

(Ellis & Goodyear, 2010, 189)

Ecology

The discipline of ecology studies the relationships between organisms and their environments. This conventional ('textbook') definition is widely used. We think it is useful as a starting point for opening up a discussion about an applied science of educational ecology, both here in the book and in practice in universities where leaders are trying to find ways of refocusing attention on how educational arrangements actually function. One can start to develop ecological concepts and language to analyse, discuss and make decisions about these arrangements. One can take a more sophisticated, systemic and systematic approach to providing leadership for difficult areas such as the integration of education, IT and facilities planning. Part of the function of this chapter is to share some ecologically inspired ideas from recent work on educational issues, to help build foundations for an applied science of educational ecology. Chapter 9 then goes on to suggest some relevant methods of inquiry.

Before going further, we need to point out that the 'textbook' definition is potentially misleading. It suggests that organisms and environments exist separately and are mutually exclusive: that each can pre-exist the other. On the contrary

> the words *animal* and *environment* make an inseparable pair. Each term implies the other. No animal could exist without an environment surrounding it. Equally, although not so obvious, an environment implies an animal (or at least an organism) to be surrounded.
>
> (Gibson, 1986, 8)

On this view, the proper focus of ecology is on 'the whole-organism-in-its-environment ... not a compound of two things, but one indivisible totality ... a developmental system' (Ingold, 2000, 19). Failing to take a strong ecological perspective – failing to take that 'indivisible totality' as the unit of analysis – risks a deep misunderstanding of the dynamics of the developmental system itself. Similarly, it could be a mistake to think of the 'organism-in-its-environment' as a bounded entity, a complex but delimitable thing, rather than as a developmental process. It may be *easier* to share descriptions of complex entities moving, over time, from one fixed state or configuration to another. It is easy to slip into such language in everyday discussions. But a closer look makes it clear that flux is the norm. We will return to this towards the end of the chapter.

Ecology began as a study of relations between non-human animals and their environments, understanding how animals made themselves 'at home'. (The etymological roots of 'ecology' are from the Greek: *oikos* (household) and *logos* (knowledge). *Oikos* suggests notions of dwelling or habitat.) The sub-discipline of 'human ecology' emerged in the 1920s as academics from several disciplines realised the potential of studying relations between 'human animals' and their physical environments. For example, H.H. Barrows argued for human ecology to take the central place in geographical research and teaching (Barrows, 1923). Extending ecological thinking to also include the social environment opened up opportunities for a line of work on 'social ecology' (e.g. Dogan & Rokkan, 1969) and similar moves have been made in cognate fields, including anthropology, archaeology, psychology, organisational studies and economics (e.g. Butzer, 1982; Bailey & Barley, 2011). Over the past century, the study of human–environment relations has developed a range of methods, tools and theoretical ideas. Two specific areas are particularly important when finding foundations for educational ecology. One of these is ecological psychology and we treat this at greater length later in the chapter. The other brings into consideration relations between human beings and the environments *they* have created. Ecological studies of non-human animals originally attended to the 'natural' biophysical environment. Over time, greater recognition has been given to human impact on the environments of other organisms, as manifest, for example, in forest clearing and the spread of agriculture, pollution and urbanisation. Consequently, 'environment' now has to be understood as including the artificial as well as the natural, human-built structures as well as structures that owe nothing to human activity or influence. (We are not ignoring the environmental engineering activities of non-human animals – beavers, birds, bees and others.)

'Urban ecology' is a further specialisation of ecology which examines how human and non-human animals inhabit urbanised spaces. We mention this because an ecological perspective on education needs to have theoretical ideas and methods that can take proper account of artificial structures – including the kinds of *built structures* that provide physical 'learning spaces' as well as technological systems. How humans have evolved to learn in and from natural environments is part of the story, but educational ecology also needs to be able to discuss how our species has learned to re-engineer the environment to open up new possibilities for both productive and epistemic activity. Kim Sterelny (2003, 2012) traces a distinctive line in human evolution that leads to a phenomenon he calls 'epistemic niche construction'. Many animals create and exploit ecological niches and some animals reconfigure their environment to enhance the learning opportunities of their young. (Modern) human animals stand out in the extent to which they create epistemic niches – informal learning environments – for apprenticeship learning by the young: opportunities for what Barbara Rogoff and colleagues call 'learning by observing and pitching in' (e.g. Rogoff, 2014). Andy Clark takes this a few steps further. As a species we

> do not just self-engineer better worlds to think in. We self-engineer ourselves to think and perform better in the worlds we find ourselves in. We self-engineer worlds in which to build better worlds to think in. We build better tools to think with and use these very tools to discover still better tools to think with. We tune the way we use these tools by building educational practices to train ourselves to use our best cognitive tools better. We even tune the way we tune the way we use our best cognitive tools by devising environments that help build better environments for educating ourselves in the use of our own cognitive tools (e.g. environments geared toward teacher education and training). Our mature mental routines are not merely self-engineered: they are massively, overwhelming, almost unimaginably self-engineered.
>
> (2011, 59–60)

The next four sections of this chapter flesh out the kinds of work that can be done by educational ecology as an applied science. We pull the threads together at the end of the chapter, but for now we offer the following definition: 'Educational ecology is an applied science that studies and shapes learning systems. A learning system is a dynamic coupling of people and the multifarious resources on which they are drawing in order to learn.'

Ecological perspectives in education

The rest of this chapter summarises some key ideas and insights from ecologically inspired writing in education and the learning sciences. For convenience, and to make this more digestible, we have organised the account in four sections that move in scope from larger to smaller units of analysis. We recognise that there is a danger in this form of organisation, in that it could make it easier to ignore processes that move up and down scale levels. Fortunately, most of the authors on whose work we are drawing also recognise this danger. The first section considers how universities sit in their broader ecologies. It is an outward-looking perspective, though one which raises many questions for understanding internal arrangements. We draw particularly on the recent writing of Ron Barnett (especially Barnett, 2018). The second section takes the ecology of each university as its unit of analysis – looking inwards, and considering how management and leadership might draw on ecological ideas, especially about self-improving systems and feedback loops, in organising their work. We update our earlier contributions (Ellis & Goodyear, 2010) and also draw on Bain & Zundans-Fraser's recent book on the self-organising university (Bain & Zundans-Fraser, 2017). The third section takes us 'down' further, to a focus on specific teaching and learning activities and learning environments. This is where 'activity systems' most comfortably meet ecological thinking. From educational writing, we have selected work by Rose Luckin on her Ecology of Resources model (Luckin, 2010). We complement this with some ecological writing from science and technology studies and human–computer interaction, particularly Nardi & O'Day (1999). In the fourth of these sections, attention shifts to individual people and their learning activity. We single out the pioneering contribution of Urie Bronfenbrenner, bringing ecological considerations to the study of human development (e.g. Bronfenbrenner, 1979). Seen from the perspectives of ecological psychology and cognitive ecology, 'individual students' turn out to be more complicated. We follow Bateson, Gibson, Clark, Hutchins, Ingold and others in showing why it is important to question the taken-for-granted boundaries around people, minds and mental activities. Although this attention to minds and cognition may seem very 'micro', its implications flow back out to all levels of educational management and leadership.

Universities in their wider ecosystems

Barnett: the ecological university

Over the last 30 years or so, Ron Barnett has become one of the most prolific, widely read and influential commentators on universities and the challenges they face (see, e.g., Barnett 1990, 1997, 2007). Barnett hints that his latest book (Barnett, 2018) may represent the apogee of his thinking on the topic, and this gives us reason to take seriously his decision to mobilise the rich set of concepts and values associated with ecology. Naturally enough, he also urges caution:

> The term 'ecosystem' is rather honorific. The term 'system', after all, betokens robustness in the world and definite boundaries and even some manipulability. Ecosystems, however, are precisely not like this; they are always inchoate. They have little, if anything, in the way of definite boundaries. They are more like clouds, always changing their formations and irrevocably permeable. However, even while being outwardly inchoate and formless, they still retain some degree of inner cohesion, with their elements clinging together. They have, as we may put it, a thin ontology, but they have a presence none the less.
>
> (Barnett, 2018, 55)

We are tempted to modify this a little: it may be the case that how inchoate or fluffy the ecosystem looks depends upon where one looks at it from, and what work one is doing. For example,

> If one conceptualises 'the environment' as a monolithic whole, perhaps the way it looks when viewed from an airplane, or else the way it looks when understood through the peephole of a momentary vector of sense-perceptions, it begins to seem arbitrary, chaotic, or hostile. In a certain sense, it seems

static, as if it has an anatomy but no physiology. But … the lifeworld has a great deal of living structure … actively maintained by agents while also providing preconditions for their own cognition.

(Agre & Horswill, 1997, 139)

As we explained in the Introduction, Barnett points to the 'dual headedness' of ecology – as both a descriptor for systems and a disciplinary field. He uses the strong value orientation of ecological concerns as a way of arguing for ameliorative action: if the ecology of a university system is damaged, we should do something about it; if universities can contribute to the reduction of ecological damage in the world, so they should. And he uses the analytic ideas most associated with ecological thinking as tools for understanding universities and their changing roles in the world. He emphasises five aspects of ecological thinking and action: the *interconnectedness* of things, potential *diversity, impairment, responsibility* and *restoration*.

Recognising the *interconnectedness* of things is easy in principle, but following through on its implications is much harder. This is the case in relation to practical educational work and also in relation to explaining and predicting educational phenomena. (A great deal of research on educational technology, pedagogical approaches and learning space design is framed in terms of simple causal or correlational relationships (Goodyear et al., 2018). Requests by educators and educational leaders for evidence-based guidance also tend to expect answers that are cast in simple terms.) Taking a systems approach can offer a better understanding of the complexity of the underlying phenomena, and as we show in Chapter 9, difficult choices have to be made in finding the boundaries of complex systems and in defining the constitution and dynamics of such systems. But such work must and can be done, as long as the risks are understood.

Reduction of *diversity* within an ecosystem is just one sign of *impairment*. If universities are favouring the education of one social class, or disproportionately recruiting and promoting white male staff or responding preferentially to the interests of multinational companies, then something is badly wrong: the health of the higher-education ecosystem suffers, and with it so does society. The same may be true when diversity is reduced in pedagogical methods, assessment strategies or curriculum offerings. This is not to say that increasing diversity within an ecosystem is always good. However, diversity reduction without a proper understanding of its consequences will always be a source of risk, particularly of the capacity to cope with future environmental change.

Other signs of impairment may be associated with loss of ecological balance or the disruption of important flows, of information or resources, for example. Whatever the symptoms and causes, recognition of ecosystem impairment triggers concern about responsibility – what has caused this and who should do what to fix things? Like Barnett, we see some of the power of an ecological disposition coming from this inbuilt drive to recognise *responsibility* and take *restorative action*. It makes no sense to look at a withering educational ecology and shrug one's shoulders. An ecological disposition is committed to restorative action, whether this is damage being done to a university or damage a university is doing to the webs of activity within which it sits.

Like other ecologically inspired authors, Barnett acknowledges the importance of processes and relationships that flow across levels of scale. However, the analysis he presents in *The ecological university* is, we think, particularly useful in acknowledging larger spaces of engagement and wider flows. He shows how contemporary universities are enmeshed in seven 'ecological zones'. Table 8.1 provides a summary of what he means by this.

The university as an ecosystem

Ellis & Goodyear: educational ecology and sustainable innovation

In Ellis & Goodyear (2010), we suggested that the key aspects of an ecology of learning included:

- maintenance of an ecological balance around the concept of learning;
- the development of self-awareness of how parts of the educational ecology are related to the whole;
- the ongoing pursuit of feedback to inform self-awareness – especially about roles and functions within an ecology;
- the capacity of self-correction required to ensure (re)alignment in a rapidly changing world.

We argued that the point of ecological balance for a university most easily rests – amongst the trinity of learning and teaching, research and service – with *learning*, as it is in learning that the other aspects of university work can find a home. Learning can enfold teaching, research and service to the community. Maintaining an ecological balance on learning requires all the parts of the university to act in ways that demonstrate self-awareness of their function and purpose in relation to the mission of the institution. Every part of the university needs to be imbued with an understanding of 'good learning' (Knight & Trowler, 2001). In order for the parts of a university to understand how they are functioning, in relation to the work and purpose of the whole, they need to engage in systematic processes of collecting feedback from stakeholders about the effectiveness of their operations. Student feedback is central to this, but feedback from other internal and external stakeholders is important too. (Crucially, this needs to include both (a) feedback on a broad range of valued outcomes, not just those that are easy to measure and (b) evidence that supports the joint construction of process models – to create a shared understanding of *how outcomes are actually achieved*.) In a context of rapid change, self-correction by the parts of a university in order to align their operations to the mission of the university as a whole is constantly required in order to maintain an ecological balance focused on learning.

Table 8.1 Barnett's seven ecological zones

Ecological zone	The university engaging with the world in/through this space/zone
Knowledge ecology	Universities are (still) important nodes in the production and circulation of knowledge; they can affect the health of various systems and fields of knowledge; insofar as knowledge can affect the well-being of the world, universities have, and should act upon, opportunities for improving knowledge ecologies
The ecology of social institutions	There are many kinds of social institutions in the world, distinguished in part by their core values; even though institutions shaped by neoliberal economics and the instrumental use of knowledge may dominate, other institutions exist (and there can be diversity of values within any one institution). So, universities can find institutional partners who are not wholly driven by neoliberal economics (etc.): partners who can benefit directly from a university's help, or who can help universities achieve more good in the world.
Persons	Universities engage with individuals in a variety of ways and there are broad arrays of competing conceptions about what forms of relationship (between university and persons) are worthwhile, appropriate, dangerous, misguided, etc.
The economy (considered as an ecology)	There are many economies, rather than one global economy; universities have (recently) become major players in some local economies; through interactions with various economic systems, universities can question the health of those systems and broaden the sets of things which are valued.
Learning	This is to be understood in two senses – the learning ecology of a society and the learning environments of each individual person/student. Universities can play diverse roles in meshing with the learning of organisations, communities and individuals.
Culture	Barnett struggles with the university's relationship to culture (understood mainly in terms of artistic works), feeling that the university's only legitimate role is as critic (and certainly not as endorser of a canon). He says the university cannot escape being enmeshed in whatever society (social elites?) value as culture, but it seems he is stymied. In the gap he leaves, we might say that universities can/should play a distinctive role in drawing attention to what is valued in other cultures (including their artistic products).
The natural environment	Barnett wants to expand our sense of the ecological – moving well beyond its taken-for-granted attachment to the 'natural' world. Hence the six ecological zones described above. However, the natural also remains important and universities need to find ways of contributing to the health of the natural world: not just through 'shallow' sustainability and restoration projects, but through advancing a 'deep ecology' commitment to the well-being of the whole of existence.

Bain & Zundans-Fraser: the self-organising university

Bain & Zundans-Fraser (2017) view with some scepticism the ability of universities to improve the quality and productivity of teaching and learning activities. More specifically, they argue that few if any universities have made internal arrangements that can improve matters at scale, rather than in small, discrete sub-areas. Their diagnosis reveals two problems. Both are sector-wide and only one can be fixed by redesign within a university.

The first problem is essentially a matter of professionalism, or the lack of it in university teaching. In short, teaching in universities is not subject to the pressures experienced in professionalised fields, wherein there are mechanisms to enable improved practice and censure poor practice. The second problem concerns the internal arrangements universities typically make to enhance teaching quality. Bain & Zundans-Fraser analyse these as an (at best) loosely coupled 'effort chain', within which each of the mechanisms concerned turns out to be unfit for purpose.

> Not only do universities lack the models of practice at scale required to impact learning and teaching quality, they lack the internal analytic and evaluation systems, methods and tools to measure what they are doing in valid and reliable ways (Bain and Drengenberg 2016). This is not because of a lack of research and practical guidance. Extensive longitudinal research exists related to efficacious practice … and approaches for implementing protocols derived from these practices. The issue is whether universities have the capacity to design themselves in ways that employ an understanding of the learning and teaching context to produce professionally controlled practice for the benefit of all faculty and students. To alter these circumstances requires an understanding of what learning and teaching means with sufficient clarity to establish differences or distinctions in the quality of practice at scale.
>
> (Bain & Zundans-Fraser, 2017, 5)

Turning first to the matter of professionalism, Bain & Zundans-Fraser draw on the work of Bowker & Star (2000) to help define the elements that constitute a professional field and enable improvements in practice. The fundamental element is 'comparable and visible professionally controlled practice'. 'All professional fields are built upon an understanding of context derived from the use of research-based protocols for professionally controlled practice' (Bain & Zundans-Fraser, 2017, 3).

Table 8.2 helps unpack this. Mature professions like medicine and engineering display all three of these characteristics. A large part of their ability to improve working practices over time comes from the interworking of such mechanisms. This is not to say that changes in practice are faultless or to ignore the fact that very poor practice can occur and persist. Rather, the point is to note that governing (controlling, self-regulating, cybernetic) mechanisms

Table 8.2 Professionally controlled practice

Comparability	The use of evidence-based approaches across multiple settings and practitioners
Visibility	Work processes should be observable and observation can distinguish between better and poorer practice
Professional control	A managed professional process enabling standardisation and differentiation of practice while also allowing a degree of professional flexibility; control understood as 'dynamic management and evaluation of comparable and visible practice'

Source: based on Bain and Zundans-Fraser (2017, 3)

are needed, and need to work effectively, for better practice to prosper and poor practice to lose favour. (Some of the catastrophic failings in professional work come about when 'visibility' is impaired, as when bad practice is hidden away by managers prioritising minimisation of reputational damage in the short term.)

Professionalising university teaching, so that it can be improved through the self-governing mechanisms that empower other professions, is clearly a major challenge: one that cannot be tackled by universities acting alone. It needs sector-wide effort, at national and international levels.

It *is* possible to tackle the second problem that Bain & Zundans-Fraser identify through university redesign. In diagnosing the failure of current arrangements to reliably improve practice at scale – across the whole of a university, for example – Bain & Zundans-Fraser dissect the 'effort chain' involved. Table 8.3 provides a concise summary of their critique of each of the five main entities on which universities typically rely for improvements in teaching. While we may not wholeheartedly agree with the critique, it is clear that university leaders have serious work to do in convincing stakeholders that current arrangements *can* deliver better teaching and learning, and in moving forward.

To make our point rather brutally, we have only to look at the role of *feedback* in higher education practice. In a flourishing ecology, feedback mechanisms enable a number of beneficial processes to operate, improving resilience, restoring balance and allowing evolutionary rather than catastrophic responses to changing external conditions. Other than in some rare situations where leaders and practitioners have made great efforts to improve practice, feedback in tertiary teaching and learning is a mere ritual. The feedback that staff who are marking assignments give to their undergraduate students is rarely actionable; it is often too late, beside the point and unread. Staff and students need a better understanding of how to give, read and use feedback if it is to have a discernible effect on subsequent learning, let alone on the students' ability to make their own judgements about the quality of work (Winstone et al., 2017; Boud et al.,

Table 8.3 Diagnosis of why university teaching and learning enhancement efforts rarely work at scale

Standards	Externally imposed standards, associated with state requirements for accreditation and/or from professional bodies are rarely grounded in ways that can have a reliable effect on practice; they are too general to operationalise; 'standards falter because they lack underpinning evidence-based protocols for visible and comparable practice that would give meaning to them' (p. 5). To be effective, standards need to have a 'clear line of sight to professionally controlled evidence-based protocols for practice' (p. 6).
Governance	In universities, learning and teaching governance processes are not informed by evidence-based protocols for practice or by research on learning. 'There is no body of evidence showing a discernible effect of quality assurance approaches on learning and teaching in higher education ... governance efforts create a quality illusion ... although all they really do is amplify the fundamental lack of professional control in the standards of practice they are seeking to meet' (p. 6)
Teaching evaluation	Student evaluations of teaching measure whether they were happy with what they were offered; students rarely have the expertise to know whether they were offered teaching appropriate to their needs. ('This is analogous to asking patients about their doctors' bedside manners without attending to the quality of their medical practice' (p. 8).)
Promotion frameworks	As with standards (above), promotion criteria are rarely expressed with the precision, or the grounding in evidence-based practices, needed to make meaningful distinctions.
Learning and Teaching centres	Most of the effort by L&T centres is directed to a small minority of willing academics; centres are not equipped or motivated to operate strategically, at scale. They 'influence learning and teaching through elective, selective, and exemplary approaches that are incompatible with whole-of-organizational change' (p. 12).

Source: after Bain and Zundans-Fraser (2017, 5–12)

2018). Conversely, it is becoming clear that students' ratings of their teachers' teaching commonly suffer from fatal problems of validity and reliability. Such feedback data has been playing a significant role in academic promotions cases in recent years, yet there is growing evidence that it is not fit for purpose (Uttl et al., 2017).

In a more positive vein, Bain & Zundans-Fraser offer a 'learning and teaching context cycle' coupled with six university (re)design elements which collectively frame a way forward to a sustainable self-improving systems. The cycle loops through:

1. Attribution and efficacy: connecting models of teaching and learning to their outcomes
2. Standards: enabling professional standards to discriminate between good and poor practice; requires adoption of protocols for comparable and visible evidence-based practice
3. Workable distinctions in the day-to-day practices of learning and teaching, allowing evidence-based comparison of what works well, for whom, where and why.
4. Emergent feedback: use of actionable, real-time, knowledgeable, feedback from all parties
5. A shared model of learning and professional practice.

The body of Bain & Zundans-Fraser's book explains and illustrates the six design elements that enable a university to become self-organising:

1. Mobilising the community around commitments to, and a model of practice for, learning and teaching
2. Instantiating that model with evidence-based approaches to learning and teaching
3. Modifying the governance structure to form a network of self-similar teams at each level of the management
4. Releasing and harnessing emergent feedback: feedback emerging all the time, rendering learning and teaching visible and comparable; feedback usable at all levels in the hierarchy
5. Reframing agency and leadership, at all levels, around a shared schema for learning and teaching. (Ideas about agency in university teaching have evolved without an understanding of professional practice.)
6. Implementing technologies that embody the chosen working methods of the learning and teaching community.

What Bain & Zundans-Fraser have identified is a strategy for using the culture and infrastructure of a profession together with redesign of a university's main learning and teaching structures and processes to give universities the capacity to act as self-regulating systems that can improve over time as well as demonstrate and explain such improvements. This is one way of implementing a key element in the conception of an ecologically balanced university that we outlined in Ellis & Goodyear (2010). Clearly, its successful implementation depends on significant action at several levels in the higher-education ecosystem, including at the levels of national regulation, professional standards and identity, and internal mechanisms.

Activity systems, learning environments and the ecology of resources

Moving down one level further, we arrive in territory which is much more familiar to researchers and practitioners in educational technology: the level at which a class or course group tackles an educational task with the aid of people and resources in a definable 'learning environment'. The term 'learning environment' readily affords the generation of ecological ideas and terminology. For example, Hannafin & Hannafin (1996) use the 'ecology/ecosystem' metaphor to evoke the complexity and interdependence of the many components and activities that make for success in a distance learning environment.

> Learning environments operate as ecosystems. Individual elements must function autonomously as well as interactively. In biological terms, each independent organism benefits from the mutualistic, symbiotic relationships among other organisms in the ecosystem in order to attain system homeostasis, or equilibrium. In learning environments, learners as well as facilitators observe, measure, test, listen and probe to assess the integrity and effectiveness of the environment and make needed changes. This may require the learner and facilitator to examine and adjust strategies, technologies or learning activities to achieve balance. It requires active teaching and learning to develop understandings of how each element, as well as the overall system, is functioning . . . Ecosystems are judged successful when they promote equilibrium among their components and interact in ways that support their functions. Balance must be attained initially in order for the ecosystem to evolve, and must be maintained in order for it to survive and prosper.
>
> (Hannafin & Hannafin, 1996, 52–3)

Luckin: the Ecology of Resources model

Rosemary Luckin's Ecology of Resources model has been developed through reflection on lessons learned, over a number of years, through a series of substantial practical educational technology research and development projects. It emerges, in part, through a growing realisation that

> the *arrangement* of the resources within a setting impacts upon the way that the resources are used to support learning within that setting. ... [and that].. the design of technology can influence a learner's interactions with the resources in their environment beyond those solely provided by the technology.
>
> (Luckin, 2010, 74; emphasis added)

Luckin's Ecology of Resources model is underpinned by socio-cultural perspectives on learning, with a particularly strong contribution coming from activity theory (see Chapter 7, above). She is particularly interested in how IT-based tools, as well as more able people, can scaffold a learner's activity, extend their capabilities and enhance the progress of their learning. Looking at how learning contexts can be designed and redesigned, Luckin suggests analysing current and proposed contexts through identifying key elements that are of three main kinds. She labels these 'Knowledge & Skills', 'Tools and People' and 'Environment'. Figure 8.1 provides a simplified illustration.

Figure 8.1 places a single learner at the centre of the ecology, in line with Gibson's assertion (1986, 7), that an environment is always the environment of a single organism. (This does not make it harder to take a design stance aimed at creating a productive learning context that will work for many and diverse learners. Rather, it is saying that, *at learn-time*, each learner inhabits their own environment.) The other distinctive contribution of Luckin's model is its foregrounding of 'filters' – which act to modify the learner's access to, and experience of, the set of elements in each of the three categories. Filters can have positive and negative effects. In some cases, they may deny the learner access to what would otherwise be a useful resource or idea. In other cases, they may help prevent overload and confusion. As Figure 8.1 implies, elements in the three categories of 'Knowledge & Skills', 'Tools and People' and 'Environment' can influence each other directly but they are not directly available to the learner.

Luckin points out that analysis of a learning ecology needs to pay careful attention to the ways the various elements identified influence one another. In other words, the ecology functions through relations between its constituent elements, not (just) through the aggregate functioning of the elements independently (2010, 124–134).

The three categories of 'Knowledge & Skills', 'Tools and People' and 'Environment' contrast with those we use in ACAD (activity-centred analysis and design – see Chapter 7). 'Environment', in Luckin's model, refers to the spatial setting (e.g. a classroom, workplace or home). 'Tools and People' are combined because they can each play a similar role in relation to someone's learning: either can be a source of scaffolding. Indeed the *role* that an element plays determines which of the three categories it sits within (Luckin, 2010, 120). 'Knowledge and

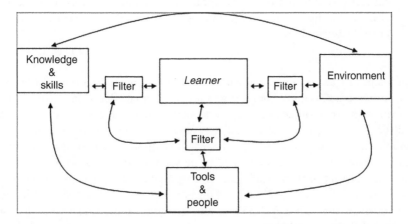

Figure 8.1 Luckin's Learner-centred Ecology of Resources model (adapted from Luckin, 2010, 93–4)

skills' refers to what is to be learned, what has already been learned and what could be useful in the current situation. In ACAD, we separate 'tools' from 'people', placing the former in the 'physical' and the latter in the 'social' primarily because we are using a design-led ontology. As designers, we have more control over what tools do than over what people do. They behave differently and it is right that they should do so. Moreover, from this same design-led ontological position, 'environment' only matters through the manifestation of its physical and social elements; hence it is not needed as a separate (additional) term. Finally, ACAD splits 'knowledge and skills' into (i) the task (in its broader epistemic context) and (ii) that which is inscribed or embodied in physical artefacts and/or known by other people.

We make these contrasts to highlight some of what is distinctive about Luckin's model and the ACAD model, not to criticise the former. ACAD's simple ontology makes sense at design time, and – as we said in Chapter 7 – the three kinds of design components become deeply entangled at 'learn-time'. It is driven by quite a strong materialist or realist view of the world. Luckin's model has the potential to span design, enactment (learn-time) and post-hoc evaluation and to sustain conversations between design specialists, learners and teachers, in part through its closer adherence to a view of the world that has currency in the everyday practices and language of formal education. In combination with ideas about co-created services (Chapter 6) and the tools and methods to be outlined in Chapter 9, we suggest that ACAD can also help sharpen discussions about the integration of education, IT and facilities planning.

Nardi & O'Day: information ecologies

> We define an information ecology to be a system of people, practices, values, and technologies in a particular local environment. In information ecologies, the spotlight is not on technology, but on human activities that are served by technology.
>
> (Nardi & O'Day, 1999, 49)

Nardi and O'Day are concerned with a broad range of applications of information technologies, not just those to be found in formal education settings. Like Luckin, they draw on activity theory to help frame relations between people and the tools they use. Like Luckin they also focus on what we are calling the 'middle range' of settings – neither the macro of whole organisations and global relations, nor the micro of the individual person's mind. While both macro and micro are relevant to them, their gaze and arguments fit more comfortably with the meso, with the kinds and scope of phenomena that we described in Chapter 7 as activity systems. Nardi & O'Day also share the commitment to ecological values that Barnett emphasises:

There is an urgency in the notion of ecology, because we all are aware of the possibility of ecological failure ... we feel a sense of urgency about the need to take control of our information ecologies, to inject our own values and needs into them so that we are not overwhelmed by some of our technological tools.

(Nardi & O'Day, 1999, 56)

Accompanying this sense of peril and the need to act, Nardi & O'Day suggest some additional resonances of the ecological metaphor: healthy diversity (in contrast to the homogeneity of 'community'), continual evolution and the need for time to let things develop properly. This leads them to make three suggestions about strategies for evolving healthy information ecologies which, in our view and theirs, include ecologies dedicated to learning:

- work from core values; from heart as well as head;
- pay attention to – and talk about – the *meanings* assigned to technologies that are in (or coming into) your ecology;
- ask open-ended questions about the use of current and new technologies.

They also explain the importance of a scarce and fragile resource that was salient in some of our interviews with chief information officers: home-grown expertise. They use an image of expert gardeners and gardening to make the point:

Gardeners are people who can translate concepts and mechanisms back and forth between the domain of work and the technology itself. They occupy a special niche in information ecologies, because they bridge the specifics of the domain, with its unique problems and challenges, and the capabilities of the tools used in the domain ... Gardeners know the work, and they know their fellow workers and their problems and frustrations. Gardeners work right alongside everyone else, performing many duties in addition to gardening. This gives them the ability to respond to local needs with sensitivity and understanding.

(Nardi & O'Day, 1999, 141)

We come back to this in Chapter 9, where we argue that more attention needs to be paid to roles that work across internal organisational boundaries and to structures that might help improve what 'gardeners' and other 'third space' workers are able to do (Whitchurch, 2013).

The ecology of human development

In this fourth and final sub-section we tighten the focus again, to the level of the individual person/learner. But in so doing, we also introduce some 'level-spanning' ideas and language.

Urie Bronfenbrenner can be credited with first introducing a serious, eco-logically informed vein of analysis into thinking about education and human development. Bronfenbrenner's key book (1979) lays out the foundations for a psychology of human development that acknowledges relations between the developing person and their environment, social as well as physical. Crucially, Bronfenbrenner brought into this framing the influence of *distal* environments, opening up possibilities to include broader social, economic, political and cul-tural phenomena in explanations of how local ('micro') settings affect develop-ment. He frames his approach in the following way.

> The ecology of human development involves the scientific study of the pro-gressive, mutual accommodation between an active, growing human being and the changing properties of the immediate settings in which the devel-oping person lives, as this process is affected by relations between these settings, and by the larger contexts in which the settings are embedded.
>
> (Bronfenbrenner, 1979, 21)

Although much of his analysis of key processes in human development focuses on dyads – such as interactions between a mother and her child – Bronfenbrenner's broader understanding of relations between environment and human activity succeeds in drawing attention to how ideas, objects, people and their activities in other settings influence how the members of the dyad relate to one another and behave. More generally, this richer or more extensive ecological view opens up possibilities for explaining how activities unfolding in one setting, whether the activities of a dyad, or an individual or a group, are shaped by structures and processes in other settings. His characterisation of the nature of human develop-ment is both broad and rich and it is also imbued with a strong ecological sense of the developing person and the environment shaping each other.

> Human development is the process through which the growing person ac-quires a more extended differentiated, and valid conception of the ecolog-ical environment, and becomes motivated and able to engage in activities that reveal the properties of, sustain, or restructure that environment at levels of similar or greater complexity in form and content.
>
> (Bronfenbrenner, 1979, 27)

Bronfenbrenner's conception of the ecology of human development distin-guishes between four kinds or levels of system. He refers to the levels as micro-, meso-, exo- and macro-systems. Table 8.4 provides Bronfenbrenner's definitions of the four systems levels.

The other key part of his theoretical framing of the ecology of human devel-opment uses four conceptual building blocks: *molar activities, settings, roles* and *interpersonal structures.*

Table 8.4 Bronfenbrenner's definitions of four levels of system influencing human development

Micro-system	'a pattern of activities, roles and interpersonal relations experienced by the developing person in a given setting with particular physical and material characteristics'
Meso-system	'comprises the interrelations among two or more settings in which the developing person actively participates (such as, for a child, the relations among home, school and neighbourhood peer group; for an adult, among family, work and social life).'
Exo-system	'refers to one or more settings that do not involve the developing person as an active participant, but in which events occur that affect, or are affected by, what happens in the setting containing the developing person'
Macro-system	'refers to consistencies, in the form and content of lower-order systems (micro-, meso and exo-) that exist, or could exist, at the level of the subculture or the culture as a whole, along with any belief system or ideology underlying such consistencies'

Source: Bronfenbrenner (1979, 22–26)

'Activity' is a crucial construct in Bronfenbrenner's theory: not just any activity but what he refers to as 'molar' activity. Molar activity is an '*ongoing* behavior possessing a *momentum* of its own and perceived as having *meaning or intent* by the participants in the setting' (Bronfenbrenner, 1979, 45, emphasis added). Bronfenbrenner distinguishes between 'molar activity' and molecular behaviour – or simple 'acts' Molecular behaviour and acts are short-lived and of minimal importance, rather like the subordinate *actions* and *operations* of activity theory. 'Ongoing', in Bronfenbrenner's definition, implies significant duration: more than a momentary event. 'Momentum' leads to persistence or resistance to interruption before the goal of the activity is accomplished; intent provides momentum. Whereas activity theory insists that every activity is defined and initiated by its object (in the sense of purpose or goal), Bronfenbrenner is more nuanced: 'The question of perceived aim is thus always relevant for defining an activity, *if only by default* ... activities vary in the degree and complexity of the purposes that animate them' (Bronfenbrenner, 1979, 46 emphasis added).

In contrast, his definition of 'setting' is narrower: 'a place where people can readily engage in face-to face interaction – home, day care center, playground, and so on' (1979, 22). This is a more constrained and grounded notion than Luckin's 'environment', which we described above and to which it otherwise bears a strong resemblance. Bronfenbrenner was writing at a time when young children, who are in the front of his mind when he speaks about development, had very little access to communications technologies. Writing today, he might have expanded his definition of the setting, but it is clear that he recognised the need to take into account the effects of entities remote from the immediate setting.

> Activities differ in the *extent to which they invoke objects, people, and events not actually present in the immediate setting.* Such invocation may be accomplished through conversation, story telling, fantasy, pictorial representation, or a variety of other media. To the extent that activities refer to events occurring in other places at other times, they reflect an expansion of the actor's phenomenological world beyond the immediate situation. Thus it is possible to speak of an 'ecology of mental life' with a potential structure isomorphic with that of the ecological environment.
>
> (Bronfenbrenner, 1979, 47, original emphasis)

On this view, when someone speaks about their activities in another setting, they are showing they can create a 'mental mesosystem' (47).

Two further terms of Bronfenbrenner's remain to be defined: roles and interpersonal relations. A *role* is 'a set of activities and relations expected of a person occupying a particular position in society, and of others in relation to that person' (85). A *relation* obtains when 'one person in a setting pays attention to or participates in the activities of another' (56). In combination, roles and interpersonal relations constitute the social aspects of the environment in which human development unfolds, complementing the various artefacts and other things that constitute the physical environment. As mentioned, Bronfenbrenner is particularly interested in developmental activities involving roles and relations in which emotional attachments are strong – notably, dyads consisting of parent and child – though it is clear that his ideas generalise to other settings and relations, particularly those that involve mimetic learning, apprenticeship learning or 'learning by observing and pitching in' (Collins et al., 1989; Sterelny, 2003, 2012; Billett, 2014; Rogoff, 2014).

> Learning and development are facilitated by the participation of the developing person in progressively more complex patterns of reciprocal activity with someone with whom that person has developed a strong and enduring emotional attachment and when the balance of power gradually shifts in favour of the developing person.
>
> (Bronfenbrenner, 1979, 60)

It is tempting to wonder whether Bronfenbrenner's four systems levels can also be applied to the development of other 'learning organisms'. More specifically, can they be applied to social institutions such as universities, government agencies or corporations? Can such entities be understood as 'learning organisations' acting and developing in micro-systems, influenced by meso-, exo- and macro-systems? For example, is it helpful to think of a university (as a self-organising system in Bain & Zundans-Fraser's sense) as developing, in part, through transitions across, and relationships between, two or more settings in which it participates? Or is that stretching the metaphor, and Bronfenbrenner's constructs, too far? As we explain in Chapter 9, rather than anthropomorphising the university, it might be safer to think of the activities of teams of people and their ecological relationships. Understanding how a curriculum development team, or a team developing new learning spaces, is influenced by, and modifies, its various ecosystem layers, becomes a significant strategic goal.

Hutchins and cognitive ecology

Bronfenbrenner's insistence on an ecological understanding of human development, with its corollaries for how psychological research should be done, was radical in its time. This is easy to underestimate. As he put it at the time, psychology's

> emphasis on rigor has led to [lab-based] experiments that are elegantly designed but often limited in scope. This limitation derives from the fact that many of these experiments involve situations that are unfamiliar, artificial, and short-lived and that call for unusual behaviors that are difficult to generalize to other settings. From this perspective, it can be said that much of contemporary developmental psychology is *the science of the strange behavior of children in strange situations with strange adults for the briefest possible periods of time.*
>
> (Bronfenbrenner, 1977, 513, original emphasis)

This led Bronfenbrenner to advocate rigorous research into human development 'in the wild'.

The final set of ideas we want to introduce in this chapter, to help think about ecology and learning at the level of the individual person, come from research on 'cognition in the wild' – which has driven the formation of an area of cognitive science now known as cognitive ecology (Hutchins, 1995, 2010). While our starting point is the individual person, it will soon become clear that (a) the boundaries of personal cognition (and learning) are not easy to draw, and (b) we are looking at a close coupling of person+environment, realised as a developmental process.

Cognitive ecology is the study of cognitive phenomena *in context* (Hutchins, 2010). Its distinctive nature can best be understood in its opposition to the highly individualistic and mentalistic understandings of cognition that have dominated psychology and to those areas of cognitive science that have taken a strongly computational, symbol-processing approach. Rather than seeing cognitive processes as internal to the individual, Hutchins's ecological perspective sees them as partly internalised, but he is careful to moderate the meaning of this term:

Internalization has long connoted some thing moving across some boundary. Both elements of this definition are misleading. What moves is not a thing, and the boundary across which movement takes place is a line that, if drawn too firmly, obscures our understanding of the nature of human cognition.

(Hutchins, 1995, 312)

One cannot understand an organism without understanding how it interacts with other organisms and things in its environment. Similarly, one cannot understand cognition without understanding the web of connections between mind, brain and world, including tools and other artefacts, and other people. If one restricts one's understanding of cognition to what happens within the envelope of a person's skin or skull, then much becomes invisible and inexplicable. In other words, cognition cannot be understood in terms of internal symbolic events. The information loops involved in cognition shift from body to world and back again.

It is within this coupling of individual and environment, in the flow itself, that ecological psychologists locate meaning and intelligent action ... From this ecological perspective, learning is a process of becoming prepared to effectively engage dynamic networks in the world ... it is one thing to 'know' something in order to pass a standardized test and quite another to function in those situations in which the knowledge has value and still another to choose to engage in those situations.

(Barab & Roth, 2006, 4)

Everyday discourse about learning, teaching, assessment and curriculum matters in higher education is suffused with terms that come from a 'folk psychology' of learning and capability. An unexamined image at the heart of this folk psychology is the individual learner: a private (virtually disembodied) mind, to be filled and/or sharpened (Bereiter, 2002; Moore, 2013; Dall'Alba et al., 2018; Wang & Zheng, 2018). The folk psychology mobilised in such discussions maps neatly to Macfarlane's (2017) notion of the student as individual customer to be managed. If we can draw on richer ecological understandings of learning, development and capability, it becomes easier to identify points of contact between education and infrastructure planning and to draw upon more realistic models of what capable, knowledgeable individuals are actually able to do in the world.

For example, in his exposition of cognitive ecology, Hutchins (2010) makes a point that is vitally important for higher education. It speaks to academia's privileging of 'private disembodied thought' or 'armchair reflection'. It raises deep questions about how we understand human capabilities – such as how people *actually* accomplish work – which in turn raises questions about curriculum, pedagogy, assessment and design for learning.

Increased attention to real-world activity will change our notions of what are the canonical instances of cognitive process and which are special cases of more general phenomena. For example, private disembodied thinking is undoubtedly an important kind of thinking, but perhaps it receives more attention than it should. This mode of thinking is common among academics and can sometimes be induced in experimental subjects, but it is relatively rare in the global cognitive ecology. It is also deceptive. Far from being free from the influences of culture, private reflection is a deeply cultural practice that draws on and is enacted in coordination with rich cultural resources. The focus of intellectual attention is already shifting to the relations among action, interaction, and conceptualization. Perception, action, and thought will be understood to be inextricably integrated, each with the others. Human cognitive activity will increasingly be seen to be profoundly situated, social, embodied, and richly multimodal. The products of interaction accumulate not only in the brain but throughout the cognitive ecology.

(Hutchins, 2010, 712)

Educational ecology: foundations

Near the start of this chapter we offered the following working definition of educational ecology: 'Educational ecology is an applied science that studies and shapes learning systems. A learning system is a dynamic coupling of people and the multifarious resources on which they are drawing in order to learn.' To put some flesh on the bare bones of this definition, we can draw some key foundational ideas from each of the four sections above. From Barnett's new book (Barnett, 2018) we take the idea that activities within a university are enmeshed in seven much wider ecological zones. Universities can, and should, play a role in improving the health of these ecological zones – recognising also that what happens in those wider spaces has practical implications for work within each university, including the work of imagining desirable futures. From the second section we take ideas about the university as a self-organising, self-improving system, noting that the capacities for self-regulation and self-improvement depend upon timely flows of actionable knowledge and the means to make and explain evaluative judgements about the quality of the educational work being done. From the third section, on activity systems and the ecology of resources, we push for clearer recognition of the importance of materials and their properties: for a better understanding of how the physical (material, digital, hybrid) environment and its tools, artefacts, spaces, and so on function in educational ecologies. Associated with this is an argument for recognising how the health of such ecologies depends upon the attentions of skilled and committed 'gardeners'. The final set of ideas needed to constitute educational ecology involves reimagining the acting and learning student: setting university discourse free from the limitations of individualistic folk psychology.

Educational ecology to inform educational leadership within a university

We are offering the idea of an applied science of educational ecology as a potentially useful approach to many of the issues that emerge in understanding and guiding educational activities – in schools as well as universities, workplaces and organisational learning, informal as well as formal learning. Like other authors who have been using ecological ideas to talk about education and/or learning and development, we think the approach has wide application. That said, our principal interests, like those of the leaders we interviewed for the first part of the book, are in tertiary education, with a particular concern for how universities can organise themselves more appropriately to foster learning that permeates the institution. We offer the following to help focus on such matters:

- At the heart of educational ecology as an applied science is *learning*. Learning is a capacious construct, large enough to enfold research and service.
- Learning makes most sense when it is understood as an activity in, and an outcome of, the functioning of an activity system.
- For university leaders, it is more realistic and more productive to think about the provision of support for a manageable range of activity systems than to think in terms of the aggregated or averaged needs of thousands of individual students.
- From a design and planning perspective, the needs of activity systems can be understood using the tripartite structure of social, set and epistemic architectures. The social architecture includes how students, teachers and other participants interact. The set includes material, digital and hybrid structures that 'furnish the stage' on which the life of an activity system plays out. The epistemic includes the key tasks that students tackle, and the structures of knowledge and knowing that motivate and give meaning to those tasks.
- A university is home to a multiplicity of activity systems, at any one time. Some of these consist of students working on tasks. Others consist of academic and professional staff working to provide better support for student learning (e.g. through better library provision, better-integrated IT systems, etc.).
- Within the complex ecologies of a university, a focus on learning can help each constituent part nurture: mechanisms of self-awareness, an understanding of how its actions influence others (and the whole), demand for better feedback and the ability to self-correct. Among other benefits, this focus can help with early recognition of, and remedies for, ecological damage, including when ecological balance is threatened.

When investigating how the ecology of a university is functioning, the choice of departure point will depend on a number of factors, including scale of inquiry (e.g. whole of university, or a course of study, or an assessment task). But in general, each investigation will need to consider carefully, and be explicit about, the appropriate unit(s) of analysis, ecological boundaries, within-system and between-system relationships and the dynamics of change. Careful choices also need to be made about perspective and time-frame. Whose viewpoints, experience and interests are to be foregrounded? Over what timescale do the key processes unfold? How does the life cycle of programme or project decision-making determine deadlines for investigative work, evidence and recommendations? These will look different at the levels of a course, learning space or element of IT infrastructure than at the whole-of-institution levels which concern top-level university leaders.

Questions of life cycle and timescale also raise matters of continuity and disruption in university affairs. For example, in a number of universities and university systems around the world, the appearance of massive open online courses (MOOCs) was represented as either an existential threat or an unprecedented golden opportunity, or both. Looked at over the longer term, to take into account an extended period in which universities had been experimenting with, and making sense of, the problems and possibilities of digital technologies, MOOCs have been assimilated into mainstream functioning. Like learning management systems (LMSs) before them, MOOCs came to be understood as a class of decision-making problem that university managements could work upon: MOOCs (and LMSs) could be assimilated into a university's ecology without significant damage and indeed management attention and action was needed to make this happen. On the longer view, it may turn out that the main effects of these 'disruptive' innovations are felt through a broadening of the remit of management decision-making (e.g. taking digital educational technologies more seriously) rather than through disrupting university business models.

Summary of Chapter 8

Chapter 8 began by offering a working definition for educational ecology as an applied science, emphasising the investigation, design and evolution of learning systems. It reviewed selected elements from the literature on educational ecologies and ecological thinking in education, moving from the large to the small in scope and scale: from how universities mesh with seven ecological zones to how human capabilities and learning can be understood ecologically. The chapter closed with some foundational ideas for an applied science of educational ecology, drawing out particular points of relevance for university leaders.

In the next chapter, we introduce some ways of approaching enquiries into the functioning of educational ecologies, paying particular attention to models that support participatory and collaborative forms of enquiry and problem-solving, as well as design-inspired forms of management and leadership.

References

Agre, P., & Horswill, I. (1997). Lifeworld analysis. *Journal of Artificial Intelligence Records*, 6, 111–145.

Bailey, D. E., & Barley, S. R. (2011). Teaching-learning ecologies: mapping the environment to structure through action. *Organization Science*, 22(1), 262–285.

Bain, A., & Drengenberg, N. (2016). *Transforming the measurement of learning and teaching in higher education.* New York: Routledge.

Bain, A., & Zundans-Fraser, L. (2017). The self-organizing university: designing the higher education organization for quality learning and teaching. Singapore: Springer Nature.

Barab, S., & Roth, W.-M. (2006). Curriculum-based ecosystems: supporting knowing from an ecological perspective. *Educational Researcher*, 35, 3–13.

Barnett, R. (1990). *The idea of higher education.* Buckingham: SRHE/Open University Press.

Barnett, R. (1997). *Higher education: a critical business.* Buckingham: SRHE/Open University Press.

Barnett, R. (2007). *A will to learn: being a student in an age of uncertainty.* Maidenhead: SRHE/Open University Press.

Barnett, R. (2018). *The ecological university: a feasible utopia.* London: Routledge.

Barrows, H. H. (1923). Geography as human ecology. *Annals of the Association of American Geographers*, 13(1), 1–14.

Bereiter, C. (2002). *Education and mind in the knowledge age.* Mahwah, NJ: Lawrence Erlbaum Associates.

Billett, S. (2014). *Mimetic learning at work: learning in the circumstances of practice.* Heidelberg: Springer.

Boud, D., Ajjawi, R., Dawson, P., & Tai, J. (eds). (2018). Developing evaluative judgement in higher education: assessment for knowing and producing quality work. London: Routledge.

Bowker, G., & Star, S. (2000). *Classification and its consequences.* Cambridge, MA: The MIT Press.

Bronfenbrenner, U. (1977). Toward an experimental ecology of human development. *American Psychologist*, 32(7), 513–531.

Bronfenbrenner, U. (1979). *The ecology of human development: experiments by nature and design.* Cambridge, MA: Harvard University Press.

Butzer, K. (1982). *Archaeology as human ecology: method and theory for a contextual approach.* Cambridge: Cambridge University Press.

Clark, A. (2011) *Supersizing the mind: embodiment, action, and cognitive extension.* Oxford: Oxford University Press.

Collins, A., Brown, J. S., & Newman, S. (1989). Cognitive apprenticeship: teaching the crafts of reading, writing and mathematics. In L. Resnick (ed.), *Knowing, learning and instruction* (pp. 453–494). Englewood Cliffs, NJ: Lawrence Erlbaum Associates.

Dall'Alba, G., Sandberg, J., & Sidhu, R. K. (2018). Embodying skilful performance: co-constituting body and world in biotechnology. *Educational Philosophy and Theory*, 50(3), 270–286.

Dogan, M., & Rokkan, S. (eds). (1969). *Social ecology.* Cambridge, MA: MIT Press.

Ellis, R., & Goodyear, P. (2010). *Students' experiences of e-learning in higher education: the ecology of sustainable innovation.* New York: RoutledgeFalmer.

Gibson, J. (1986). *The ecological approach to visual perception.* Hillsdale, NJ: Lawrence Erlbaum Associates.

Goodyear, P., Ellis, R., & Marmot, A. (2018). Learning spaces research: framing actionable knowledge. In R. Ellis & P. Goodyear (eds), *Spaces of teaching and learning: integrating perspectives on research and practice* (pp. 221–238). Singapore: Springer Nature.

Hannafin, K., & Hannafin, M. (1996). The ecology of distance learning environments. *Training Research Journal, 1,* 49–70.

Hutchins, E. (1995). *Cognition in the wild.* Cambridge, MA: MIT Press.

Hutchins, E. (2010). Cognitive ecology. *Topics in Cognitive Science, 2,* 705–715.

Ingold, T. (2000). The perception of the environment: essays in livelihood, dwelling and skill. Abingdon: Routledge.

Knight, P., & Trowler, P. (2001). *Departmental leadership in higher education.* Buckingham: SRHE/Open University Press.

Luckin, R. (2010). *Re-designing learning contexts: technology-rich, learner-centred ecologies.* New York: Routledge.

Macfarlane, B. (2017). *Freedom to learn: the threat to student academic freedom and why it needs to be reclaimed.* London: Routledge.

Moore, T. (2013). Critical thinking: seven definitions in search of a concept. *Studies in Higher Education, 38*(4), 506–522.

Nardi, B., & O'Day, V. (1999). *Information ecologies: using technology with heart.* Cambridge, MA: MIT Press.

Rogoff, B. (2014). Learning by observing and pitching in to family and community endeavors: an orientation. *Human Development, 57*(2–3), 69–81.

Sterelny, K. (2003). *Thought in a hostile world: the evolution of human cognition.* Oxford: Blackwell.

Sterelny, K. (2012). *The evolved apprentice: how evolution made humans unique.* Cambridge, MA: MIT Press.

Uttl, B., White, C. A., & Gonzalez, D. W. (2017). Meta-analysis of faculty's teaching effectiveness: student evaluation of teaching ratings and student learning are not related. *Studies in Educational Evaluation, 54,* 22–42.

Wang, M., & Zheng, X. (2018). Embodied cognition and curriculum construction. *Educational Philosophy and Theory, 50*(3), 217–228.

Whitchurch, C. (2013). Reconstructing identities in higher education: the rise of 'Third Space' professionals. London: Routledge.

Winstone, N. E., Nash, R. A., Parker, M., & Rowntree, J. (2017). Supporting learners' agentic engagement with feedback: a systematic review and a taxonomy of recipience processes. *Educational Psychologist, 52*(1), 17–37.

9

Educational ecology

Ways and means

The main purpose of this chapter is to share some ideas about promoting and supporting educational ecology within a university.

> Human environments and – even more so – the capacities of human beings to adapt and restructure these environments are so complex in their basic organization that they are not likely to be captured, let alone comprehended, through simplistic unidimensional research models that make no provision for assessing ecological structure and variation … environmental structures, and the processes taking place within and between them, must be viewed as interdependent and must be analysed in systems terms.
>
> (Bronfenbrenner, 1977, 518)

We are assuming, if you have reached this point, that the ecological conception we have been promoting is proving sufficiently persuasive, or sufficiently intriguing, to merit further investigation; that our argument for applied ecology as a way of filling the gap between education strategy and student experience has potential. So this chapter takes a practical turn. We offer two main things. The first part of the chapter sketches some approaches to analysing how an educational ecology is functioning: how it is achieving what it achieves; how its internal processes generate its outcomes. We have selected four example approaches, while also listing a number of other good candidates. Each of the approaches involves work that is done *in* an organisation, rather than *to* an organisation. Each has ways of including stakeholders in the processes of analysing what is going on and designing ways of improving things. The second part of the chapter addresses the thorny problem of how to relate research and practice. We take a very practical approach to this matter also. Starting with some of the perennial difficulties of using educational research to improve educational processes and outcomes, we go on to describe a structure for building stronger relations, more trust and better mutual understanding between those who research and those who can make educational change happen. While we are sympathetic to the view that every academic can benefit from spending some of their time engaged in the scholarship of teaching and learning we are also convinced that good research depends on disciplinary resources: sharp methods, a broad-based, up-to-date understanding of the science of learning, and effective methods for dissemination, for example. Some universities have managed to sustain internal research and development (R&D) units with the mandate, skills and resources needed to do this kind of work and to keep up with developments in the global research community. The tradition of 'institutional research' in North American universities is a case in point (Terenzini, 1993, 2013; Haskell, 2017). But in many countries, including Australia and the UK, such R&D units are rare, and questions keep being raised about their viability. As we see it, the challenge is to nurture research capabilities of a scale and scope commensurate with the needs of a whole university, while also being able to ensure that the research carried out is well aligned with institutional priorities. We describe a model based on 'Research–Practice Partnerships' (Penuel & Gallagher, 2017) as an illustration of a way forward. Neither the first or second parts of the chapter aims to offer recipes for success. Rather, we have tried to offer concise introductions to ways of working, and to recommend good sources of practical guidance on each approach. How these developments connect back to educational strategy and the integration of leadership across education, IT and facilities is revisited in the final chapter.

Framing ecological approaches to quality enhancement and innovation

Many of the recurrent practices of teaching in higher education merit closer scrutiny and most are open to improvement. But habits can be hard to unsettle and some university work takes on the appearance of ritual: part of what holds the educational apparatus together and makes it recognisable and navigable, but not necessarily fit for its avowed purpose. (See, for example, our comments in Chapter 8 on feedback.)

Then there are things that manifest as actual problems. Problems can emerge in a number of ways. They may become obvious to a teacher through direct experiences in the classroom, or through their students' performance in final exams. Or they may emerge from careful scrutiny of university-wide data and reflection on the meaning of unexpected patterns. Once a problem is revealed, it may or may not have an obvious solution. Some serious diagnostic and redesign work may be needed before anything can be done to improve the situation. In short, there are routine practices that call for inspection and improvement when time allows, and there are problems that demand attention. Problems and solutions can be simple or complex. It may be easy to get agreement on what the problem is, but hard to see what can be done about it. Conversely, a complex problem may have a simple, self-evident solution. As Figure 9.1 illustrates, the difficulties involved in analysing a problem and creating a solution are not necessarily correlated, and, in principle, addressing educational problems can sit anywhere in the space suggested by the figure. In this chapter, we are particularly concerned with work upon problems that sit in the top-right quadrant. As we will argue below, progress with problems in this quadrant needs some sophisticated methods and tools.

The suggestions in this chapter are probably more relevant to the work of a team of people than to the solo teacher (though we hope solo teachers also find

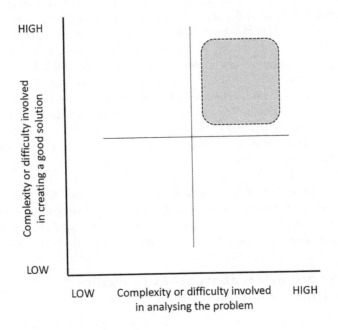

HIGH

Complexity or difficulty involved
in creating a good solution

LOW

LOW   Complexity or difficulty involved   HIGH
                   in analysing the problem

Figure 9.1

value here). For example, we have quite a bit to say about the need to develop a consensus about the nature of a problem and the best way of solving it. Also, we think the work of teams on larger problems is more likely to need, and garner, some support from those in leadership positions, which will be better directed if there is a shared understanding of methods of problem analysis and solution.

The bottom-left quadrant of Figure 9.1 represents problems whose nature and solution are self-evident. No special methods are needed to gain a consensus here on what is wrong and what to do about it. The upper-left quadrant is for problems that are readily diagnosed, but where finding a good solution is more complex: where it's far from obvious how to proceed. The lower-right quadrant is the inverse situation. Here, problems are tricky to analyse, but once they are understood, it is immediately clear what should be done. The horizontal axis of Figure 9.1 relates to the sophistication of the tools and methods needed for *analysis*. The vertical axis relates to the sophistication of the tools and methods needed for *design*. It may seem that we are labouring the point, but it is important to develop a feel for the level of sophistication needed in analysis and design and to realise that a problem that is difficult to analyse does not necessarily need all the paraphernalia of a design-based approach for its solution. A full-blown design process does not need to be underpinned by a thorough, in-depth investigation and mapping of an educational ecology, if agreement has been reached on the problem.

Insider approaches to analysis (and design)

Valuable work on educational problems (and their solution) *can* be done by 'outsiders'. External consultants can be valuable, particularly if they spot things that have been taken for granted for so long that they have become invisible, or if they can import valuable knowledge gained in other places. This 'external' gaze doesn't have to depend on bringing in expensive consultants. Colleagues from other disciplines, faculties or universities can also bring valuable insights and provide translatable case studies from their own experience. Being on the outside looking in can generate useful new perspectives.

That said, there are some very strong arguments for 'insider' research. If a programme team carries out some diagnostic work on its own courses, and/or the learning environments used by its students, then the models they create of how the course works are likely to be richer, more nuanced and more likely to be understood, applied and maintained. The same is true of (re)design. Indeed, analysis and design can fuse into a single, iterative process, in which the people who care most about the programme use candidate design solutions to test provisional representations of the problem(s) they are analysing.

Structured approaches to design, using more sophisticated tools and methods, are gaining attention in higher education, though off a low base. (Such tools and methods have been widely used and improved in other sectors, notably industrial and military training, for sixty years or more. In universities they have, until quite recently, been the preserve of specialists in instructional design or instructional systems development.) In the last five years or so, some simple but evocative tools and methods for design have been created and successfully promoted among university teachers, particularly in the UK and Australia. Bower & Vlachopoulos (2018) provide a useful review.

These complement an array of approaches to researching and enhancing local educational practices. Carvalho and Goodyear (2018) identified over 20 distinct approaches to analysing and designing new programmes, products and services that have been tried out in the context of educational innovation. Some of these bear close family resemblances, but each has distinguishing characteristics. Some of these have been used widely in education for decades (see for example, action research and action learning), while others are more recent and/or more niche (e.g. 'lean start-up' or community-based design research). Table 9.1 provides an overview and follow-up references.

We have limited space here, so we will focus on just four of these approaches: soft systems methodology (SSM), realist formative evaluation, formative intervention and participatory design-based research. These share some ancestry – for example, in Kurt Lewin's action research and in activity theory. Each lends itself to collaborative analysis and design – where a team, community or network with a stake in a shared future commits to researching a complex system and taking steps to improve its vitality. We have also picked these four examples because they can be used with (and by) groups of students, as well as with and by senior

Table 9.1 'Insider' approaches to analysis & design

	Approach	Source
E	Action learning	Pedler, 2011
	Action research	Lewin, 1952
E	Community-based design research	Bang et al., 2016
	Creative communities	Manzini, 2005
	Design anthropology (emic; etic)	Gunn et al., 2013
E	Design-based implementation research	Fishman et al., 2013
E	Design-based research	Kelly et al., 2008
E	Expansive learning	Engeström & Sannino, 2010
E	Formative interventions	Engeström et al., 2014
	Formative/developmental evaluation	Patton, 2010
	Lean startup	Gong & Janssen, 2015
	Participatory design	Schuler & Namioka, 1993
E	Participatory design research	Bang & Vossoughi, 2016
	Participatory action research	Whyte, 1991
E	Practice-based research	Levy, 2003
	Rapid prototyping	Connell & Shafer, 1989
	Second order cybernetics;	Sweeting, 2016
E	Self-managing learning ecologies	Ellis & Goodyear, 2010
	Soft systems methods	Pries-Heje et al., 2014
E	Social design experiments	Gutiérrez & Vossoughi, 2010
	Theory-based/driven evaluation	Coryn et al., 2011
	Transformation design	Burns et al., 2006

Note: E in column 1 denotes an approach originating in, or best exemplified by, research and practice in education.

management teams and their staff members. They have a nicely recursive quality that helps strengthen connections between research, education and community engagement (Fung, 2017; Carvalho & Goodyear, 2018).

Soft systems and wicked problems

There has been a steady stream of work on soft systems methodology (SSM) for more than 50 years; it is hardly a new field. We make no apology for starting this part of the chapter with it, partly because there have been a number of recent developments in the application of SSM to understanding and improving teaching and learning in higher education (Ison & Blackmore, 2014; Markauskaite & Goodyear, 2017; Goodyear & Markauskaite, forthcoming).

SSM was developed at Lancaster University by Peter Checkland and colleagues, as part of an exploration of the possibility and potential of using systems thinking approaches in the domains of management and organisational studies (see, e.g., Checkland, 1999). An early insight was the need to distinguish the 'hard' approaches that had been proving successful with well-structured problems in engineering from a 'softer' kind of approach that could help with the ill-structured, 'wicked' problems found in management.

Understandably, Checkland stressed the point that 'soft' did not mean 'sloppy' or lacking in rigour. Indeed, he notes that what distinguishes SSM is not the 'softness' of the problems to which it may be applied, but its ontology and epistemology.

> Hard systems thinking assumes that the world is a set of systems (i.e. is *systemic*) and that these can be *systematically* engineered to achieve objectives. In the soft tradition, the world is assumed to be problematic, but it is also assumed that *the process of inquiry* into the problematic situations that make up the world can be organized as a system. In other words, assumed systematicity is shifted: from taking the world to be systemic to taking the process of inquiry to be systemic ...
>
> (Checkland, 1999, A49)

We find that this sits very comfortably with the notion of ecology as a way of seeing and being in the world. Checkland notes four key ideas in the evolution of SSM:

- All real-world problem situations involve human beings seeking or wanting to take *purposeful action* (c.f. 'activity' in Chapter 7, above).
- Accounts of purposeful activities can be built from any number of viewpoints; a group of people who want to understand and act helpfully in relation to such activities have to agree on a *shared viewpoint*, in order to make progress.
- Therefore, models of activity are not judged by their representational fidelity so much as by their value in supporting discourse and argument about what should be done; they are *resources for structuring debate* about different ways of seeing the situation.
- At the heart of the SSM process is a *learning cycle* in which models of activity structure a debate about change.

Part of the motivation for SSM, and what helps distinguish its utility, is the realisation that well-structured problems represent only a fraction of what managers need to deal with, and that serious tools and methods are needed that can help with wicked problems or what Checkland preferred to call 'problem situations'. On this reading, once a (well-structured) problem is properly identified, it is usually trivial to specify the means for its solution. But many *problematic situations* exist, in which stakeholders have a sense that things are not right, but what exactly is wrong eludes precise definition, and will not stand still (Goodyear & Markauskaite, forthcoming).

SSM is operationalised in a number of ways, but at its heart the process goes through several iterations of a learning/enquiry cycle, in which the key stages are:

- Collect perceptions of the problem situation from a range of stakeholders; create the richest possible picture of the situation being studied.

- Establish one or more 'root definitions' that capture the essence of the system(s) involved.
- Build and test candidate conceptual models of the system.
- Compare the conceptual models with reality.
- Implement feasible and desirable changes.

SSM is strongly associated with the use of various diagramming and representational techniques. While these may not be essential to the general approach, SSM practice suggests that creating shared representations of problematic situations and what might be done about them is a valuable way of building consensus. Organisational life often depends upon use of ambiguous language to postpone conflict. Working together on a shared representation of what is, and what should change, can provide a useful source of discipline when serious decisions about complex changes have to be made (and lived with).

Realist formative evaluation

This second approach is also tailored to explaining how a complex learning system (or project, or intervention) actually functions. The primary aim of *summative* evaluation is to provide an account of the value of a project's outcomes once it has concluded. In contrast, *formative* evaluation is intended to provide information that can shape a project as it moves forward. Realist evaluation – sometimes called realistic evaluation – is an approach to evaluation that attempts to explain how a project, programme or other kind of intervention has the effects that it does (Pawson & Tilley, 1997). While conventional summative evaluation may be able to answer questions like 'did it work?' or 'was it good value for money', realist evaluation is designed to answer more complex questions of the form: 'what works, for whom, in what contexts and why?' Realist(ic) evaluation is firmly grounded in realist conceptions of how to do good (social) science. In essence, it aims to explain *outcomes* through an understanding of *mechanisms* that function in certain *contexts*. It gives a central role to theorising about causation – what mechanisms are responsible for creating specific desired or unwanted outcomes, and how do the contexts in which the mechanisms are found condition their operation? In this regard, it resembles other approaches to theory-based evaluation (Chen & Rossi, 1992; McLaughlin & Jordan, 1999; Strömdahl & Langerth Zetterman, 2002).

Realist formative evaluation can therefore be understood as an approach to evaluation that aims to guide the development of a project (or other kind of intervention) during its lifetime, by providing explanations of relations between outcomes, mechanisms and contexts. It can be most useful when it tackles explanations of prevailing circumstances – how things currently work, for good and ill – and also how the changes brought about by a project actually function. Indeed, a project can be seen as having (beneficial) effects when previously existing mechanisms that generated problematic outcomes are dislodged by new mechanisms. In this sense, the analytic and explanatory part of realist formative evaluation does the kind of analytic work we described in Chapter 7: it can be a very useful, disciplined, approach to analysing and explaining how existing educational activity systems are functioning.

The book by Pawson & Tilley (1997) provides a practical, accessible and authoritative introduction to realist evaluation. In the space we have here, we can pick up on the following points (215–219) as maxims to guide realist evaluation:

- attend to how and why interventions can cause change;
- dive below the surface of observable inputs and outputs;
- focus on how existing causal mechanisms are removed or countered by newly introduced mechanisms;
- understand the contexts in which existing and new mechanisms are activated;
- get a clear understanding of outcomes and how they are produced;
- to generalise about how interventions work, identify the configurations of contexts–mechanisms–outcomes;
- regard interactions between evaluators and project stakeholders as a two-way teaching and learning process;
- recognise that projects live within open systems: the world is always changing.

In our view, a particular strength of realist evaluation is that its roots in scientific realism inject a helpful discipline with respect to what constitutes a satisfactory explanation. At the heart of such explanations are *generative mechanisms*.

> Social interventions only and always work through the action of mechanisms, through a process of weaving resources and reasoning together. Without this being the first item on the research agenda, all subsequent work on program outcomes will remain a mystery.
>
> (Pawson & Tilley, 1997, 69)

Put another way, new programmes do not cause their outcomes. They create opportunities for the people involved in the programme to act differently; changes in their activity lead to the outcomes. A new flexible learning space doesn't cause improved learning outcomes, but it may provide users of the space with opportunities and constraints that lead them to act differently. A moment's reflection may make this seem no more than a common-sense observation, but much of the prevailing discourse about learning spaces and other educational innovations reinforces a simpler but wrong-headed view that new spaces or tools cause better educational outcomes.

Another reason that we have selected realist evaluation as an approach worth considering is that there has been a flurry of interest recently in using realist methods to evaluate innovations in medical education, including the use of educational technologies (see especially Wong et al., 2010, 2012; Ericson et al., 2017; Sholl et al. 2017). Much of this work takes a summative approach and is based on systematic reviews of the literature. While this has some promise for extending and adding nuance to our understanding of 'what works, for whom, in what circumstances' its retrospective nature means that it cannot, of course, play a formative role in guiding innovation projects during their life cycle.

Formative interventions

The term 'formative intervention' is closely associated with the work of Yrjö Engeström and colleagues, and is underpinned by (cultural historical) activity theory (CHAT). Engeström distinguishes the formative intervention approach from other approaches to intervention in educational and workplace settings, stressing the importance of recognising the *agency* of those affected by, and bound up in, such interventions. The contrast is most starkly drawn with randomised controlled trials (RCTs) but Engeström also takes proponents of design experiments and design-based research (DBR) to task for similarly neglecting the *agency* of those who inhabit the ecologies into which researchers insert their new designs (Engeström, 2011; Engeström et al., 2014). On this view, the agency of participants is not to be seen as an awkward but minor source of error or 'noise' in the implementation of an intervention; it is a vital part of how an intervention works, and that fact needs to take a central place in interventionist methodologies.

Engeström (2011) highlights five areas of weakness in DBR approaches: vagueness about the unit of analysis, problematic assumptions about the nature of causation, lack of attention to the (upfront) processes through which new designs come into being, ignoring the way that interventions involve 'contested terrain', and privileging of the researcher's agency and goals over those of the teachers and students: researchers in DBR projects typically retain control and decide on closure.

Until recently, the DBR literature did not have much to say about issues of power, subversion, struggle and control. (See the subsection on participatory design research, below.) Yet sociologically informed research on, and evaluation of, educational and community interventions points to the importance of the strategies that people devise when participating in interventions: 'resistance and subversion are not accidental disturbances that need to be eliminated. They are essential core ingredients of interventions and they need to have a prominent place in a viable intervention methodology' (Engeström, 2011, 603).

The essence of the formative intervention approach resides in the following four characteristics. First, the whole *activity system* is taken as the unit of analysis (see Chapter 7). This means that

> interventions need to be embedded and contextualized in the participants' meaningful life activity. An intervention that limits itself to the transformation of actions and ignores the motivational dynamics stemming from the object of the activity may be technically effective in the short run but is unlikely to have durable formative influence in the long run.
>
> (Engeström, 2011, 608)

Second, *contradictions* – 'historically accumulating structural tensions' (609) have to be seen as the primary source of development and change. In social systems generally, the fundamental contradiction is between the use value and exchange value of commodities. In higher education, we can point to the contradiction between studying to learn useful skills and knowledge and studying to get a qualification; between learning because of its intrinsic rewards and learning in order to pass the exams. By implication, the analytic work done by those practising formative intervention needs to include understanding the historical dynamics of the activity system. Interventions need to build on the energies generated by contradictions.

Thirdly, the *agency of participants* needs to be seen as an important part – perhaps the most important part – of any causal explanation of the intervention. It is not just that human agents interpret the intervention, they also experience and are driven by contradictory motives and they take on intentional transformative action. (As we argued in discussing realist evaluation above, it is not the intervention that causes change, it is the people involved in the intervention who cause change.) Finally, in successful formative interventions, the transformation of practice involves significant conceptual change: typically, the *expansion* of concepts that currently prevail in the setting to open up new ways of understanding the object of activity.

These ideas about formative intervention have been worked out through both deeper consideration of developmental theory and practical experience in helping groups of people (in workplace and/or educational settings) find ways of making change. The best-known examples come from interventions carried out through the *Change Laboratory* (e.g. Virkunnen & Newnham, 2013).

Participatory design-based research

'Design-based research', or DBR, has evolved a set of methods for creating, trialling and incrementally improving an educational innovation. DBR has a strong commitment to working in the everyday educational settings of schools and universities. It grew out of a tradition of developing and testing technology-based learning innovations in much more controlled, lab-like settings. It can be understood as a reaction to experiences in educational technology R&D in the 1970s and 1980s, where sophisticated systems that worked well in the lab failed to work in the 'real world' of education (Kelly et al., 2008). In part, DBR seeks to discover why an innovation that works 'in theory' (or in ideal circumstances) fails to deliver 'in practice'. Researchers taking a DBR approach therefore spend a good deal of time and energy trying to understand the additional supports, system tweaks, and so on that are needed to replicate and repeat success in complex classroom settings. They also commit to incremental improvement over time, though the constraints of project funding and life cycles often mean that DBR activity goes through only a few iterations.

Although DBR is committed to making a difference in real-world classrooms, and is concerned to address issues of scaling-up and sustainability, it would be fair to say that it is strongly directed by the researchers' need to contribute to the advancement of theory (Sandoval, 2014; Wozniak, 2015). Indeed, a criticism of DBR is that it is more concerned with testing the theoretical ideas that inspired the innovation than with understanding the ecology into which the innovation was dropped.

While DBR has been in fashion for 20 years or more, *participatory* design-based research is newer. This means that it is still taking shape, and there are very active debates about its nature and purposes. Simplifying somewhat, we can say that there are weaker and stronger interpretations of participatory DBR. By 'weaker' we mean that some interpretations of the idea go no further than the kinds of routine practices of co-design and co-configuration that we sketched in Chapters 6 and 7. Students always modify the tasks they are set and the environments in which they work, even if some of these modifications may seem rather trivial and are carried out spontaneously (co-configuration) rather than in a more planful way (co-design). Engaging students seriously in co-designing curriculum, assessment tasks and learning environments has been researched quite extensively (e.g. diSalvo et al., 2017; Janssen et al., 2017). It has taken on a new lease of life recently in higher education in the Students as Partners movement (see, e.g., Matthews et al., 2018).

Some versions of this co-designing and partnering activity fall under what we are calling the 'stronger' interpretation of participatory DBR. Under this interpretation, students and other key stakeholders take on proactive roles and the scope of what may be changed is radically stretched, to include some of the aims and activities of social innovation and the design of relational services that we introduced at the end of Chapter 6.

In an understandably evangelical introduction to a recent special issue on participatory DBR, Bang & Vossoughi (2016) put it like this:

> change is not just about conventional forms of what we typically label learning and practice but is also about transformative social change. In our view, transformative social change involves the interweaving of structural critiques with the enactment of alternative forms of here-and-now activity that open up qualitatively distinct social relations, forms of learning and knowledge development, and contribute to the intellectual thriving and well-being of students, teachers, families, and communities.
>
> (Bang & Vossoughi, 2016, 175)

Participatory DBR is close kin to some other well-established forms of community-based research and engagement, such as participatory action research and community-based design (Zavala, 2016). Although this stronger version of participatory DBR is mainly being developed in and around schools and school communities, with school-aged students and their families, we can see a number of connections to higher-education practice, some of which are reflected in work on Students as Partners. For example, participatory DBR can engage students from traditional under-represented communities in work aimed at creating learning environments, curricula and/or assessment tasks that are better suited to their needs. In addition, for students from all backgrounds, participation in DBR can help develop some of the skills, understandings and dispositions needed to be a more autonomous learner: being better able to shape their future learning environments to better suit their emerging needs and the requirements of the new problems on which they find themselves working. Beyond that, a number of universities are setting up programmes that provide students with opportunities to engage in community transformation projects of various kinds, providing opportunities to learn what is involved in working with others to bring about valued change. (Fostering 'moral know-how'.)

An important point here is to recognise the temptations of encouraging students to learn so-called 'design thinking' skills and methods, decoupled from authentic engagement in change. There is a faddish interest, within several areas of education, in 'design thinking', reduced to working step by step through an idealised design process, but without the possibility of actually making change. This strikes us as a watering-down of opportunities – to experience the full range of design thinking, including radically reframing problems as presented, and to gain from sustained involvement with diverse others in understanding and making change. If PDR is watered down so that it is impossible for students to experience having 'consequential impacts in the here and now' (Bang & Vossoughi, 2016, 174) or understanding that design and intervention work can be a routine part of human activity (Gutiérrez et al., 2016), then they are being seriously short-changed. As Zavala (2016) notes, participation in authentic, consequential, community-oriented design activity can help students appreciate how design practices themselves are 'negotiated and emergent', that designing a successful campaign for change depends upon extensive action-research, that the nature of participation affects the relationships formed with others and that the capabilities developed through such participation can transform one from being an individualistic 'reactionary activist' to a collectivist, proactive, 'anticipatory organiser'.

We now need to move on, from describing example approaches to analysis and design – approaches to doing educational ecology – to consider forms of infrastructure that can support such work in the longer term. That is, we move from a treatment of methodology and tools to a consideration of how appropriate structures might be created, within a university, to foster smarter and stronger work on design and analysis for educational enhancement.

Research–practice partnerships

In many areas of educational activity, and in many parts of the world, there is a widely lamented gulf between educational research and educational policy and practice. There are also numerous diagnoses of why this is the case. In this section, we focus on strategies to bridge the gulf, paying particular attention to an approach that centres on 'research–practice partnerships', or RPPs. Penuel & Gallagher (2017) provide a useful and very readable book-length account of RPPs. However, their experience is largely of working with school districts in America. So in this section, we offer a translation of some of their key ideas, to better fit the higher-education context, drawing as we do so on our own recent experiences with the Centre for Research on Learning and Innovation (CRLI) at The University of Sydney.

A common complaint about educational research is that it lacks the methodological rigour of research in some other fields, notably in health, and that it produces findings that do not give firm guidance about what practitioners should do. In response, some countries have developed databases or clearing houses for evidence about 'what works', and some high-profile researchers have created franchises based on meta-analyses of studies of different educational strategies. While there is some merit in these developments, we need to note that:

- The vast majority of such work is schools-oriented, and there is very little guidance available that can readily be drawn upon for educational practice at university level.
- There is a growing conviction that asking 'what works' always oversimplifies the problem, and that research needs to tell us about 'what works, for whom, in what circumstances, and why'. (As with realist evaluation, introduced above.)
- Most educational leaders are not looking for impact studies about 'what works'. They are more interested in tools or frameworks that can help them with new ways of thinking about local problems (Penuel et al., 2016).

RPPs are intended to bridge the gap between research and practice – including policy formation and other kinds of educational leadership activity. (To avoid having to repeat 'policy and practice' we'll just say that educational practice includes policy and leadership.). RPPs are a way of bringing research and practice closer, establishing shared agendas and creating 'soft infrastructure' that helps sustain and disseminate successful innovations.

RPPs are *long-term* relationships between educational researchers and educational practitioners (and through them to students as co-designers). They are based on *mutually agreed* goals and a shared understanding of problems and possibilities, including a shared understanding of what the researchers can actually bring to the table, and what opportunities and constraints are real and pressing for the educational organisation(s) and people involved. They involve *building relationships between people* and organisations, and developing shared understanding and trust, and not just exchange of knowledge. They centre on, and are driven by, *problems of practice.*

RPPs require *long-term relationships.* Many educational innovation and research and development projects have a lifespan of one to three years. To get funding, they usually need to be based on a proposal that has already defined both the problem and a solution strategy. There is rarely the time, or funding, to allow researchers and practitioners to come together to explore and build a joint understanding of what the problem actually is, or how best to approach it, or get a sense of each other's skills, or learn to trust one another. Moreover, when the end of the project approaches the researchers have to start looking elsewhere, for new funding and new partners. As often as not, when the researchers walk away, the fine-tuning and informal professional development work they have been doing come to an abrupt stop, and previously successful innovations can falter or fail. Many research–practice encounters take the form of brief, one-sided transactions: either the educational organisation with a problem hires in some researchers as short-term consultants or the researchers treat educational organisations as mere sites for data collecting. Neither of these is an RPP. It is better to think of an RPP as an open-ended, joint commitment to working together. This allows time for listening and shared learning, formation of trust, understanding each other's priorities and needs, working on joint activities in ways that are not constrained by single projects or one-off grants.

RPPs are *focused on problems of practice*. They are driven by a commitment to use-inspired research and the creation of actionable knowledge.

RPPs are *mutualistic*. Both parties work towards a shared goal, and understand and acknowledge each other's priorities. They are characterised by joint deliberation and negotiation. While problems of practice motivate the partnership, educational leaders and practitioners also need to understand the incentives and constraints that shape the researchers' lives and careers. For example, being able to gather data in a way that permits publication of findings in top journals needs to be understood as a serious, legitimate priority for the researchers. It is not icing on a cake. Successful RPPs do not leave this mutualism to chance. Instead, they use *intentional strategies* of various kinds to support and protect it. These include such things as memorandums of understanding (MoUs), governance mechanisms that advance the needs of all parties, and on-the-ground activities through which researchers and practitioners gain sharper understandings of their needs, strengths and issues. 'In a partnership, the partners understand their shared aims, their individual aims, and how each partner has accommodated the other to engage in joint work together' (Penuel & Gallagher, 2017, 22).

Penuel & Gallagher (2017, 23ff.) identify three main types of RPP. We describe each of these briefly here, not as fixed models but as ways of stimulating some further thinking about what kind of RPP may suit specific organisational needs and circumstances. The three types are: research alliances, design-based RPPs and networked improvement communities.

Research alliances

Research alliances are typically place-based and link an educational organisation to a research institute. For Penuel & Gallagher (2017) a defining characteristic is that, in a research alliance, the researchers study, but do not design, the educational organisation's policies and practices. In this way, the researchers can provide the organisation with an independent voice and with evidence collected and presented in a disinterested way. The ongoing nature of the relationship allows for proper accountability, which also helps secure more stable or predictable funding. A research alliance usually has a board or other kind of governing mechanism which helps set the long-term vision and approve and monitor annual plans, and so on.

Design-based RPPs

Design-based RPPs differ from research alliances in that the researchers *are* proactively involved in designing educational interventions. They are committed to making their inventions work in practice. Over the last 20 years or so, most DBR studies have been relatively small scale, but Penuel and colleagues have developed methods for designing, testing and iteratively improving educational innovations at scale. They distinguish their approach as design-based implementation research, or DBIR (Fishman et al., 2013). Working iteratively – especially with an annual education cycle – and at scale means that DBIR really requires ongoing, mutually beneficial relationships between design researchers and educational practitioners. Hence it is an instance of an RPP.

Networked improvement communities (NICs)

NICs have been championed by the Carnegie Foundation for the Advancement of Teaching, which has been active in higher education as well as schooling (Bryk et al., 2015). A NIC is typically a network of organisations that comes together around a shared educational problem. Researcher and practitioner roles tend to be more blurred than in other forms of RPP. Educators play an active role in developing and testing strategies for improving practice. NICs following the Carnegie model adopt methodologies that have been developed in the health sector for improving practice; they also study their own improvement practices (working on 'improving improvement'). Some key NIC architectural elements are hubs and network nodes. A NIC hub brings together researchers, educators, network facilitators and people with methodological expertise in implementation and improvement science. Since the operation of a NIC usually involves several iterations of improvement strategies over several years – with strategies being tested and refined through grassroots action – skills are needed to keep the NIC on track and productive. Key participants in the network nodes play a crucial role in maintaining momentum and direction. NICs use methods from industry and business management as well as from the health sector. Among other things, they make use of 'small tests of change' and 'change packages' to enable problem investigation and scale up of solutions; they create and maintain a 'working theory of practice improvement' as a shared representation of how the NIC's improvement goals will most likely be attained, and they use an approach called 'practical measurement' to generate better and more actionable data to inform changes to future practice.

An unresolved problem with NICs comes from their distributed character. The fact that they are not restricted to one organisation is a source of strength but also a vulnerability, in that issues of accountability and ongoing funding become more problematic. For as long as a NIC can achieve its goals through volunteer effort and the disposable energy of enthusiastic educators, all is fine. But sustaining a NIC through difficult periods – and ensuring the vital hub is properly resourced – need serious financial commitments.

Difficulties encountered by RPPs

This brings us to a major difficulty with RPPs more generally, though it is one that university leaders can address. This is the question of predictable funding over the long term, on a scale that gives both researchers and educational practitioners the confidence to invest their precious time in what are necessarily lengthy, and sometimes difficult, processes of relationship-building and joint learning. It takes time, and the setting aside of prejudices, for university teachers who have no formal training in educational research and no understanding of developments in the learning sciences to come to a proper understanding of what researchers from those areas can and cannot offer. It takes time for those researchers to understand the complexities and constraints of educational innovation in the wild spaces of university teaching. They too have to resist temptations to make premature judgements about what is worth doing, or doable. It takes time to find the 'sweet spots' where 'problems of practice intersect with important gaps in knowledge' (Penuel & Gallagher, 2017, 128).

Many university leaders are committed to protecting a place for 'engaged scholarship' which integrates research, educational work and service for the benefit of the community as well as the university. Funding an RPP is a good vehicle for this.

Improving flows of information, insights and problems between research and practice

> Research in the human sciences, it may be argued, is less designed to dictate what one does than to provide information that agents, both teachers and students, can use in making informed decisions about what to do in the multiple and varied contexts in which they work
>
> (Olson, 2004, 25)

Whatever organisational structures may be created to help align educational priorities with internal R&D, there remains the question of the roles and skills of personnel involved. In this last section, we introduce one further idea, which can be implemented at smaller or larger scales. This is the notion of translational research and translational developers. The roots of this idea are in the health sector and in IT systems design. The essence of the argument is that information will not simply flow, as if under some kind of gravity or pressure, from research to its application. Rather, skilled people are needed who have the job of connecting research and users and translating, or transforming, knowledge as it passes in each direction. More accurately, the role adds value by helping researchers better understand the needs of research users and research users better understand how they can apply research-based knowledge.

The development of translational research in the health sector arose from a realisation that work needed to be done to overcome obstacles on the path of knowledge application 'from bench to bedside'. In other words, results from cutting-edge medical research were moving too slowly, or too unevenly, through to application in healthcare settings (Waldman & Terzic, 2010). Given the length of the path from initial research to safe application, translational work of different kinds needs to be done at different points in the journey. The infrastructure for R&D in the health sector is much more extensive than in education: different roles with different skillsets can be founded at several points on the research to application path.

Donald Norman has picked up on this problem in the context of technology design and development (e.g. Norman, 2009) and Ellis & Fisher (2017) have explored it more thoroughly in relation to the design of complex learning spaces. Both papers emphasise the value of bi-directional translation and transformation. It is not simply that people working on new digital tools or learning spaces can benefit from knowing about potentially relevant research evidence, but also researchers can benefit from knowing more about the needs and priorities of research users (practitioners) working at the application end. More generally, there is value in supporting people and processes that do 'boundary work' – crossing between communities and proactively connecting people, ideas and resources (Star & Griesemer, 1989; Wenger et al., 2002; Cremers et al., 2017).

Recognising and acting upon these kinds of blocks and bottlenecks is widely acknowledged as an important breakthrough in the health sector, to the point where investment in translational research centres is now routine and where training programmes are available to develop the specialist skills needed by dedicated personnel.

We are not suggesting that the answer for universities is to invest in structures and personnel duplicating what works in the health sector. The ecologies are different, as are the causal mechanisms that connect interventions to outcomes. Rather, we are suggesting that relying on a flow of educational research evidence from researchers to journals to teachers is inefficient and ineffective and that educational leaders have known this for decades. A rational response is to learn from what works elsewhere, adapt to meet local circumstances, and fund, monitor and manage appropriately.

Connecting this back to the practical suggestions made earlier in this chapter, deputy vice-chancellors (education) could set up frameworks for RPPs, within which translational development roles fit neatly. Or to test the water, they can recruit and resource translational developers, and/or help existing academic and educational development staff take on such roles in a more structured way. Crucially, this needs to be underpinned by a realistic appreciation of the complexities and dynamics of educational ecologies, as well as fluency with the kinds of tools and methods we identified in the first part of the chapter. And if our argument about the critical importance of filling the ignorance gap between high-level educational strategy and actual student experience is at all persuasive, then attaching translational development functions to other key players in the mid-levels of the organisation, such as associate deans for learning and teaching, is also likely to make sense (Floyd & Preston, 2018).

Summary of Chapter 9

This chapter has built upon the foundational ideas for educational ecology that we shared in the previous chapter. To move towards implementation of ecologically informed research and development – for quality enhancement and/or educational innovation purposes – university leaders need to give shape to appropriate structures and find resources for ways of working that are informed by good evidence that is locally applicable. Given the focus we have recommended on service design and activity systems, in Chapters 6 and 7, these methods need to be capable of explaining how local systems *actually* work: how they produce the outcomes that they do. It is no longer adequate to correlate grades and student satisfaction ratings with proxy indicators of educational inputs, or to attempt summative evaluations that prove the wisdom of introducing pet educational innovations. There are many tried-and-tested methods for bringing people together to construct robust shared understandings of how things currently work, and concrete plans (designs) for how they might best be improved. We have sketched four of these: soft systems methodology (SSM), realist formative evaluation, formative interventions and participatory design research (PDR), and have identified a dozen or more others. In the second part of the chapter we argued that continuous improvement needs long-term relationships between those whose focus is on educational practice and those whose research can inform and be informed by that practice. Research–practice partnerships (RPPs) offer one way of framing how such partnerships can be supported and managed. RPPs can involve people tasked with translating between research and practice, although such translational developers can also find homes within other kinds of organisational structure.

References

Bang, M., Faber, L., Gurneau, J., Marin, A., & Soto, C. (2016). Community-based design research: learning across generations and strategic transformations of institutional relations toward axiological innovations. *Mind, Culture, and Activity, 23*(1), 1–14.

Bang, M., & Vossoughi, S. (2016). Participatory design research and educational justice: studying learning and relations within social change making. *Cognition and Instruction, 34*(3), 173–193.

Bower, M., & Vlachopoulos, P. (2018). A critical analysis of technology-enhanced learning design frameworks. *British Journal of Educational Technology.* doi:10.1111/bjet.12668

Bryk, A., Gomez, L., Grunow, A., & LeMahieu, P. (2015). *Learning to improve: how America's schools can get better at getting better.* Cambridge, MA: Harvard University Press.

Bronfenbrenner, U. (1977). Toward an experimental ecology of human development. *American Psychologist, 32*(7), 513–531.

Burns, C., Cottam, H., Vanstone, C., & Winhall, J. (2006). Transformation design. RED paper 2. London: Design Council.

Carvalho, L., & Goodyear, P. (2018). Design, learning and service innovation. *Design Studies, 55*, 27–53.

Checkland, P. (1999). *Systems thinking, systems practice.* Chichester: Wiley.

Chen, H., & Rossi, P. (1992). *Using theory to improve program and policy evaluations.* Westport, CT: Greenwood.

Connell, J., & Shafer, L. (1989). *Structured rapid prototyping.* Englewood Cliffs, NJ: Prentice Hall.

Coryn, C. L., Noakes, L. A., Westine, C. D., & Schröter, D. C. (2011). A systematic review of theory-driven evaluation practice from 1990 to 2009. *American Journal of Evaluation, 32*(2), 199–226.

Cremers, P. H. M., Wals, A. E. J., Wesselink, R., & Mulder, M. (2017). Utilization of design principles for hybrid learning configurations by interprofessional design teams. *Instructional Science, 45*(2), 289–309.

DiSalvo, B., Yip, J., Bonsignore, E., & DiSalvo, C. (eds). (2017). *Participatory design for learning: perspectives from practice and research.* New York: Routledge.

Ellis, R., & Fisher, K. (2017). Translating translational research on space design from the health sector to higher education – lessons learnt and challenges revealed In L. Carvalho, P. Goodyear, & M. de Laat (eds), *Place-Based Spaces for Networked Learning* (pp. 225–241). New York: Routledge.

Ellis, R., & Goodyear, P. (2010). *Students' experiences of e-learning in higher education: the ecology of sustainable innovation.* New York: RoutledgeFalmer.

Engeström, Y. (2011). From design experiments to formative interventions. *Theory & Psychology, 21*(5), 598–628.

Engeström, Y., & Sannino, A. (2010). Studies of expansive learning: foundations, findings and future challenges. *Educational Research Review, 5,* 1–24.

Engeström, Y., Sannino, A., & Virkkunen, J. (2014). On the methodological demands of formative interventions. *Mind, Culture, and Activity, 21*(2), 118–128.

Ericson, A., Löfgren, S., Bolinder, G., Reeves, S., Kitto, S., & Masiello, I. (2017). Interprofessional education in a student-led emergency department: a realist evaluation. *Journal of Interprofessional Care, 31*(2), 199–206.

Fishman, B., Penuel, W. R., Allen, A.-R., Cheng, B. H., & Sabelli, N. (2013). Design-based implementation research: an emerging model for transforming the relationship of research and practice. *Yearbook of the National Society for the Study of Education, 112*(2), 136–156.

Floyd, A., & Preston, D. (2018). The role of the associate dean in UK universities: distributed leadership in action? *Higher Education, 75,* 925–943.

Fung, D. (2017). *A connected curriculum for higher education.* Retrieved from London: www.ucl.ac.uk/ucl-press/browse-books/a-connected-curriculum-for-higher-education

Gong, Y., & Janssen, M. (2015). Demystifying the benefits and risks of lean service innovation: a banking case study. *Journal of Systems and Information Technology, 17*(4), 364–380.

Goodyear, P., & Jones, C. (2002). Implicit theories of learning and change: their role in the development of eLearning environments for higher education. In S. Naidu (ed.), *eLearning: technology and the development of teaching and learning.* London: Kogan Page.

Goodyear, P., & Markauskaite, L. (forthcoming). The impact on work and practice of wicked problems and unpredictable futures In J. Higgs, D. Horsfall, S. Cork, & A. Jones (eds), *Practice futures for the common good.* Leiden: Koninklijke Brill NV.

Gunn, W., Otto, T., & Smith, R. (eds). (2013). *Design anthropology: theory and practice.* London: Bloomsbury.

Gutiérrez, K. D., Engeström, Y., & Sannino, A. (2016). Expanding educational research and interventionist methodologies. *Cognition and Instruction, 34*(3), 275–284.

Gutiérrez, K., & Vossoughi, S. (2010). 'Lifting off the ground to return anew': documenting and designing for equity and transformation through social design experiments. *Journal of Teacher Education, 61*(1–2), 100–117.

Haskell, C. (2017). Institutional research as a bridge: Aligning institutional internal data needs and external information requirements a strategic view. *Higher Education Evaluation and Development, 11*(1), 2–11.

Ison, R., & Blackmore, C. (2014). Designing and developing a reflexive learning system for managing systemic change. *Systems, 2*(2), 119–136.

Janssen, F. J., Könings, K. D., & van Merriënboer, J. J. (2017). Participatory educational design: How to improve mutual learning and the quality and usability of the design? *European Journal of Education, 52*(3), 268–279.

Kelly, A., Lesh, R., & Baek, J. (eds). (2008). *Handbook of design research methods in education: innovations in science, technology, engineering and mathematics learning and teaching.* Mahwah, NJ: Lawrence Erlbaum Associates.

Levy, P. (2003). A methodological framework for practice-based research in networked learning. *Instructional Science, 31*(1–2), 87–109.

Lewin, K. (1952). *Field theory in social science.* New York: Harper & Bros.

Manzini, E. (2005). Enabling solutions for creative communities: social innovation and design for sustainability. *Designmatters, 10*(1), 45–52.

Markauskaite, L., & Goodyear, P. (2017). *Epistemic fluency and professional education: innovation, knowledgeable action and actionable knowledge.* Dordrecht: Springer.

Matthews, K., Dwyer, A., Hine, L., & Turner, J. (2018). Conceptions of students as partners. *Higher Education.* doi:10.1007/s10734-018-0257-y

McClaughlin, J., & Jordan, G. (1999). Logic models: a tool for telling your program's performance story. *Evaluation and Program Planning, 22,* 65–72.

Norman, D. A. (2009). The research–practice gap: the need for translational developers. *Interactions, 17*(4), 942.

Olson, D. (2004). The triumph of hope over experience in the search for 'what works'. *Educational Researcher, 33,* 24–26.

Patton, M. (2010). Developmental evaluation: applying complexity concepts to enhance innovation and use (3rd edn). New York: Guilford.

Pedler, M. (ed.) (2011). *Action learning in practice* (4th edn). London: Gower.

Penuel, W., Briggs, D., Davidson, K., Herlihy, C., Sherer, D., Hill, H., . . . Allen, A.-R. (2016). *Findings from a national survey of research use among school and district leaders.* Boulder, CO: National Center for Research in Policy and Practice,

Penuel, W., & Gallagher, D. (2017). *Creating research–practice partnerships in education.* Cambridge, MA: Harvard Education Press.

Pries-Heje, J., Venable, J., & Baskerville, R. (2014). Soft design science methodology. In J. Simonsen, C. Svabo, S. Strandvad, K. Samson, M. Hertzum, & O. Hansen (eds), *Situated design methods* (pp. 77–95). Cambridge, MA: MIT Press.

Sandoval, W. (2014). Conjecture mapping: an approach to systematic educational design research. *Journal of the Learning Sciences, 23*(1), 18–36.

Schuler, D., & Namioka, A. (1993). *Participatory design: principles and practices.* Hillsdale, NJ: Lawrence Erlbaum Associates.

Sholl, S., Ajjawi, R., Allbutt, H., Butler, J., Jindal-Snape, D., Morrison, J., & Rees, C. (2017). Balancing health care education and patient care in the UK workplace: a realist synthesis. *Medical Education, 51*(8), 787–801.

Star, S., & Griesemer, J. (1989). Institutional ecology, 'translations' and boundary objects: amateurs and professionals in Berkeley's Museum of Vertebrate Zoology, 1907–39. *Social Studies of Science, 19*(3), 387–420.

Strömdahl, H., & Langerth Zetterman, M. (2002). *Theory-anchored evaluation: an attempt to increase ownership in evaluation in higher education.* Stockholm: KTH Learning Lab.

Sweeting, B. (2016). Design research as a variety of second-order cybernetic practice. *Constructivist Foundations, 11*(3), 572–578.

Terenzini, P. T. (1993). On the nature of institutional research and the knowledge and skills it requires. *Research in Higher Education, 34*(1), 1–10.

Terenzini, P. T. (2013). 'On the nature of institutional research' revisited: plus ca change...? *Research in Higher Education, 54*(2), 137–148.

Virkkunen, J., & Newnham, D. (2013). *The Change Laboratory: a tool for collaborative development of work and education.* Rotterdam: Sense Publishers.

Waldman, S. A. & Terzic, A. (2010). Clinical and translational science: from bench-bedside to global village. *Clinical and Translational Science, 3*(5), 254–257.

Wenger, E., McDermott, R., & Snyder, W. (2002). *Cultivating communities of practice.* Cambridge, MA: Harvard Business School Press.

Whyte, W. F. E. (1991). *Participatory action research.* Thousand Oaks, CA: Sage Publications.

Wong, G., Greenhalgh, T., & Pawson, R. (2010). Internet-based medical education: a realist review of what works, for whom and in what circumstances. *BMC medical education, 10*(1), 1–12.

Wong, G., Greenhalgh, T., Westhorp, G., & Pawson, R. (2012). Realist methods in medical education research: what are they and what can they contribute? *Medical Education, 46*(1), 89–96. doi:10.1111/j.1365–2923.2011.04045.x

Wozniak, H. (2015). Conjecture mapping to optimize the educational design research process. *Australasian Journal of Educational Technology, 31*(5), 597–612

Zavala, M. (2016). Design, participation, and social change: what design in grassroots spaces can teach learning scientists. *Cognition and Instruction, 34*(3), 236–249.

10

Conclusions

This book falls into two halves. In the first half of the book we shared key points from our interviews with university leaders and identified a major problematic area. This manifests itself in a number of ways:

- the difficulty of joining up thinking about educational, digital and facilities strategies: the lack of constructs and terminology to support co-ordinated leadership and planning across education and learning space;
- the privileging of quality assurance and compliance over quality enhancement and innovation;
- a focus on simple measurable *outputs*, such as retention rates, grades achieved, employment rates and student satisfaction, and an under-developed capacity to analyse and explain *processes*.

As the quotation below from Penuel & Gallagher indicates, it is not unusual for educational organisations to find themselves confronting complex problems that have multiple origins, and being reduced to searching for simple, low-cost solutions. It is time to move on.

> The education research and development system, moreover, produces interventions that are hardly ever comprehensive enough to solve problems with multiple root causes. And, unlike in medicine, there are few mechanisms or resources allocated specifically to support the spread and implementation of evidence-based innovations. These conditions feed our never-ending search for low-cost solutions that oversimplify the problems we face in education.
>
> (Penuel & Gallagher, 2017, 147)

In the second half of the book, we offered four sets of ideas that we believe can be assembled into a paradigm for tackling complex problems of the kind identified through our interviews. The elements we drew together can be thought about and are talked about using a variety of labels, but we find appealing the idea of educational ecology as an applied science.

It is clear that ecological ideas are enjoying a resurgence in the literature of higher education. We reviewed some of this work in Chapter 8 and identified four strands of thinking from which the foundations of such an enterprise can be built:

- that universities are enmeshed in a number of much wider ecological zones; that what happens in these zones influences the internal dynamics of each university and that universities have a moral responsibility to act in ways that improve the health of each of these zones (Barnett, 2018).
- that universities can be understood as self-organising, self-improving systems and that capacities for self-improvement can be strengthened by enabling and encouraging each part of the university to become better at learning about learning (Ellis & Goodyear, 2010; Bain & Zundans-Fraser, 2017).
- that the physical environment (material, digital and hybrid) plays a very significant, often underestimated, role in enabling learning, and that people who have the combination of disciplinary and local knowledge needed to look after such environments are rare and valuable (Nardi & O'Day, 1999; Luckin, 2010).
- that students are not best understood economically (as 'managed customers') or through the lens of individualistic folk psychology (Bronfenbrenner, 1979; Clark, 2011; Hutchins, 2010; Macfarlane, 2017).

As we explained in Chapters 6 to 8, concepts and methods associated with educational ecology can shed new light on perennial and apparently intractable problems of leadership; notably those where the absence of a shared understanding of how complex learning systems function makes alignment between learning and teaching, IT and facilities problematic. Table 10.1 captures some headline points. But this also needs to be understood in a dynamic way. It is not simply that a joint understanding of educational ecologies can fill the conceptual and terminological gap that the IT and facilities leaders identified as a major source of problems. It is also the case that *joint investigations* into how local learning systems are actually functioning can identify what needs to be done – why, how and by whom – if the systems themselves are to become stronger. Without a shared conceptual and methodological framework, leaders are likely to drown in a flood of uninterpretable learning analytics data.

How to realise an applied science of educational ecology within each university was addressed in two steps. In Chapters 6 and 7 we introduced a way of conceptualising student learning activity that helps bridge between the higher-level concerns of education, IT and facilities strategies and the realities of teaching and learning processes. Activity – what students are *actually* doing – is the core concept here. There is very little systematic research on how students actually do what they do when they are learning: much of their learning activity is unsupervised or only lightly supervised and the key processes are invisible or barely visible to those who teach them. Yet it has been a tenet of university practice for decades that *what the student does* is the key to what they learn (Biggs & Tang, 2007).

Table 10.1 Mapping educational ecology to the five organisational elements

Element	How concepts and methods from educational ecology strengthen work on each organisational element
Strategy	The ultimate purpose of educational strategy is to improve learning opportunities, experiences and outcomes. Strategy is realised through course designs and learning environments. Understanding student learning activity as epistemically, physically and socially situated provides a way of linking designs, environments, activities and outcomes. The absence of a shared conception of these connections makes it extremely difficult to align educational, IT and facilities strategies and to monitor their effectiveness.
Governance	Understanding activity systems as fundamental units of analysis for educational planning provides sharper focus for governance. Without this, it is unclear who should be represented where, and what data should be gathered to inform decisions. Ecologically inspired local research plays an essential role in explaining how the university's various learning systems function, and whether they can and should be improved.
Policy	Policies have real effects insofar as they inform and constrain action that shapes learning tasks and learning environments. Understanding how policy documents help situate real-world educational activity contributes to improving and rationalising policy frameworks.
Management	Management cannot focus on the needs of every student, nor can it be properly informed by statistical averages and stereotyped 'users'. Taking activity systems as fundamental units of analysis and action makes management problems more tractable and alignment across functional areas more feasible.
Funding	Working with a manageable number of activity systems and learning environments makes costing and cost comparisons easier. Innovative arrangements can be modelled as reconfigurations of existing activity systems and environments. Taking an ecological approach helps identify the interconnections between all the elements needed to make a novel intervention/project succeed; it affords holistic approaches to budgeting.

So in Chapter 7 we introduced activity theory and activity-centred analysis and design (ACAD) to help understand what student learning activity consists of, and how it is physically and socially situated. We proposed activity systems as the best unit of analysis for finding out, and representing, how every significant episode of learning happens. Activity systems can be small or large, short-lived or enduring, focused on student learning, faculty planning, university management and more. Talking about activity systems makes it possible for all university stakeholders to speak in a common language. It also enables us to see how the integration of educational, IT and facilities work can be realised through engagement in the collaborative design of services for activity systems: the topic of Chapter 6.

Our other step in realising educational ecology came in Chapter 9, where we outlined two more of the necessary parts of an applied science: methodology and organisational infrastructure. Methodological approaches like soft systems and formative intervention share the virtues of (a) engaging all the people who 'have skin in the game' in processes of local inquiry and enhancement and (b) connecting analysis and redesign – understanding how a local activity system functions and what can be done to improve it. Some approaches, like participatory design research, include strategies that help students themselves to improve their own learning environments (short term), engage with local communities on issues of concern (medium term) and acquire the skills, ideas and confidence (the 'moral know-how') needed to lead such work into the future.

Lest this be seen as over-ambitious or idealistic, we would argue that such approaches are providing tools and structure for a movement that can be glimpsed in many places in contemporary higher education. They align with some core goals in movements like 'Students as Partners' and in work on the 'Connected Curriculum' (Cook-Sather et al., 2014; Healey et al., 2016; Fung, 2017; Tong et al., 2018).

Over recent decades, Western universities have been very good at picking up and reproducing modish language about their purposes and methods – engaged enquiry, T-shaped graduates, being and becoming, and so on. They have been less good at 'tooling up' to deal with the complexity of analysing how their educational ecosystems actually function and of systematically redesigning for sustainable improvement. Lack of shared concepts, language and other tools is one part of the story. Much of the rest is down to organisational structures, responsibilities and leadership.

> The traditional structures and ways of working in higher education run the risk of falling too far behind the pace of change. If we want our institutions to be the center of accessible education, then the most important next steps for higher education may be to rethink organizational structures and establish innovation teams. Guided by the principles of complexity science and working collectively, CIOs, provosts, directors of academic innovation, and others tapped to lead innovation can and should develop the frameworks that both speak to academic values and help us all adapt to a changing context.
>
> (Eshleman, 2018, 57)

For example, it would be good to see some reforms in the professional development programmes and key performance indicators for university leaders. At a minimum, these should reflect and encourage success with *joint planning and integration* across education, IT and facilities: to promote joined-up thinking about innovation, quality, new course and curriculum designs, IT and learning spaces. In time, we might see university leaders and their teams emerge as advocates and expert practitioners in the applied science of educational ecology.

References

Bain, A., & Zundans-Fraser, L. (2017). *The self-organizing university: designing the higher education organization for quality learning and teaching.* Singapore: Springer Nature.

Barnett, R. (2018). *The ecological university: a feasible utopia.* London: Routledge.

Biggs, J., & Tang, C. (2007). *Teaching for quality learning at university: what the student does* (3rd edn). Buckingham: Open University Press.

Bronfenbrenner, U. (1979). *The ecology of human development: experiments by nature and design.* Cambridge, MA: Harvard University Press.

Clark, A. (2011) *Supersizing the mind: embodiment, action, and cognitive extension.* Oxford, Oxford University Press.

Cook-Sather, A., Bovill, C., & Felten, P. (2014). *Engaging students as partners in learning and teaching: a guide for faculty.* San Francisco, CA: Jossey Bass.

Ellis, R., & Goodyear, P. (2010). *Students' experiences of e-learning in higher education: the ecology of sustainable innovation.* New York: RoutledgeFalmer.

Eshleman, K. (2018). Emergent EDU: complexity and innovation in higher ed. *EDUCAUSE Review, May/June 2018,* 56–57.

Fung, D. (2017). *A connected curriculum for higher education.* Retrieved from London: www.ucl.ac.uk/ucl-press/browse-books/a-connected-curriculum-for-higher-education

Healey, M., Flint, A., & Harrington, K. (2016). Students as partners: reflections on a conceptual model. *Teaching & Learning Inquiry,* 4(2), 1–13

Hutchins, E. (2010). Cognitive ecology. *Topics in Cognitive Science, 2,* 705–715.

Luckin, R. (2010). *Re-designing learning contexts: technology-rich, learner-centred ecologies.* New York: Routledge.

Macfarlane, B. (2017). *Freedom to learn: the threat to student academic freedom and why it needs to be reclaimed.* London: Routledge.

Nardi, B., & O'Day, V. (1999). *Information ecologies: using technology with heart.* Cambridge, MA: MIT Press.

Penuel, W., & Gallagher, D. (2017). *Creating research–practice partnerships in education.* Cambridge, MA: Harvard Education Press.

Tong, V., Standen, A., & Sotiriou, M. (eds). (2018). *Shaping higher education with students: ways to connect research and teaching.* London: UCL Press.

Review questions to explore educational strategic readiness

In Chapter 5, we summarised the ideas and concerns of university leaders in the areas of education, IT and facilities as a way of exploring the maturity of educational strategizing – expressed in terms of capability and alignment. We used the combined experience of the interviewees to create a set of key questions that can guide deeper investigations into university readiness, including the capacities needed to deal with ongoing change in the sector.

Key questions

These are intended to work as *orienting* questions. That is, posing each question is likely to lead to further questions – 'what does that mean in our university?', 'what evidence and insights would we need to answer that?', and so on.

Overarching questions:

1. What levels of agreement are there about terminology related to new course designs and integrated learning space? What is the level of institutional understanding about how new course designs and integrated learning spaces can enable the education mission of a university?
2. To what extent are the organisational elements of education strategy, governance, policy, management and funding each holistically designed and informed?
3. To what extent are the organisational elements of education strategy, governance, policy, management and funding aligned in relation to the education mission of the university?
4. What change is occurring or being aimed at? What is the time scale? How will it affect the relevant people – that is what different perspectives will arise (students, academics, professional staff, senior management, different disciplines?)
5. What disruption will the change invoke? How will that impact be managed and continuity of service be achieved?

Each of the organisational elements revealed through the analysis of the interview transcripts can be investigated further, using the following types of questions.

Strategy questions:

1. When did the university last complete a project of *simplifying programme structures* around a disciplinary core that maximises student choice, pathway flexibility, study opportunities and modular acquisition of credentials and credit? How successful was it?

2. To what extent has the university identified measures of quality and innovation in education *processes* that are likely to lead to the desired outcomes? What evidence is there providing links between these and desired outcomes: both programme-level and course-level outcomes?

3. To what extent are *opportunities for key strategic outcomes* (such as work-integrated learning, transferable knowledge and skills) embedded in the curriculum and broader student experience?

4. What *new measures have been identified* to bring stronger coherence and quality to the student experience? How do these help with issues such as measuring transferable graduate attributes and success in areas like retention?

5. Are the educational (or learning and teaching) strategic elements and directions described in sufficient detail to guide priorities, initiatives and decision making? Are they described in a language that is understood by the broader institution?

Governance questions:

1. To what extent does education governance involved in new course designs have oversight of the direction of development of physical and virtual learning space?

2. How representative is governance membership of stakeholders? How up-to-date are governance members with innovation in learning and teaching?

3. How 'joined up' are the deliberations of governance committees responsible for new course designs and learning spaces?

4. To what extent are the relevant governance committees successful in engaging the university community, particularly across multiple disciplines?

5. To what extent do the relevant governance committees facilitate and encourage a balance between quality assurance and innovation in new course design and integrated learning spaces?

Policy questions:

1. To what extent does the current policy framework of the university promote a flexible approach to programme, course and credential design?

2. To what extent does the policy framework strike a balance between ensuring quality and encouraging innovation in learning and teaching?

3. To what extent does the current policy framework enable an innovative and appropriate use of physical and virtual learning space in the design of programme and course goals, learning and teaching activities, assessment and outcomes?

Management questions:

1. To what extent has engagement with the university community through governance eased management issues?
2. What additional initiatives need to be put in place at the level of each project to promote cultural change that supports educational innovation involved in new course design?
3. To what extent are educational innovations shaping and leading development in physical and virtual learning space and vice versa? Is ongoing digital disruption being planned for?
4. To what extent is there appropriate staff development support accompanying innovative projects designed to improve course design and better integrate learning spaces?
5. How collaborative and aligned are the IT and facilities staff when engaged in designing and providing learning space to meet the needs of new course designs provided by faculties?

Funding questions:

1. To what extent are the requirements of new course designs shaping investment in the learning space provision at the university?
2. Is there/has there been sufficient funding allocated to enable a simplification of the programme structure of the university as described in the strategy questions above?
3. To what extent is there agreement on the scale and allocation of funds to physical and virtual learning space services and support to university programmes (i.e. aligned with the stated strategic educational (learning and teaching) outcomes)?
4. Is there commensurate funding for the accompanying staff development required when embarking on new course designs in integrated learning spaces?
5. Does the university funding strategy recognise the full life-cycle costs of integrated learning space provision for programme delivery?
6. To what extent is there agreement on how to measure the outcomes of providing new learning spaces for new course designs?

Researcher ratings

University Code	Strategy Capability	Strategy Alignment	Governance Capability	Governance Alignment	Policy Capability	Policy Alignment	Management Capability	Management Alignment	Funding Capability	Funding Alignment
FF	1	1	1	1	2	2	1	1	1	1
Y	1	1	1	1	1	2	1	1		
AA	1	1	1	1	2	1	1	1		
II	1	1	1	2	1	1	1	2		
HH	1	2	2	2		1	1	2	1	1
V	1	1	1	1			2	2		
DD	2	2	2	1	1	2	2	2		
GG	2	2	2	1	2	2	2	2		
JJ	2	2	3	2	2	3	2	3		
CC	2	2	2	1			2	1	2	1
T	2	1	1	1			1	1	1	1
K	2	2	2	2			2	2	3	2
O	2	2	2	2			3	2	3	3
N	2	2	2	2	4	3	3	3	2	1
U	2	2	2	2			3	3	3	3
R	2	2	2	1			2	1	2	1
B	3	2	3	2			3	2	2	3
MM	2	1	1	1			2	2	2	2
F	3	3	3	2			2	2	3	3
L	3	1	2	2	1	2	2	1	2	1
C	3	2	2	2			2	1	3	2
EE	3	3	4	2	5	5	2	2	2	1
KK	3	2	3	2	4	3	2	2	1	1
M	3	2	2	1	4	3	2	2	3	2
D	3	2	3	2			3	2	4	2

(Continued)

University Code	Strategy Capability	Strategy Alignment	Governance Capability	Governance Alignment	Policy Capability	Policy Alignment	Management Capability	Management Alignment	Funding Capability	Funding Alignment
X	3	3	3	3	3	3	3	3	2	2
W	3	5	5	4	5	5	4	4	3	3
J	3	3	4	3			3	4	3	3
H	3	3	3	3			3	2	2	2
A	3	3	3	3			3	3	3	3
LL	4	3	3	2			3	2	3	3
E	4	2	3	3			3	3	3	3
BB	4	2	4	3	3	4	4	4		
G	4	3	4	3			3	3	3	3
P	4	4	4	3	3	3	3	2		
Z	4	2	3	2	3	2	2	2		
L	4	2	1	2			2	1	1	2
S	5	5	5	5	4	3	5	4	5	4
Q	5	5	5	4	5	4	4	3		

Note: ratings are based on interview transcripts and available university documentation.

Index

Note: Page numbers in **bold** refer to tables.